In Search of the Lost Decade

In Search of the Lost Decade

Everyday Rights in Post-Dictatorship Argentina

———

Jennifer Adair

UNIVERSITY OF CALIFORNIA PRESS

University of California Press, one of the most distinguished university presses in the United States, enriches lives around the world by advancing scholarship in the humanities, social sciences, and natural sciences. Its activities are supported by the UC Press Foundation and by philanthropic contributions from individuals and institutions. For more information, visit www.ucpress.edu.

University of California Press
Oakland, California

© 2020 by Jennifer Adair

Library of Congress Cataloging-in-Publication Data

Names: Adair, Jennifer, 1977– author.
Title: In search of the lost decade : everyday rights in post-dictatorship
    Argentina / Jennifer Adair.
Description: Oakland, California : University of California Press, [2020] |
    Includes bibliographical references and index.
Identifiers: LCCN 2019019904 (print) | LCCN 2019980965 (ebook) |
    ISBN 9780520305175 (cloth) | ISBN 9780520305182 (paperback) |
    ISBN 9780520973282 (ebook)
Subjects: LCSH: Argentina—Politics and government—1983–2002. |
    Argentina—Economic conditions—1983– | Argentina—Social
    conditions—1983–
Classification: LCC F2849.2 .A29 2020 (print) | LCC F2849.2 (ebook) |
    DDC 982.06—dc23
LC record available at https://lccn.loc.gov/2019019904
LC ebook record available at https://lccn.loc.gov/2019980965

Manufactured in the United States of America

28   27   26   25   24   23   22   21   20
10   9   8   7   6   5   4   3   2   1

For Julián and Elio

CONTENTS

ACKNOWLEDGMENTS

In historical terms, this book examines a brief period: the roughly six-year government of Raúl Alfonsín following Argentina's return to democracy in 1983. The making of this book took much longer, with many people and institutions to thank along the way. I am grateful to them all.

I first arrived in Buenos Aires in 2004, when the study of Argentina's recent history had opened in new ways after the 2001 economic crisis and the mass popular protests that ensued. Among other outcomes, the uprisings forced a reassessment of the nation's authoritarian past and its lingering effects on the democratic present. I had the privilege to witness these debates up close while working with the organization Memoria Abierta, an alliance of human rights groups dedicated to preserving the memory of the dictatorship that ruled from 1976 to 1983. My time at Memoria Abierta gave me a crash course in Argentine history. Through their labor and activism, the inspiring archivists, historians, and artists who worked there demonstrated how history and memory operate in daily life, along with the firm conviction that engaging the past can make change. This book began there, through the friendships and projects cultivated over the years.

As the ideas that inform this book took shape, I was fortunate to be mentored by a generous group of scholars and teachers. Katie Hite, Leslie Offutt, and Matilde Zimmermann first sparked my interest in Latin American history and politics at Vassar College. Their courses, scholarship, and one formative trip to Cuba convinced me to study history, while their guidance continues to light the way. The Department of History at New York University was an ideal academic home for many years, due above all to the unwavering encouragement of my advisers and their intellectual example. Greg Grandin supported this project from the beginning and at every turn helped make it better. He found elegant ways to distill and express complicated ideas and pushed me to understand Latin America's tradition of social rights with greater clarity. I owe much more than I can express to his generosity, his incisive readings, and the instruction of his politically engaged scholarship. Some of my favorite moments in graduate school were spent in Sinclair Thomson's seminars, where he modeled the rigor and creativity of the most gracious mentors. His enthusiasm for this project and the care of his always detailed and lucid comments mark this book. I was lucky to be at the beginning stages of fieldwork when Barbara Weinstein joined the Department of History. The depth of her intellectual engagement with Latin American history and the combination of her brilliance, steady counsel, and warmth have been invaluable ever since. In Buenos Aires, Elizabeth Jelin encouraged this project years ago when it was still a vague inkling. Her observations and criticisms sharpened my investigation into post-dictatorship Argentina and continually pushed me to go beyond facile conclusions and straw men. She generously opened her personal archives and helped see this project to completion. I also benefited enormously from the feedback of Ada Ferrer, whose seminars and scholarship left lasting impressions.

My peers in the history department made NYU a vibrant and fulfilling place to study. Many of the friendships made there continue to enrich my life. Thanks to Lina Britto, Joaquín Chávez, Anne Eller, Aldo Marchesi, Yuko Miki, Daniel Rodriguez, Federico Sor, Franny Sullivan, Christy Thornton, Josh Frens-String, and Ana María Quesada, among others. Martín Sivak generously set up interviews and contacts in Buenos Aires and offered useful comments on several chapters. Ernesto Semán dedicated countless hours to talking through the ideas for this book and helped shape the direction that it ultimately took. I will always be grateful for that time and his friendship. Michelle Chase and Carmen Soliz read and then re-read multiple versions of several chapters and improved many of the arguments. Lisa Ubelaker Andrade deserves special mention. Much of this book was first written, in dissertation form, side by side in multiple cafés throughout Buenos Aires. She has been a sounding board and confidant for this project and many more. I struggled with where to place her in these acknowledgments, since she has been a part of this book at practically every stage. Thanks, pal.

Navigating the archives in Argentina often presents challenges to researchers. This book would not be possible without the expertise of the dedicated archivists and staff at several research institutions, public archives, and libraries. I thank the archivists at the Archivo General de la Nación/Departamento Archivo Intermedio for leading me to the letters that are the subject of the fifth chapter. The Comisión Provincial por la Memoria in La Plata holds the records of the Dirección de Inteligencia de la Policía de la Provincia de Buenos Aires (DIPPBA). In addition to materials that have shed new light on the coordination of state terror and repression, the archive also contains invaluable repositories of the more mundane aspects of local and municipal history in the outskirts of Buenos Aires following the dictatorship. During the early stages of this project, Laura Lenci graciously explained how the archive functioned and helped me to process the original request for materials that inform the book. I also thank Magdalena Lanteri, among others, at the Comisión, who later facilitated a fruitful search for materials related to the 1989 hyperinflation and food riots. Fr. Armando Dessy granted me access to the archives of the Obispado de Quilmes and patiently answered my questions about the history of Quilmes and the diocese. The staff at the newspaper *El Sol* in Quilmes kept the office open a little later on several occasions. My friend Federico Lorenz facilitated contact with the Archivo Nacional de la Memoria. I thank the staff members there, who permitted me the time to examine files from the National Commission on the Disappearance of Persons (CONADEP) related to the PAN food program. Librarians at the Biblioteca y Archivo Histórico de la UCR and the Instituto de Investigaciones Gino Germani at the Universidad de Buenos Aires provided helpful assistance and access to campaign materials and oral testimonies. Sebastián Szkolnik's research acumen was critical, especially for the processing of source materials for the fourth and final chapters. I also extend my thanks to photographers Daniel Rodriguez and Enrique Rosito, who granted me permission to include their photographs in the book.

In Buenos Aires, I spoke with dozens of individuals and former members of the Alfonsín administration, who shared their expertise and helped me navigate the political and social life of the 1980s. Among others, I would like to especially thank Aldo Neri, Leopoldo Moreau, and Jesús Rodríguez. Several individuals also opened up their archives and lent me personal materials for this study. Ricardo Mazzorín offered his insights into Argentine political economy and allowed me access to the records that form the basis for the fourth chapter. Catalina Vera took time during her busy schedule to locate rare manuals from her days working on the PAN food program. On several occasions, Patricia Aguirre made herself available to discuss Argentine social programs and food politics and aided in the location of PAN records and program participants.

Many friends and colleagues commented on and edited the book along the way. I always looked forward to conversations with Marian Schlotterbeck and Alison Bruey, who ensured that this book would see the light of day. Rania Sweis's editorial skills improved the prose in many places. Isabella Cosse and Mercedes García Ferrari created a productive and friendly workshop space during an intense writing phase. Isabella in particular continues to provide inspiration and a model of creative historical thinking and intellectual generosity to emulate. The book's arguments and structure benefited enormously from conversations over the years with Benjamin Bryce, Emilio Crenzel, Marina Franco, Laura Golbert, Mark Healey, Elizabeth Jelin, Gabriel Kessler, Federico Lorenz, Natalia Milanesio, Jimena Montaña, David Sheinin, and Brenda Werth. Talks and presentations at Bates College, Bowdoin College, Universidad de Buenos Aires, Universidad de San Andrés, and Universidad Torcuato di Tella also helped refine many arguments.

The Bates College Department of History and Department of Politics provided a welcoming setting of generous colleagues, including Lydia Barnett, Paul Eason, Karen Melvin, Caroline Shaw, and Clarisa Pérez-Armendáriz. They read and offered feedback at many crucial moments. I had the good fortune to complete this book as a member of the Department of History and the Latin American and Caribbean Studies Program at Fairfield University. I extend thanks to my fantastic colleagues, who create a stimulating academic environment in which to share and sharpen projects. As the book progressed, I benefited as a fellow in the Humanities Institute Seminar, which facilitated additional writing time, workshops, and fruitful research collaborations with students, who reminded me of the value of readable histories. Gwen Alfonso, Rachelle Brunn-Bevel, Jocelyn Boryczka, Lydia Willsky-Ciollo, Liz Hohl, Maggie Labinski, Alexa Mullady, Silvia Marsans-Sakly, Sunil Purushotham, and Giovanni Ruffini read, discussed, edited, and made time for welcome happy hours and camaraderie. Michelle Farrell has been a stalwart colleague, intrepid travel companion, and gracious writing buddy. Our "office hours" on the Metro North kept this project on track and made it richer through her friendship.

I would also like to thank the institutions and financial support that made the research and writing of this book possible. Grants and fellowships from New York University, the Tinker Foundation, the Fulbright-Hays Doctoral Dissertation Fellowship, and the Mellon Foundation/American Council of Learned Societies supported fieldwork and writing during the dissertation phase. Faculty summer research grants from Bates College, Fairfield University, and the National Endowment for the Humanities facilitated additional research trips to Buenos Aires. The final stage of writing was supported by an NEH fellowship, which provided time away from classroom and administrative duties. Any views, findings, conclusions, or recommendations expressed in this book do not necessarily represent those of the National Endowment for the Humanities. At the University of California Press, Kate Marshall and Enrique Ochoa-Kaup provide the most supportive environment for their authors. I am ever grateful to Kate for her keen eye and ongoing enthusiasm for this project. Benjamin Bryce, Eduardo Elena, Jessica Stites Mor, and one anonymous reviewer read the manuscript for UC Press. Their observations made this a better book. All errors, of course, are my own.

Many more friends and family provided sustenance, housing, work spaces, and comfort over the years. Dave Giles, Rachel Lears, Anne Lebleu, and Tom Pyun have seen this book from start to finish. They have been there through all of the ups and downs in between, reminding me with their love and their lifelong friendships of the rich world beyond this project. To them, thank you. The affection and friendship of Jane Brodie, Wendy Gosselin, and Maxine Swann have been a beacon for over a decade now and one of the many felicitous results of this book. Members of the *club de cultura para todos*—Sergio Adrada Rafael, Álvaro Baquero-Pecino, Michelle Farrell, Geoff Shullenberger, Leonard Nalencz, and Charlotte Whittle—transformed New York into an inviting place to rediscover. In Buenos Aires, Maria Laura Guembe first welcomed me to the city, opening her house to multiple red suitcases. Maria Alejandra Pavicich has been a source of solace and steady humor through it all. Walter Altman, Alan Cibils, Martha Farmelo, Graciela Karababikian, Federico Lorenz, and Lisa Ubelaker Andrade always make Buenos Aires feel like home. I thank my husband Julián's family, especially Teresa Azcárate and Irene Troksberg, who shared their memories of 1980s Argentina. They created a warm space in their family for me and now provide infinite love for their grandson. My sister Kadi, brother-in-law Matt, and nieces Ava and Lucy made this journey fun and meaningful. It has been a thrill to see them grow with this book. My parents Jim and Nancy taught me the power of history and then encouraged me to study it. Their support and motivation have been steadfast, their love boundless. They too deserve credit for seeing this project through, for showing an interest—sometimes unwittingly—in the Alfonsín years, and for providing a home to always return to.

My biggest gratitude is due to Julián Troksberg, for whom a few phrases at the end of these acknowledgments cannot suffice. Our life is interwoven with this book. From Buenos Aires, to Portland, Maine, to New York City, he endured more alfonsinismo and the Radical Party than he ever thought possible with enthusiasm, love, and patience. If this book exists, it is because of his reflections and insight, generously shared in the midst of his own creative work, which in turn helped improve mine. My greatest joy has been to build our future together. We welcomed our son Elio as this book was in its final stages. His arrival brought us much happiness and inspiration for new projects to come. This book is for them, and for all of the adventures that await us.

Introduction

On May 1, 1989, María, a high school teacher from Buenos Aires, wrote a letter to President Raúl Alfonsín as he embarked on his final months in office. The country was in the midst of a crisis of hyperinflation, and elections were set for two weeks away. Earlier in the day, María had heard the president's last address to Congress, and she felt compelled to write to him. "My friend," she began, then recounted how she and her husband, an adjunct university instructor, had worked hard over two decades of marriage, weathering continual financial difficulties and the sensation of "always having to start over." María emphasized that she had no "political affiliations" that would cloud her judgment, lest the president think she was writing to ask for political favors. She recalled her happiness at casting her vote for Alfonsín in 1983, after seven years of military dictatorship. Though she did not regret the decision, she was barely able to mask her exasperation when she asked, "But why did you take away our hopes[?] . . . [W]hy did you abandon us?" After mentioning her adolescent daughters and her concerns about their desire to quit their studies and leave Argentina, she concluded her letter with a mix of resignation and renewed appreciation, "So no matter, Mr. President, thank you, thank you so much for helping me recover my dreams and hopes in 1983, and thank you for the democracy that allows me to live and to write you this letter, even though it does not allow for me to get sick."[1]

When Raúl Alfonsín was inaugurated on December 10, 1983—following a brutal period of military dictatorship that had disappeared thousands—he offered this succinct but compelling definition of democracy: "With democracy," he said, "one eats, one is educated, one is cured." This equation of political rights with physical and social well-being resonated in a country where many understood political

terror and social deprivation to be bound up with one another. Alfonsín had cam-
paigned on a pledge to address the junta's human rights violations, as well as to
fight hunger, improve welfare, and make education more readily available. But
when he took office he assumed the burden of a national debt of over US$43 billion
and rising rates of poverty, particularly in heavily populated Buenos Aires and its
environs. Partly as a result of these challenges, his government's ambitious social
agenda stalled, overwhelmed by rampant inflation and debt. In 1989, during a
crisis of hyperinflation, food shortages led to riots and supermarket lootings
throughout the provinces of Buenos Aires, Rosario, and Córdoba, forcing Alfonsín's resignation six months before his term was to expire.

This is a book about how Argentines defined a just, democratic society after years
of military rule and fiscal emergency. It begins with the effervescence of new democracy and vows to eliminate hunger and ends with food shortages and supermarkets
aflame. Whereas many observers tend to interpret these events as a history of failure,
this book restores a sense of process and possibility to Argentina's democratic restoration and to the Alfonsín government's attempts to stave off social emergency during a decade of simultaneous political openings and a looming neoliberal world
order. As María's letter makes clear, Argentines took seriously Alfonsín's pledge that
democracy would feed, educate, and heal. Her message also crystallizes a key contribution of this book, which argues that the bold promise of the Alfonsín government
had its roots in a holistic definition of democracy that saw political, social, and
human rights as mutually reinforcing and capable of ending the armed forces' long
reign over Argentine public life. Over the course of the 1980s, individuals measured
the Alfonsín government not only in terms of its attempts to prosecute the crimes of
the armed forces and to restore political institutions, but also in terms of its ability to
fulfill demands for material well-being. The book chronicles these everyday meanings of rights—often expressed as demands for basic needs such as food, welfare, and
full employment—and the lived experience of Argentina's democratic return, which
took shape far beyond the ballot box.

BEYOND "TRANSITIONS TO DEMOCRACY"

In Search of the Lost Decade moves from the presidential palace to the streets, from
the family table to the marketplace, and back again to examine the making of what
many social scientists consider the most emblematic of Latin America's "transitions
to democracy." Until now, there have been few social histories of this period, during
which nearly the entire continent moved away from violent civil wars and vicious
dictatorships to constitutional governance.[2] An influential body of scholarship
focused on electoral process and elite decision making has long been the standard
against which the region's constitutional returns have been judged.[3] The first writings on Latin America's redemocratization were published years before dictator-

ships ended in Argentina, Brazil, Uruguay, and Chile. The demise of the Greek military regime in 1974 and the death of Francisco Franco in 1975, which initiated Spain's transition to democracy, sparked great interest in the possibility of the return of competitive governments in South America.[4] State terror and authoritarianism prompted intellectual networks in European and North American think tanks and universities and exile communities throughout the hemisphere to reevaluate the possibilities for political democracy in Latin America as understood up to that point. Their debates, publications, and exchanges produced the idea of "transitions to democracy" and theories about the conditions necessary to emerge from authoritarian rule, many of which hinged on the consolidation of political institutions and the taming of the armed forces.[5] These formulations constituted real-time guideposts for the direction of democratic openings in the 1980s and 1990s.

Though their concerns varied, intellectuals and activists saw the restoration of political democracy as the primary way to protect citizens in-country from human rights abuses and to ensure the end of military dictatorships. As Guillermo O'Donnell reminds us, "The horror of the repression suffered at both the macro and the micro levels, as well as the memory of the huge mistake committed by those who scorned democracy because they wanted to jump immediately into a revolutionary system, seemed to all of the authors during that first wave of writings on transitions to be reason enough to give a process-oriented focus to our studies."[6] To be sure, there were compelling reasons for the more limited, institutional focus of these works. The staggering violence of authoritarian rule lent pressing urgency to the task of theorizing democratic returns. But it also had the effect of narrowing the field of the politically possible in the aftermath of dictatorships and of constraining the protagonists of transitions to a limited set of individuals, institutions, and questions.

In Search of the Lost Decade moves beyond the more narrowly defined institutional spaces of constitutional restoration and complicates the very notion of a "democratic transition" by grounding political transformation in the quotidian realms of neighborhood, home life, and marketplace, among others. The key actors here include self-described "ordinary Argentines," church officials, internal food producers, welfare recipients, government ministers, and the president himself. By widening the scope of the democratic return to include a broader range of protagonists, events, and concerns, we can grasp the less commonly known, but no less decisive, social forces and agendas that shaped the reemergence of a democratic public sphere in Argentina after years of military rule.

EVERYDAY RIGHTS

Observers often point to human rights as a towering achievement of post-dictatorship Argentina. In 1985, it became the first democratic nation to prosecute its armed forces, in historic trials that resulted in initial convictions for five of the nine junta leaders who had ruled from 1976 to 1983. The *Nunca Más* investigative commission inspired similar efforts in Chile, Guatemala, and postapartheid South Africa. Advances in genetic testing innovated by the world-renowned Argentine Forensic Anthropology Team helped to identify victims in the aftermath of genocidal violence in Guatemala and El Salvador, and more recently of state violence in Mexico. Argentine jurists worked to enshrine human rights protections in international law and to establish conventions against torture and forced disappearance.[7] On the home front, the human rights movement quickly evolved into a political force of its own. Activists have fought for decades against impunity and bitter reversals of justice and in favor of remembrance. These "labors of memory," to borrow Elizabeth Jelin's phrase, have made reckoning with Argentina's authoritarian past a benchmark of civil society, and human rights a language of the post-dictatorship era inaugurated in 1983.[8]

The domestic and global reach of the Argentine human rights movement is undeniable. But we have not yet fully understood the broader social meanings of *rights-speak* and the work that it did in the years immediately following the end of the dictatorship. Most accounts that trace the rise of local and transnational human rights regimes in the 1970s and 1980s define human rights in connection with their liberal democratic origins, placing emphasis on political liberties and individual protections from state violence.[9]

By contrast, a principal finding of this book demonstrates that human rights became a multivalent political language that revived historic struggles for social justice dating to the emergence of state-led welfare at midcentury. Given the violent imprint of authoritarianism, which left behind legacies of torture and disappearance, the centrality of social questions to the making of the democratic return has so far been left out of the story of post-dictatorship Argentina, with most scholars foregrounding changes in the formal political sphere.[10] Yet the social realms of democratic restoration take on greater urgency when considering the aftermath of dictatorship in Argentina. The regime was responsible for some of the most heinous crimes of Latin America's long Cold War. But widespread social violence also accompanied state terror. The transition from state-led development to neoliberalism initiated by the regime was felt in the form of a punishing assault on the livelihoods of many, made manifest in attacks against organized labor, a rollback of social protections, and the struggle to fulfill basic needs. Understanding human rights in relation to questions of material well-being and social justice offers a more nuanced picture of post-dictatorship Argentina and the making and unmaking of democratic expectations. It also enables us to see that the roots of those democratic expectations were grounded not only in the immediacy of the dictatorship, but also in the memory of a benefactor state that proved less viable as the decade continued.

The promises and pitfalls of democratic return and the ways that individuals made sense of political change in their daily lives often emerged through struggles over food: who lacked it, who provided it, who set prices, and what Argentines ate. Raúl Alfonsín's campaign pledge to end hunger—at once rousing and banal—took root in an alarming reality. State terror had led to a direct increase in hunger among the most vulnerable sectors between 1976 and 1983. In Argentina, a food-producing nation that historically prided itself on its ability to provide for its citizens, food and consumption had mediated the boundaries between individuals, the state, and the market since the emergence of Peronism in the 1940s.[11] The promise of food for all—though far from a fulfilled reality—formed a cornerstone of the modern welfare state, one that linked the most basic of material needs to a functioning democratic system. These values came under fierce attack during the military regime. Though Argentina remained one of the most food-secure nations in Latin America throughout the 1980s, new anxieties about the hunger caused by the dictatorship rattled a belief in Argentina as a land of plenty with the ability to keep its citizens physically safe and well fed. Over the course of the decade, individuals defined food as a fundamental "human right" at the heart of democratic restoration. Food was thus a litmus test of democracy.

But this is not a book about food per se. Rather, it draws from the new food history of Latin America to examine the less commonly explored tensions between rights and political economy during the years immediately following the end of the dictatorship.[12] The story that follows uses food as a narrative thread to render more intelligible the everyday meanings of rights shaped by the ordinary, intimate, though no less political contests in which the dramas of the democratic return played out. The daily struggle against inflation, the rush to beat fluctuating currency boards, and the challenge of feeding families competed with headlines of military trials, rebellions, and palace intrigues. But it was in the supermarkets, banks, and breadlines where citizens engaged most closely and consistently with the promise of individual and collective well-being offered by the new democracy, and where those ideals were most fiercely tested, challenged, and transformed over the decade.[13] Anchored geographically in Buenos Aires and the surrounding suburbs, this book's six chapters document how a moral economy of democracy evolved in relation to state programs to alleviate hunger, regulate the price of basic staple goods, and fortify the foundations of a faltering welfare state. When supermarket riots erupted in 1989, they signaled not only the abrupt end of the Alfonsín presidency, but also the radical remaking of the expectations of just six years before, as well as a diminished belief in a type of democratic state that could provide for and protect the physical integrity of its citizens.

Despite political openings across Latin America, the 1980s have been referred to as a "lost decade" because of the twin effects of recession and rampant indebtedness. In this view, economic stagnation and stalled monetary reforms paved the way for the widespread application of neoliberal policies throughout the region. One immediate consequence of the 1989 food riots was to hasten the gutting and privatization of public enterprises during the government of Carlos Menem (1989– 1999). In the name of Peronist "productive revolution," Menem infamously undid the legacies of his party and political movement, ushering in a decade of free-market fundamentalism and widening social inequalities. The painful consequences of those recipes are by now well known. In late December 2001 Argentina defaulted on its debt and plunged half of the population into poverty. Widespread popular rebellion against globalization and the local political class met with state repression that resulted in an estimated forty deaths. The economic collapse that inaugurated the twenty-first century resulted in not just the ousting of one president—as had happened during hyperinflation in 1989—but also the quick succession of a series of five presidents in one month.

The narrative of post-dictatorship Latin America tends to draw a straight line from the violence of state terrorism in the 1970s to the consolidation of a neoliberal worldview in the 1990s, capped off, in the Argentine case, by the economic crisis at the beginning of the twenty-first century. Indeed, the authoritarian projects of Latin America's Cold War dictatorships relied on the instrumental use of state violence in the 1970s to lay the foundations for the neoliberal policies that were consolidated by constitutional governments two decades later. Often absent in this telling, however, is the dramatic tension of the decade that came in between the brutality of the 1970s and the massive social severing of the 1990s. Lost in the narrative of the recent past is the actual "lost decade."

In Search of the Lost Decade slows this history down, demonstrating that the rise of a neoliberal worldview was neither as seamless nor as inevitable as previously believed. The years immediately following the end of the dictatorship in Argentina saw citizens and state actors grappling with the contradictions of a shifting economic order while uncomfortably coming to terms with the expiration of earlier state-led development models. This perspective offers an important corrective to studies that reduce political change to economics or that see austerity as unilaterally imposed on Latin America from the outside. Instead, by zooming in on the everyday realms in which the democratic transition was lived, this account grasps the gradual undoing of the Alfonsín government's comprehensive rights agenda, which eventually legitimated proposals for the full-scale implementation of neoliberalism over the course of the 1990s.

DICTATORSHIP AND DEMOCRACY IN TWENTIETH-CENTURY ARGENTINA

A guiding premise of this book maintains that Argentina's "transition to democracy" in the 1980s was not much of a transition at all, but rather a new phase of ongoing contests to define the contours of democracy, rights, and citizenship in the twentieth century. Raúl Alfonsín's 1983 electoral victory originated in the central conflicts of modern Argentine politics, namely the nation's frequent periods of military rule, which attempted to keep at bay the more unruly aspects of both representative democracy and mass political participation. Argentina's first experiment with democracy, which expanded civic rights through voting, electoral reform, and greater popular participation in politics, came to an end in 1930 with a military coup. For the next fifty years, the country alternated between extended periods of military rule and weakened democratic governments. Each successive decade saw the collapse of at least one constitutional government and the installation of de facto civilian-military regimes guided by fealty to the armed forces, the Catholic Church, and the nation's landowning, export-oriented elite.[14]

Juan Domingo Perón, the former labor secretary who came to power through open elections in 1946 and oversaw the unprecedented expansion of social welfare protections and the labor movement, was the only freely elected president to fulfill his term between 1930 and 1952. Under Perón, democracy in Argentina was redefined along emancipatory, fundamentally social lines and as a rebuff of the liberal governments that had come before. Despite opposition to Peronism and the often-factious public arena in which it operated, Peronist ideals of social justice continued to animate popular movements for the rest of the century. The 1955 military coup that overthrew Perón and sent him into exile coincided with the acceleration of the Cold War in Latin America and the radicalization of politics and daily life. By the mid-1960s the Argentine military and the civilian governments that supported it had shown their willingness to persecute political enemies in accordance with an evolving national security doctrine. The military governments that followed intensified a pattern of authoritarianism that was lurching forward in increments of ever-more-repressive regimes.

Following his eighteen years in exile, Juan Perón's return to the presidency in 1973 generated wide-ranging expectations for order and revolutionary change. His sudden death, nine months after taking office, brought his third wife, María Estela Martínez de Perón, to the presidency and dashed any hopes for the end of political turmoil. Politically weak and ineffectual, the government of "Isabel," as Perón's widow was known, authorized the creation of right-wing paramilitary death squads, which began campaigns of repression, torture, and disappearance. State terror was accompanied by rampant economic chaos. In 1975, the draconian economic package announced by the minister of economy, Celestino Rodrigo, rapidly devalued the peso, provoked food and fuel shortages, and gave Argentines their first taste of prolonged inflation. Yet even in the midst of this unrest, Argentina remained the last civilian government in the Southern Cone and the final stronghold of revolutionary movements throughout a region where right-wing dictatorships had recently taken hold in Chile and Uruguay.[15] That government did not last long. On March 24, 1976, the armed forces orchestrated a coup that launched the darkest period in contemporary Argentine history.

Outside of Argentina, "Dirty War" is the label often used to describe the criminal regime that came to power in March 1976. That designation is a misnomer, however. The armed forces did not wage battle against equally matched foes; instead, they wielded a state-sponsored apparatus of surveillance and repression to systematically terrorize, torture, and disappear their civilian victims. For seven years (1976–1983), the regime epitomized the brutality of Latin America's Cold War, authoritarian dictatorships.[16] The ruling junta, comprised of representatives from the army, navy, and air force, baptized their mission the "National Reorganization Process." In step with the virulent anticommunism of neighboring Southern Cone dictatorships, the regime also revived homegrown traditions of conservative Catholic doctrine; anti-Semitism; and a form of nationalism that idealized Argentina's white, European past. Along with their vocal supporters in the Church, the armed forces railed against the excesses of liberal democracy and the corrupting influences of popular social movements, which they blamed for Argentina's moral decline. They described their project in messianic terms: the salvation of Argentine bodies and souls in the service of the ultimate restoration of Argentine prosperity and Christian civilization. Yet contrary to most accounts of the regime as fundamentally antidemocratic, the junta envisioned its own long-term project for Argentine democracy. As Paula Canelo has demonstrated, members of the armed forces sought to "de-Peronize" the masses, turn back the clock on the achievements of collective political action, and restore the frameworks of elite-led republicanism.[17] This they vowed to achieve by rooting out subversion by any means necessary.

The regime distinguished itself by its savagery. Prisoners were abducted from their homes, workplaces, and schools and disappeared into a vast network of clandestine detention centers, where they were subjected to torture and execution. Hundreds of pregnant women gave birth in captivity. Before the women were killed, their babies were torn from them, and the majority were put up for illegal adoption. The notorious "death flights," in which drugged prisoners were thrown alive from planes, transformed the murky waters of the River Plate into a cemetery along the shores of Buenos Aires. A trail of secret prisons dotted the landscape of many urban centers and residential neighborhoods. Survivors of the Navy Mechanics School (ESMA), the regime's most infamous detention center, located in a well-heeled section of Buenos Aires, vividly recall the cheers coming from the nearby stadium during Argentina's 1978 World Cup victory, which rattled the walls of their cells. *Nunca Más*, the landmark 1984 investigative report, which provided a chilling breakdown of the regime's crimes and its victims, estimated the total number of disappearances at close to nine thousand.[18] Human rights organizations have long placed that figure much higher, at thirty thousand. Scholarly attention has recently turned to the degree of tacit social backing for the regime and the extent to which the armed forces succeeded in galvanizing support for their war against subversion.[19] In 1978, the year of Argentina's World Cup win, the popularity of the name "Jorge Rafael" peaked for newborns, in honor of the de facto president, Jorge Rafael Videla, who ruled from 1976 to 1981.[20]

By the late 1970s, the regime had murdered thousands and sent many more into exile or hiding. Yet from the depths of this loss and fear emerged Argentina's contemporary human rights movement, one of the most vocal forces to resist the regime. The Mothers and Grandmothers of the Plaza de Mayo are perhaps the most well-known organizations founded in the face of state terror, recognizable the world over by their iconic white headscarves and their tireless searches for their disappeared children and grandchildren. They joined a growing number of organizations made up of public figures, victims' family members, survivors, religious leaders, and jurists, among others, who worked to denounce the regime and its crimes and to forge links with transnational solidarity networks. Their efforts to promote the defense of human rights—defined primarily at first as protection of the body from state violence—would shape public life and debate in the decades to come. The movement also helped solidify the maxim that any future democratic government must protect the physical well-being of its citizens from state abuse, an idea later adapted by the Alfonsín government in the 1980s.

Latin America's Cold War dictatorships relied on terror to initiate radical economic transitions to neoliberalism. In Argentina, the regime and its civilian allies in the financial sector attempted to reverse several decades of import substitution industrialization (ISI) policies, which they blamed for endemic instability and political crisis. Among other measures, neoliberal boosters advocated for a retreat of the state, deregulation, and friendly conditions for foreign capital investment. Unlike in neighboring Chile, where the dictatorship of Augusto Pinochet inaugurated a wide-reaching era of free-market reforms, the Argentine junta did not fully realize its economic plan. But it did sufficiently begin to chip away at some of the foundations of mid-twentieth-century economic planning, concentrating wealth in a few domestic firms and weakening labor rights and other social protections in the process. These and other measures sparked a decade-long recession and an extended economic crisis, which shaped the parameters of governability for the rest of the century.

Over the short term, however, the junta ushered in a fleeting period of "sweet money" and consumer spending built on foundations of financial speculation and growing foreign debt. In the early 1980s, recession and an impending regional debt crisis appeared on the horizon. Tensions within the junta, along with international condemnation of its crimes, began to weaken the regime. With its reputation in tatters and more and more domestic voices calling for the end of the dictatorship, the armed forces attempted one final bid to retain power. On April 2, 1982, Argentine forces launched an ill-fated attack on the British-controlled Malvinas (Falklands) Islands, a long-disputed territory in the South Atlantic. British troops quickly defeated Argentine conscripts and exposed the junta's hollow efforts to hide its losses through widespread propaganda and a surge of nationalist pride. On June 14, seventy-four days after fighting began, Argentina surrendered to Great Britain. Within a month of the surrender, the junta announced plans for open elections and the return to constitutional rule. Just a short time before, few would have predicted the grip of the regime could be loosened. Seven years of state terror, human rights abuses, and financial boom and bust had devastated Argentina, yet the coming end of the regime brought hopes for the end of the armed forces' long hold on public life. The task of redefining the terms of democracy had begun.

ALFONSINISMO

Since his historic election in 1983, Raúl Alfonsín has been popularly known as "the father of democracy." The label marked the leader of the Radical Party as a symbol of the break between decades of ever-more-violent cycles of military rule and an era of enduring constitutionality. But the title also misleads in ways that simplify the tensions and disputes at the heart of Alfonsín's extended moment on the national stage. Often missing in recollections of the "father of democracy" is a fuller account of the democratic project that Alfonsín attempted to install and the complicated ways that its memory resonates in the present.

The roots of *alfonsinismo* emerged in the crucible of authoritarian rule. For several decades, Argentines on the left and right of the political spectrum declared the exhaustion of liberal democratic institutions in a nation where constitutional governments had been overthrown six times since 1930. But state terror reignited a widespread belief in the ability of institutional democracy to guarantee physical and social well-being. Alfonsín recognized and harnessed this shift better than any of his rivals. His hallmark phrase—"With democracy one eats, one is educated, one is cured"—has settled into nostalgia in the years since his election in 1983. At the time, it gave voice to the promise of democratic return.

The sociologist Gerardo Aboy Carlés has demonstrated that the possibility of 1983 represented a "double rupture" with Argentina's turbulent political history by putting an end to the terror of the most recent dictatorship and breaking the pattern of institutional instability that dominated the twentieth century.[21] Yet for all of its forward-looking construction of a new political frontier, Alfonsín's government actively relied on the memory of the past for its political legitimacy and foundations. He and his cohort referred to the dawn of the democratic era as inaugurating a *tercer movimiento histórico* (third historical movement), which could fulfill the earlier "democratic transitions" surrounding the movements of both Hipólito Yrigoyen and Juan Perón. Yrigoyen, the historic leader of the modern Radical

Party, had extended popular participation in politics at the beginning of the century.[22] From the earliest days of his campaign, Alfonsín exploited the memory of the Radical Party as the steadfast guardian of ethics and republican institutions. In equal measure, however, he acknowledged Peronism as a democratic force responsible for the extension of social rights and collective welfare. This interpretation of the nation's political past provided a road map for Argentina's democratic future. Accordingly, this "third way" would guide the democratic restoration, leading the way through and beyond the social turmoil and military backlash that Alfonsín and his supporters claimed had often resulted from the corporatist labor mobilization of Peronism. For Alfonsín and the intellectual architects of the newly restored democratic government, the reconciliation of a historic antagonism between political liberalism and social justice would revive the modern political foundations of the nation and put an end to the long cycle of authoritarian violence. When inaugurated on December 10, 1983, the Alfonsín government sought nothing less than a refounding of the republic. Today, however, this project is largely overlooked because it remained largely unfulfilled.

Alfonsín's election—the first that many Argentines could remember as not marred by violence or exclusion—not only signaled the return to democracy, it also marked the first electoral defeat of Peronism in forty years. This shift upended the logic of mainstream Argentine politics seemingly overnight at the onset of the new democratic era. Within Argentina, the rise of a benefactor state attuned to social justice is indelibly linked to the emergence of Peronism in the 1940s. The history that follows pushes these conversations far beyond their mid-twentieth-century origins by examining a decisive moment when the Peronist party was not in power, and state-led welfare regimes entered into worldwide crisis with the abatement of Cold War antagonisms and the collapse of socialism.

The pledges of Alfonsín's government conjured up the promises and social gains of the first Peronism. The period's legacies of expanded social welfare and rights often influenced the ways that individuals articulated their demands for new rights and protections in the years immediately following military rule. And yet the Peronist movement is decentered in this book. For readers of Argentine history, this necessitates an important exercise. Following the Justicialist Party's (PJ) electoral defeat in 1983, Peronism quickly regrouped to emerge as the most formidable challenger to the Alfonsín government and as a consolidated political party by the end of the decade.[23] This book examines these events, but often from the vantage point of actors outside of Peronism. The point of this narrative choice is to revise the sharp line that tends to be drawn between Peronist and other social agendas. By taking seriously Radical Party policy reforms in food security and welfare, we are able to understand how the centrist, "middle-class" Radical Party of Raúl Alfonsín sought to alter the dominance of Peronism through a redefinition of social rights and democracy. This also allows us to see how Peronism did not always reform itself from within, but rather in dialogue with the world around it and in conversation with other political forces. Ultimately, *alfonsinismo* helped to remake the Peronist party. The constrained political and economic climate in which the Alfonsín government operated often forced it to adopt positions that undermined its own vision for the democratic future. By the end of the decade, in the midst of hyperinflation and food riots, Peronist leaders could once again claim that they held sway in the realm of social justice, shortly before the installation of neoliberalism in the 1990s, paradoxically under the leadership of a Peronist government.

The blueprint for Argentina's democratic transition was as far-reaching and as ambitious as the structural constraints produced by military rule. In addition to the human rights abuses of the armed forces, the Alfonsín government also faced the burden of a national debt of over US$43 billion, 15 percent unemployment, and up to 25 percent of the population having "unsatisfied basic needs." These legacies came into focus only with the return to democracy. Indeed, the first two years of the Alfonsín presidency—a "democratic spring" of widespread possibility and popular support—also constituted a taking stock of what had been wrought by military rule.

In the standard narrative of the Alfonsín years, the hope and effervescence of democratic return gave way to the disillusionment of aborted justice and economic crisis. Accordingly, each promise of the new democracy was offset by a betrayal, which gradually undermined the legitimacy upon which the figure of Alfonsín—and with it the newly restored democracy—depended. The most notorious chapters in this history of promise and disenchantment began with the historic trials of the juntas and ended with the passage of impunity laws to halt prosecutions. In the fiscal realm, the bold initial attempts to renegotiate the nation's external debt receded in the face of the first privatizations of state enterprises, which defined economic life at the end of the last century. As with the return to democracy itself, the confluence of global and domestic conditions in which these events occurred was not of Alfonsín's making. But by the end of his presidency, the leader who had done so much to consolidate a more holistic vision of democracy saw its undoing based on the very measures adopted by his government. The exuberance of the "democratic spring" was equally matched by the widespread recognition that "democracy," far from being a panacea for a dolorous past, could also perpetuate and produce its own novel contradictions.

There is still much that satisfies about the narrative of hope and disillusionment that surrounds the Alfonsín government. But like the moniker "father of democracy," this history is also incomplete. We would do well to revisit the spaces in between the extremes of Alfonsín's extended moment on the national stage. We should take seriously the "failures" and more ambitious ventures, from the promise that no child would go hungry in Argentina ever again to the attempts to revive a benefactor state beyond Peronism, among others. Along with human rights prosecutions and the rule of law, these projects contained their own refoundational impulses and left their lingering imprints. The dramatic push and pull of the return to democracy, wedged as it was against the twilight of the Cold War and the dawn of the neoliberal age, saw attempts at a hegemonic project that ultimately eased the passage from one epoch to another.

OVERVIEW

The book is organized chronologically and thematically. The opening chapter investigates the breakdown of authoritarian rule. While the collapse of the military regime is often seen as a direct result of the Malvinas (Falklands) War, the chapter offers a fresh interpretation of the central role of Latin America's 1981–1982 debt crisis, which hastened the end of the dictatorship and shaped expectations for the democratic return. Chapter 2 turns to the presidential election of 1983. Raúl Alfonsín, the leader of the Radical Party, formulated a winning electoral platform that reflected a triple promise of human, social, and political rights, in the process besting Peronism, the movement most intimately linked with social justice in Argentina. Chapters 3 and 4 take an in-depth look at the Alfonsín government's attempts to fulfill campaign promises to eliminate hunger and restore economic stability. The PAN (Programa Alimentario Nacional), the flagship welfare program of the new democracy and the subject of chapter 3, attempted to curb hunger through deliveries of nonperishable goods to families in need. As the need for food grew more acute in light of the fiscal emergency, the food program exposed some of the shortcomings of the state's rights agenda, which contributed to the renovation of the Peronist party and the strengthening of a conservative sector that questioned the efficacy of a welfare state. Chapter 4 then turns to an understudied, though infamous, food scandal that shook the foundations of Argentina's democratic return. In 1988, following the government's purchase of thirty-eight thousand tons of frozen chicken from Eastern Europe, rumors of rotting poultry exploded in the media with accusations of government corruption and overreach. The incident, which came to be popularly known as the "Caso Mazzorín," served as a prequel to the neoliberal turn in the early 1990s. Chapter 5 brings together many of the book's overarching themes and is based on a close reading of over five thousand unpublished letters sent to Raúl Alfonsín from self-described "ordinary" Argentines over the course of the decade. Letter writers tested the limits of the language of human rights and laid bare the growing distance between their expectations and their daily lives in the face of a punishing economic climate and dwindling public resources. The concluding chapter analyzes the anatomy and political economy of the 1989 food uprisings. In the midst of a hyperinflationary spiral, the food riots unhinged the constituent parts of the ambitious rights agenda upon which the democratic transition had been based. The chapter also pushes Argentina's transition into the early 1990s through an exploration of how the government of Carlos Menem—in a remarkable reversal of his Peronist roots—used the specter of scarcity and social emergency to impose neoliberal policies, and with them a conception of political democracy radically divested from its social foundations.

1

The Breakdown of Authoritarian Rule

By 1981, the military junta was in trouble. During the half decade after the armed forces seized power in a bloody coup, the regime ruled Argentina through a sinister mixture of terror and economic austerity. But in 1981, the slow breakdown of authoritarian rule began. The free market reforms instituted by Finance Minister José Martínez de Hoz, which relied on speculative lending and an overvalued currency, came undone.[1] Small firms declared bankruptcy, factories shuttered their doors, and industrial workers lost jobs. Argentina's economic downturn coincided with the beginning of a regional debt crisis and Latin America's worst fiscal emergency since the Great Depression in the 1930s. The most vulnerable among Argentina's urban poor bore the brunt of the recession. Throughout the capital region surrounding Buenos Aires, *ollas populares* (soup kitchens) sprang up to address the growing need. In the Greater Buenos Aires township of Florencia Varela, one soup kitchen set up by the local diocese fed several hundred children daily, many of whose parents had recently joined the ranks of unemployed factory workers in the formerly prosperous manufacturing belts on the capital's outskirts. "These [soup kitchens] are not politically motivated, as some accuse us," the priest who ran the site declared, then went on to describe the situation in his town as unprecedented and getting worse by the day.[2]

The emergence of hunger in Argentina, a food-producing nation that had fed the world with meat and grains, represented one more alarming consequence of military rule. Even as food production and exports increased throughout the dictatorship, food access fell for the poor and marginalized sectors between 1976 and 1981, as wages were slashed and inflation climbed.[3] Yet economic crisis, as the priest who ran the soup kitchen implied, also provided an opening for oblique criticisms of the regime and new opportunities to imagine a future beyond military rule. The social emergency sparked by the junta's policies marked the beginning of the end of Argentina's most brutal dictatorship.

This chapter examines the breakdown of authoritarian rule between 1981 and 1983, a period that has received relatively little historical attention compared to the height of state terror in the 1970s and the years immediately following constitutional restoration in the 1980s. The period began with economic recession and a wave of grassroots mobilizations calling for the end of the dictatorship. It climaxed with Argentina's defeat at the hands of Great Britain during 1982's ill-fated Malvinas (Falkland) War, and it culminated in free elections and the inauguration of Raúl Alfonsín as president in December 1983. The collapse of Argentina's dictatorship is often seen as a direct result of the Malvinas War. In this view, the shock of Argentina's surrender to Great Britain jolted awake a civil society that then began to clamor for constitutional rule.[4] To be sure, the war represented a decisive chapter at the end of the dictatorship. But narratives that privilege the war tend to overlook the domestic events leading up to it and the central role that Latin America's impending debt crisis played in hastening the fall of the military regime and creating expectations for the return of democracy. Turning our attention to the reverberations of economic emergency disrupts standard accounts of the demise of the dictatorship and thus illuminates the popular demands and movements that also brought forth the eventual return to democratic life.

Though often overlooked in political analyses of the breakdown of authoritarian rule, the marches, land takeovers, soup kitchens, and neighborhood uprisings that gained force in the areas surrounding the capital played a significant role at the dictatorship's end. In the year leading up to the conflict with Great Britain in 1982, economic recession sparked an upsurge in popular mobilizations that opposed the military junta. Throughout the embattled industrial zones surrounding Buenos Aires, workers, priests, and shantytown residents, among others, made explicit connections between the material deprivations of daily life under military rule and the widespread violation of their basic economic, social, and political rights. The protests, which were gaining momentum by the time the Malvinas War began in April 1982, took their inspiration from hard-won battles for social rights and protections, most especially those achieved during the first period of Peronism (1945–1955), which had been defined by new entitlements and policies geared toward uplifting industrial workers. A central aim of the mobilizations in the early 1980s was to preserve and restore those protections, which the military regime had violently dismantled or significantly diminished. As this chapter argues, popular demands for the restoration of democracy evolved not only in relation to the immediacy of dictatorship or Argentina's defeat in war with Great Britain, but also in conversation with the memory of past struggles for social rights, which would come to shape the years following military rule.

Like the priest in Florencia Varela, protesters often expressed their grievances through anxiety about growing hunger, which fueled a moral language of outrage and exposed the military regime's empty claims to honor and prosperity. Housing issues, job loss, and an overall decline in quality of life also motivated individuals' decisions to join protests or to march against the military authorities. Taken together, these denunciations force a reassessment of the place of broader rights claims during the final years of the dictatorship. Since the early days of the regime, Argentina's tireless human rights movement had coordinated domestic and international campaigns against the junta and embedded the figure of the disappeared into the lexicon of global human rights. By 1981, popular mobilizations had begun to add new contours and momentum to campaigns against authoritarian rule. The protagonists of the uprisings analyzed here did not necessarily describe their grievances as human rights violations. Indeed, the preeminence of human rights in relation to constitutional return was not yet as fixed or as clear as it would become in the following years. Nonetheless, rights language broadly conceived lent new energy to historic demands for basic material needs in ways that linked political repression to impoverishment and boosted actions against the regime. The exposés of the socioeconomic emergency of 1981–1982 worked toward two related purposes, functioning as both condemnations of military rule and concrete calls for the restoration of political life prior to the outbreak of war in the Malvinas. In turn, the struggles to fulfill basic needs that emerged within the confines of the final years of authoritarianism informed rights claims well into the post-dictatorship era.

DEBT CRISIS AND POLITICAL OPENINGS

Since taking power in 1976, the junta had wielded a fierce repressive apparatus to annihilate its enemies and to initiate radical transformations of national economic life. For members of the armed forces, these projects mutually reinforced one another. The fiscal policies of the military regime sought to dismantle the developmentalist frameworks that had structured the Argentine economy since the 1930s.[5] Though not without their internal tensions and contradictions, the financial and military alliances at the helm of the Ministry of Economy ultimately succeeded in opening domestic markets to global capital through the liberalization of interest rates, high-risk bank lending and borrowing, reduced import tariffs, and a massive surge in public and private debt.[6] Between 1973 and 1979, private bank lending increased in Latin America from US$30 to $60 billion. In Argentina alone, debt more than doubled, from US$6 to $14 billion over that same period.[7] Yet contrary to general conceptions of the wholesale introduction of neoliberalism in Argentina, the regime never advocated outright privatization of the economy. In fact, state enterprises took on a majority of new debt in order to maintain high levels of public expenditure.[8] Nonetheless, neoliberal logics jibed with the refoundational goals of the National Reorganization Process (the junta's name for its project), which drew a straight line from populism, to economic crisis, to political and social subversion. The fiscal packages of the early years of the dictatorship combined short-term, anti-inflationary measures with a view to long-term structural readjustment. The policies aimed to displace the power of national manufacturing in favor of finance and to replace blue-collar workers with white-collar employees. Drastic economic adjustments correlated with extreme and violent attempts to reform Argentines themselves.

For a brief time, the schemes worked. The economic program of the junta led to immense short-term profits and an increase in capital flows, known better as the era of *plata dulce*, or sweet money. Many middle-class Argentines reaped the benefits of newfound prosperity as income values rose and purchasing power for the flood of imports increased. The regime wasted no time in putting the power of its propaganda mill behind the economic changes. In one television spot, a lone consumer stands next to an Argentine-made chair. When he sits down, it shatters instantly under his weight. Rattled, the man jumps up to see a flood of new chairs adorned with signs that say, "Made in . . ." crowding the screen as a calm voiceover states: "Before, competition was insufficient. We had good products, but buyers had to settle without being able to compare. Now, [the consumer] can choose from national products and imports alike." From the jubilant smile on the buyer's face as he peruses the new foreign-made chairs popping up on the screen, to the splintered pieces of wood with the "Industria nacional" sign in tatters on the floor, the choice, the ad makes clear, is no choice at all.[9]

The regime's fiscal measures lent themselves to purchases and trips abroad. However, prosperity was fleeting and was based mostly on speculation and an overvalued peso. The first signs of distress began in 1979, when the United States raised interest rates, which increased loan payments for debtor nations worldwide. Increased debt payments led in turn to more requests for loans and assistance. And since debt incurred over the 1970s was mostly in dollars, the real burden of the debt sharply increased. Mexico's eventual default on its debt in August 1982 set off a regional crisis that endured for the rest of the decade.[10] Yet even before the Mexican default, Argentines felt the effects domestically in the form of an increase in business shutdowns, job layoffs, and looming recession.[11]

By 1981, divisions had appeared within the ruling junta. The year began with a shift in leadership, with General Roberto Viola replacing Jorge Rafael Videla as de facto president. According to most observers at the time, the decision stemmed from the folly of Videla's economic policies in the face of mounting fiscal distress, in addition to international reprobation of the regime's human rights crimes.[12] Viola's economic measures fared no better than his predecessor's had, and he was ousted less than a year later on the cusp of the regional debt crisis, replaced by a hard-liner, General Leopoldo Galtieri, who vowed to restore the National Reorganization Process to its founding principles. Viola's short tenure was nonetheless significant, as the regime made several overtures to allow for the gradual regrouping of political parties and labor. Although still two years off, these events played a role in the regime's collapse and the return of democratic governance.

In the midst of economic decline and power struggles within the junta, political forces regrouped. In July 1981, the leaders of five of the country's main political parties came together to create the Multipartidaria, a coalition with designs on a transition to institutional rule, and the most forceful call from political elites for a return to democracy since the dictatorship began.[13] The group's first communiqué described its project in the context of "the most profound socio-economic crisis in the history of the country."[14] Prominent members of the Multipartidaria believed direct negotiations with the junta were essential for a political transition, even borrowing from the regime and the Catholic Church's calls for "national reconciliation." The political transition envisioned by the Multipartidaria in 1981 outlined a joint civilian and military endeavor. The coalition's first pronouncement only briefly referenced human rights and left out mention of state repression altogether. The absence of a more explicit treatment of the armed forces' crimes said something about the place of human rights in the vision of many political elites at the time, who believed that any intimation of legal redress or punishment for the armed forces would derail a return to constitutional rule.

For its part, the human rights movement, the most vocal force to denounce the regime, continued to mobilize. The Mothers and Grandmothers of the Plaza de Mayo, who had marched weekly since 1977 in the center of Buenos Aires to call for the return of their disappeared children and grandchildren, remained the most visible organizations among a wide-ranging movement made up of victims' relatives, survivors, and other public and religious figures. The year 1981 saw the Mothers' first March of Resistance, a twenty-four-hour march and vigil around the Plaza de Mayo, which drew several dozen Mothers and the watchful gaze of the authorities, who surrounded them.[15] The place of human rights during this first moment of political openings was in no way certain, however. It would take another year, when the regime's exit was assured, for massive crowds to join the marches waving the banners on human rights.

The political opportunities of 1981 also provided a space for renewed labor mobilization. The combative sector of the General Confederation of Labor, known as the CGT-Brasil, named after the street in Buenos Aires where its headquarters was located, intensified its organizing efforts with the goal of promoting an end to the dictatorship.[16] Its leader, Saúl Ubaldini, had led the first general strike against the regime in 1979, after making a name for himself at the helm of the union of beer industry workers. Equally important were cultural openings. In the year before the Malvinas War, Buenos Aires's effervescent music scene drew crowds to concert halls to hear the emerging idols of *rock nacional*. The British group Queen played to packed stadiums in Buenos Aires, Rosario, and Mar del Plata during its South American tour. At the Vélez stadium in Buenos Aires, army tanks surrounded the arena as the band belted anthems banned by the authorities. Shortly afterward, in February 1982, the folk singer Mercedes Sosa returned from exile. She celebrated her homecoming with ten days of sold-out shows and the release of a live album that became an instant hit and a marker of a decisive cultural shift.[17] Though the regime still firmly held the reins of power, these clamorings—in song and in the regrouping of political forces—reflected a national mood clearly looking toward a future beyond the regime.

POPULAR MOBILIZATION AND THE BREAKDOWN OF AUTHORITARIAN RULE

Amid these rumblings, mobilizations outside of the generally accepted centers of political and cultural activity in Buenos Aires played a vital role in forging popular expectations for the return to democratic life. Indeed, it was in the places that felt the full force of state terror—in terms of both physical violence and economic duress—that notions of a just society came together in ways that would reshape the political field at the end of the Malvinas War. This was especially apparent on the ground in the industrial townships of Greater Buenos Aires, as historic social struggles for housing, employment, and food were recast in light of the emergency caused by military rule.

The densely populated municipalities and townships of Greater Buenos Aires felt the acute impact of military rule. The areas that made up the southern industrial belt of the capital swelled between the 1930s and 1950s, spurred on by an industrial boom and a new wave of migration from the Argentine interior. Residents flocked to the expanding margins of the capital, seeking abundant factory work, social mobility, and the chance to benefit from the inclusive policies of a growing welfare state. It was in these municipalities that Peronism first flourished and the promise of new forms of social citizenship and national belonging were forged. Following the 1976 coup, low-wage earners and industrial workers bore the brunt of terror and free-market reforms.[18] The regime set out to reverse the social gains of the midcentury; between 1975 and 1980, manufacturing employment declined by 26 percent. And in the decade following the 1976 coup, fifteen thousand industrial installations went under.[19] Those workers who maintained their jobs nonetheless suffered real income losses as the soaring costs of daily life made the contradictions of the regime's policies ever more apparent. Unions, which had constituted the primary link between the working class and the promise of social citizenship since the advent of Peronism in the 1940s, also began to lose membership, declining by 23 percent between 1973 and 1984.[20]

Like the majority of industrial towns surrounding the capital, the township of Quilmes, one prominent site of mobilization located fifteen kilometers south of Buenos Aires, suffered during the dictatorship as factory workers, union organizers, and progressive members of the clergy were disappeared from their homes and factories. The local newspaper *El Sol* chronicled the effects of military rule on the urban landscape. As early as 1979, a smattering of articles noted a relatively new phenomenon taking hold in the center of the municipality. They reported a growing number of unemployed factory workers, almost always men, who took to the streets day after day, "taking odd day jobs" (*haciendo changas*) to make ends meet. The articles varied in their level of sensational and salacious detail. Uniting all of the stories, however, was a familiar arc of long careers in local factories, the shock of job loss, and the very real drama of devising new ways to support families. In manufacturing areas around the capital, industries were finding it more difficult to compete with the influx of cheap foreign goods. Factories shut down their machines, fired workers, and bolted their doors. The specific figures for Quilmes and the surrounding municipalities are difficult to come by, but to give one example, in mid-1982 the local Peugeot factory closed its doors, and forty-five hundred workers lost their jobs in one fell swoop.[21] Headlines reporting on such events remained mainstays throughout the late 1970s and early 1980s, illuminating the human toll of deindustrialization in the southern belt surrounding the city of Buenos Aires.

Against the backdrop of this crisis of labor and the working class, a growing number of protests in Greater Buenos Aires gained national attention. In Quilmes, local church leaders scheduled a day of protest for August 1981.[22] Posters announced the event as the Marcha del hambre (Hunger March) and encouraged participants to bring donations of food in a collective call for "bread and work."[23] The goal of the event, according to flyers, was to "[shine a light on] the urgent situation facing the workers of our diocese . . . to come together in solidarity, and to raise hope."[24] The bishop of Quilmes, Jorge Novak, had risen to prominence as one of the few leaders of the Argentine Catholic Church to denounce the human rights abuses of the armed forces.[25] In the weeks leading up to the Hunger March, Novak sent a letter to the police commissioner in Quilmes requesting authorization for both the march and a celebratory mass. As with other actions organized by the activist bishop, police documents reveal that security forces suspected the day would attract "agitators and/or union activists, who [would] use the event as a platform for their own aims."[26] Yet according to a memo from before the march, police were not worried that "subversive elements were involved—as of yet." The real concern of the local police was that the march would be passing by the *villas miserias* (shantytowns) and the growing population of pauperized residents recently arrived in the municipality.[27] Another result of the economic crisis of 1981 was the further growth of the slums and a burgeoning land takeover movement in the municipality, which put local security forces on edge. The police commissioner ultimately sent word that the march was prohibited. As far as the mass was concerned, however, he saw no "reasons why it should prove a problem."[28]

The Hunger March was not the first diocese event that the police had prohibited in the municipality. The year before, Bishop Novak had planned a public mass to celebrate the pope's mediation of the conflict between Chile and Argentina over the Beagle Channel, which had brought the two nations to the brink of conflict. The local police had prohibited that mass for "security reasons." The Hunger March, Novak claimed, was different, and its prohibition was even more hypocritical given the current social emergency. He wrote of the police ban of the Hunger March: "This is all the more shocking as today we read in La Nación [newspaper] the declarations of the President of the Republic, confirming 'that the Argentine people and government must denounce all discriminatory racial and religious practices to promote the defense of the rights of all human beings.'"[29] Novak's reference to the junta's notoriously cynical use of the language of rights was a commentary on the gap between the rhetoric of the regime and the reality of state terror and abuse. At the same time, the bishop's somewhat sly evocation of the simple act of "walking in the streets" for sustenance and jobs was no small matter in the context of a regime that sought to eradicate such rights. In Novak's estimation, and increasingly for many Argentines, food and work were fundamental human rights that had been systematically violated.

Though the march was banned, the mass went on as scheduled. On the day of the service, police estimated that a crowd of about 1,200 attended, while church officials and the press reported between 2,000 to 4,000 individuals gathered at the San Cayetano parish in Quilmes.[30] The choice of venue sent a clear message; San Cayetano holds a special place in the pantheon of popular religious figures as the patron saint of labor, drawing annual pilgrimages for peace, bread, and work. Before the mass, CGT representatives from the neighboring towns of Berazategui and Florencia Varela distributed packages of food and clothing among attendees. Recently unemployed workers, laywomen who coordinated soup kitchens, members of the clergy, and leaders of neighborhood associations linked arms in orations. Those gathered reflected a cross-section of individuals who felt the social emergency firsthand and who simultaneously attempted to keep at bay its more damaging effects.

The mass began in the late afternoon, and it ended with the crowd singing the national anthem.[31] Because of the size of the church, which could not hold more than a few hundred, attendees spilled into the street. The visual impact of the gathering made for an impressive sight in the midst of a regime ban on public gatherings. Police presence was strong and intimidating, and clergy later recalled that many more people were afraid to attend. Nonetheless, the mass went on peacefully into the early evening. Although the original plan for the march through the streets had been prohibited, the event accomplished the goal of assembling a crowd to denounce the mounting crisis. The singing of the national anthem also signaled that despite the local focus of the event, participants' sights were set on a broader protest against the regime.

The Hunger March generated interest and publicity beyond the municipality, drawing national attention to the social situation in Greater Buenos Aires. The newspaper *Clarín* provided extensive coverage of what it described as Novak's "dramatic and searing" sermon, which "lash[ed] out against those responsible for the current social situation."[32] During the mass, the bishop placed emphasis on one of the most visible markers of the crisis and the ostensible motivation for the day's event: hunger. "Is anyone shocked," he asked, "by the talk of hunger among us? Do we dare speak out against this social scourge which has already entered many homes in this diocese, and which is knocking on the doors of many more? Brothers and sisters, there is hunger. Today many families get by on *yerba mate* and a bit of bread and crackers."[33]

The discovery of hunger in places such as Greater Buenos Aires had already begun to touch a nerve. Though hunger had long existed in rural parts of the national territory and in more informal urban settlements, by the beginning of the 1980s it began to threaten working people in the industrial suburbs of the nation's major cities. Added to the national headlines about impending recession, troubling rumors of acute hardship accompanied the financial news. In the face of rising unemployment and a constriction of the manufacturing economy, soup kitchens sprang up in urban centers to address the growing food insecurity of large numbers of residents.[34] Most disconcerting of all, these realities were edging closer to the capital region. Novak, among many others, expressed dismay that in a food-producing country "as rich as Argentina," citizens lacked food.[35] Hunger, a hard fact of daily life for many Argentines, was a potent symbol of the social breakdown caused by military rule.[36] Researchers later found that meat consumption—an emblem of the social progress of the mid-twentieth century—dropped by almost 20 percent over the course of the dictatorship, with much steeper declines among lower-income sectors.[37] By contrast, yerba mate, the traditional tea that also acts as an appetite suppressant and forms a staple of popular diets, saw a spike in consumption over those same years.[38] *Clarín* reported that scores of Argentine children lived on the diet of the *desocupado* (the unemployed). "They have never known the taste of meat, and are fed on mate alone."[39]

Hunger reflected a socioeconomic reality in the final years of the regime. Yet it also functioned as a way to malign the armed forces without direct reference to state terror. Talk of hunger evinced a national emergency that many Argentines could relate to—and voice indignation over—even if their lives had not been directly impacted by physical violence or acute hardship. In a letter to the newspaper *Diario Popular*, a local resident expressed his frustration: "The police banned the Hunger March in Quilmes. What a shame that the police cannot ban the hunger of the people who organized the march. That would solve all the government's problems. The police can only make attempts to stop free men from exercising their rights."[40] Individuals like this letter writer used the deterioration of their material well-being to expose the recklessness of the regime and to demand a restoration of rights—a process that this writer described as inevitable. The frank letter, signed by the author, would have been unthinkable only a few years before.

Following the Hunger March, the pace of demonstrations in and around the capital accelerated. The most anti-dictatorial factions of the labor movement gained force and numbers. In November 1981, the CGT-Brasil organized a protest for "peace, bread, and work," which drew ten thousand people to the neighborhood of Liniers, home of the annual San Cayetano pilgrimage. Echoing the aims of the Hunger March in Quilmes, organizers called on participants to "pray for peace, the restitution of the rights of civility and the reactivation of the productive apparatus."[41]

Mobilizations occurred outside of traditional labor channels as well. One of the most dramatic expressions of this was a series of land takeovers that took place in the municipalities of Almirante Brown and Quilmes, where an estimated twenty thousand people occupied a stretch of land over five kilometers long. The groups included the recently unemployed, migrants from the interior, and an array of precariously employed workers—carpenters, mechanics, and others—who had been pushed out of Buenos Aires due to a combination of highway construction, shantytown eradication, and punishing rental laws, which made the capital uninhabitable for lower-income and poor sectors.[42] The new residents set out to create neighborhoods, buy plots of land, and secure municipal services, appealing directly to state authorities for their entitlement to legal protections. In effect, they sought to reinsert themselves into a society from which they had literally and figuratively been expelled. As one participant summarized, "[We] are people without a roof over our heads. We are the workers and the unemployed individuals who produce (and produced) the riches of this nation. . . . Our right to life, which is defended by the Constitution, is in serious jeopardy."[43] By placing in stark relief the most extreme forms of hardship under military rule, the land occupations buoyed the broader moment of uprisings, even as they exposed deeper, more intractable structural crises.

The demands of shantytown residents were not limited to the most marginal sectors of Argentine society, however. In the months following the land takeovers, middle- and working-class neighborhoods throughout Greater Buenos Aires revolted against a precipitous decline in public services. Beginning in 1978, the regime transferred responsibility for public services from national authorities to provincial governments. As a result of decentralization, municipalities began to outsource trash collection and street cleaning, among other essential services, to private enterprises. The companies charged exorbitant fees and converted many municipalities into centers of graft and speculation. Local citizens bore the burden of tax increases in order to maintain contracts for deteriorated services, which they increasingly refused to (or were unable) to pay. By early 1982, many municipalities were on the brink of ruin. Shopkeepers, pensioners, housewives, and students, among others, moved to the forefront of public demonstrations to denounce local authorities and cost-of-living increases. These *vecinazo* uprisings, as Inés González Bombal has shown, gained momentum after the Malvinas War, but even before the outbreak of the conflict they had revealed deep networks of neighborhood associations that functioned as intermediaries between citizens and municipal governments during the dictatorship, which were now demanding civic redress and restitution.[44] In a concise statement that would have been familiar throughout several Greater Buenos Aires townships at the time, the Federación de Sociedades de Fomento (Federation of Development Societies) of Lomas de Zamora declared, "We are suffering . . . due to the violation of official projects and agreements, and eternal promises that are never fulfilled."[45]

Seen from afar, the capital region was a crucible of unrest on the eve of the Malvinas War. To be sure, authoritarian rule did not affect all communities at the same pace or with the same severity. Yet uniting popular uprisings—from union marches, to shantytown mobilizations, to neighborhood protests—was the economic violence of the regime. Demands for housing, industrial work, public services, and an end to hunger were affirmations of the right to a dignified life, which five years of military rule had torn asunder. In late March 1982, the center of Buenos Aires was flooded with protesters—the largest number since the dictatorship began—as an estimated fifty thousand workers, human rights activists, urban professionals, and politicians joined the CGT-Brasil in a historic march and strike for "Peace, Bread, and Work."[46] Similar protests took place throughout the country. In Buenos Aires, the armed forces detained hundreds in a show of force that recalled the bloodiest moments of the regime. Though often heralded as the beginning of the end of the dictatorship, in reality the march saw the culmination of several years of local and national movements against the junta. The call to peace, bread, and work demonstrated the powerful convening force of the socioeconomic toll of the regime, one that was intimately bound up with the realities of state terror. The signs and slogans of the day transmitted an unequivocal message: "*se va a acabar la dictadura militar!*" (the military dictatorship will end). Three days later, on April 2, 1982, war erupted in the South Atlantic.

TRANSITION TO A TRANSITION

The Malvinas War opened wide a half decade of impunity, abuse, and economic mismanagement.[47] Since the nineteenth century, Argentina's claims over the remote and rocky islands had fueled various nationalist causes. The goal to wrest the territory from Great Britain was the junta's final attempt to restore legitimacy to the National Reorganization Process. The seventy-four-day conflict marked a surreal dénouement to the dictatorship. Almost immediately following the march for peace, bread, and work, the center of Buenos Aires filled again with many of the same individuals, now clamoring for an Argentine victory in the South Atlantic.

Widespread public support for the war did not translate into support for the junta, however.[48] Human rights groups used the war as an opportunity to further expose the regime's crimes. The Mothers of the Plaza de Mayo contributed one of the most enduring refrains of the conflict, which affirmed "the Malvinas are Argentine, so are the disappeared." Labor leader Saúl Ubaldini, who had been arrested during the CGT march, traveled to Malvinas to attend the inauguration of the newly installed military governor. He and other union leaders used the opportunity to highlight the fact that the working class made up the rank and file of Argentina's fighting forces. In these ways, the principal victims of the regime were inscribed into the national cause and made public. Although voices of dissent against the military's campaign were few and muffled, the regime imposed a virtual media blackout on updates from the front. British forces quickly routed the Argentine conscripts, who arrived unprepared and lacking basic supplies. The restricted news of growing losses only made the shock of Argentina's eventual defeat more bitter. Images of soldiers freezing and underfed on the frigid islands, and the slow trickle of information regarding the military's misadventure, were the final blows to a weary public, whose own domestic battles to fulfill basic needs had already discredited the junta. On June 14, 1984, Argentina surrendered to Great Britain. In July the military regime announced its withdrawal from power and plans for the return to constitutional rule.

As we have seen, the junta was already weakened before the outbreak of fighting. A week before Argentine forces launched their attack on the islands, the junta announced a plan for the reorganization of political parties, with March 1984 as the projected date for open elections.[49] Argentina's defeat in the South Atlantic sped up a process of authoritarian breakdown that had already begun, and it constrained, though it did not totally reverse, the military's ability to fix the terms of democratic return. Military loss exposed the mendacity of the junta's claims to the guardianship of the nation. Yet even in retreat, the regime still managed to wield control over the timeline of the transition.[50] Over the long months of political reorganization after the war, rumors of possible coups surfaced frequently. Given Argentina's long history of military takeovers, they were not totally unfounded. Several prominent politicians associated with the Multipartidaria, which played a prominent role in talks with military authorities, favored an extended transition to elections as a concession to the junta and as a way to ensure that the regime would actually relinquish power. Following Argentina's surrender to Great Britain, it took close to six months to settle on the official date for democratic elections. Negotiations for the transfer of power from military to civilian rule continued through the early months of 1983, with presidential elections finally set for October 30 of that year.[51]

Eventually, postwar dilemmas and the debates about their possible resolution were channeled into what would become a protracted electoral contest for the presidency. Though campaigning did not pick up full steam until June 1983, when most of the major parties elected their nominees, the opening acts of the election began almost immediately after the junta announced its withdrawal from power. On July 1, 1982, the regime lifted a ban on political organizing in place since 1976, which allowed political parties to regroup. In August 1982, parties began to recruit new affiliates, and over the following months they scrambled to build voting rosters according to revised election rules and new party statutes. By April 1983, almost three million Argentines had formally affiliated with a political party.

In the almost ten years since the nation's last open elections, the panorama of political life had shifted in significant ways. Not only had the military been discredited in defeat; but the principal political figures of the second half of the twentieth century were also no longer present. The deaths of Juan Perón in 1974 and Ricardo Balbín, the leader of the Radical Party, in 1981 opened the nation's two most powerful parties to aspiring contenders jockeying for control. Even more significant, the demographics of the voting public had also transformed, with a generation of younger voters who came of age during the dictatorship inspired by the opportunity to participate in and define a new era in national life. Voting and the heady onset of presidential campaigning were not the only signs of change after the Malvinas War, but the long years of proscription and the absence of basic political rights quickly made the ballot box one of the first battles of the coming transition.

Sixteen months passed between the end of the Malvinas War and the October 1983 elections. The postwar period was marked by nightmarish revelations of the military's crimes, the deepening debt crisis, and the acceleration of popular mobilizations. These headlines competed with alarming news of the social effects of the economic crisis gripping the nation. In Quilmes, site of the 1981 Hunger March, for example, Bishop Novak declared the diocese in a "state of emergency," launching a solidarity campaign to deal with ongoing job losses, child malnutrition, and a spike in cases of tuberculosis.[52] Novak repeated a by then familiar lament to a reporter: "This is a country that has the most fundamental resource of all: food. It is a country that should be the breadbasket to the world, with an almost infinite number of resources. It is an aberration that there are people who go to bed hungry, often without having eaten anything at all."[53] The bishop painted a vivid picture of the social violence that accompanied military rule. During the dictator-ship, the degradation of social life had been an open secret in the national press, thinly veiled or buried in the back pages of newspapers among "lifestyle" pieces. With the regime in retreat following the Malvinas War, tallying the negative impact of the dictatorship on ordinary Argentines moved to the headlines. Implicit in the widespread coverage of human rights abuses, fiscal crisis, and hunger was an assumption that the upcoming democratic government would put a definitive end to those scourges. Novak pushed expectations even further. In sharp contrast to his present surroundings of industrial decline, his commentary tapped into a long-standing trope of Argentine bounty. Many Argentines linked the imminent return of democracy to the restoration of welfare and plenitude.

The aftermath of the junta's military defeat also seemed to fix one of the most widespread and enduring assumptions about the coming transition: if authoritari-anism was responsible for five decades of political instability in Argentina, it fol-lowed that the embrace of institutional democracy would serve as the antidote to state violence and provide guarantees of a just, peaceful society. *Gente* magazine, whose editorial board had been in firm alignment with the junta, summed up the postwar sentiment: "We left behind the triumphalism of war, which many thought would change everything, and embraced the triumphalism of democracy, as if it were another magic fix-it-all formula."[54] The maxim "dictatorship versus democ-racy" eased the sense of a break with a past that many were anxious to leave behind. The drama of war and the ignominy of military surrender heightened a hopeful sense of new beginnings. Despite pronouncements about the swift remaking of political life after the war, however, there was no immediate shift in values or fore-gone conclusion about the contours of Argentina's coming democracy.[55]

And yet some baseline expectations for democratic restoration had been forged before the war, in the everyday forms in which the social and economic violence of dictatorship were experienced and addressed on the national margins. In Greater Buenos Aires, the protagonists of popular mobilizations against the regime linked civic claims and social justice through an incipient rights discourse that pushed forward calls for democratization. The Malvinas War did not remake the Argentine public life overnight. It did, however, deepen a general antiauthoritarian consensus and rights discourse that linked well-being with democratic restora-tion. The roots of this idea first emerged via the extension of welfare and social protections at midcentury. By the end of the Malvinas War, the memory of these past struggles electrified calls for the return to democracy. Combined with the refoundational impulse of the postwar moment, the principles of social rights, justice, and human dignity shaped the political field in the months leading to con-stitutional restoration.

2

The Campaign for a
Democratic Argentina

When Ana Pérez de Vera cast her vote in the presidential election on October 30, 1983, she accompanied her ballot with a letter to the candidate of her choice, Raúl Alfonsín. In her brief note, the eighty-five-year old widow and seamstress explained that she had been working since she was thirteen, and now that her vision was failing her, she hoped that Alfonsín could "find the kindness" to grant her a pension. Pérez de Vera's decision to vote for Alfonsín surprised members of her family. As she explained, "I was a strong Peronist. . . . I was for Perón and Evita." But after failing to secure a pension under the government of Isabel Perón (1974–1976), her support for the movement waivered: "[The Peronists] slammed the door in my face and now I have stomped them [le pisotié] with my vote." But her decision did not stem from frustration alone. For Ana Pérez de Vera, Alfonsín also seemed to offer her the same benefits that Peronism once had. As she followed Alfonsín's campaign on television, she was drawn in by the candidate's calls for full employment for women, pensions, and retirement funds for housewives. "I couldn't speak to him, but I felt like he was speaking to me." And so, as Ana entered the voting station in October 1983, she resolved to take a chance and to cast her vote for Alfonsín and the Radical Party. After all, she concluded, "Perón always said that it was better to do than to promise."[1]

While most accounts attribute Alfonsín's 1983 electoral victory to his pledges to restore the rule of law and uphold human rights after seven years of a criminal military regime, Ana Pérez de Vera's letter, with its references to pensions and social welfare, also suggests that Alfonsín's appeal was more wide-ranging than is generally considered.[2] Scholars of the return to democracy have tended to downplay Alfonsín's social agenda in favor of his commitment to constitutionalism.[3] For

Ana Pérez de Vera, however, these were not mutually exclusive projects. To cast a vote, she believed, would guarantee for her a measure of economic security. In addition to promises to prosecute the armed forces and rebuild institutions, Raúl Alfonsín's popularity reflected expectations that political rights, once restored, would also bring forth an era of material well-being. Yet Alfonsín's presidential win was anything but a foregone conclusion. In October 1983, his victory stunned the political field by besting the Peronist party in the movement's first electoral defeat in open presidential elections. He did so in part, as this chapter argues, by adapting a Peronist message of social rights and justice to the realities of life at the end of the military regime.

In 1983, Argentines defined democracy not only by voting, but also through the measure of the decline in their lives during the dictatorship. State terror had relied on disappearance, torture, abductions, robbery, and exile to demobilize the population. In the quotidian realm, too, the impact of the regime's economic policies had incited fear and uncertainty. The images of hungry children and struggling workers from Greater Buenos Aires discussed in the previous chapter were shocking; however, they were not isolated snapshots of impoverishment. The social toll of the dictatorship manifested itself in malnutrition, unemployment, and foreclosures, among others, cutting across broad sectors. Alfonsín issued a call for valid elections and individual political freedoms in addition to a strong state to guarantee justice and the public good. This combination represented the democratic antidote to terror and economic disarray.

As Alfonsín generated more enthusiasm over the course of 1982–1983, he addressed the suffering and economic pain wrought by military rule better than his competitors did, most especially the Peronist party, the political movement traditionally associated with social justice in Argentina. At the dictatorship's end, many Argentines linked Peronism to a legacy of instability and military repression. Alfonsín exploited this belief throughout his campaign. But he also revived a traditional Peronist message for the post-dictatorship era and in the process gained support in Peronist strongholds such as Greater Buenos Aires. He put forward a convincing platform proposing that together institutional democracy and social justice could put an end to endemic political crisis and authoritarianism. Such an undertaking involved a specific rethinking of national political life and a reconciliation of the perceived antagonisms between political liberalism and social rights. This democratic future imagined by Alfonsín, which was entwined with plans to prosecute the armed forces for their crimes and to rebuild democratic institutions, shaped his mandate and the standard against which his government would be judged. His platform reflected a bold triple promise of human, social, and political rights. Following seven years of military rule, these were ideals that many Argentines could identify with—even those whose lives had not been directly affected by state violence or impoverishment.

"THE YOUNGEST MEMBER OF THE
OLD POLITICAL GUARD"

Long before Argentines associated Raúl Alfonsín with the return to democracy, a journalist had described him in a 1979 interview as "the youngest member of the old political guard."[4] It was a fitting description. A lawyer from the town of Chascomús in the province of Buenos Aires, Alfonsín formally entered politics in the 1950s in the context of a Radical Civic Union, or Radical Party (UCR), in flux. By the mid-twentieth century, the nation's oldest political party was struggling to come to terms with its loss of footing and reach following the ascendance of Peronism. Alfonsín's initial forays into elected office revolved around the internal party splits of a diminished UCR.[5]

The beginning of Alfonsín's political career also overlapped with the final, bloody months of Juan Perón's second presidency. In June 1955, an insurrectionary band of naval officers bombed the Plaza de Mayo in the center of Buenos Aires in an attempt to topple Perón's government. In the wake of the massacre, which left three hundred civilians dead, Perón had members of the opposition arrested. Alfonsín, then a member of the Chascomús town council, was himself briefly jailed. Like most of his fellow Radicals, Alfonsín welcomed the insurrection. He sided with national party leaders such as Arturo Frondizi, Ricardo Balbín, and Oscar Alende, who supported the military coup and the de facto government of the Revolución Libertadora, the military regime that ousted Perón and sent him into an eighteen-year exile. Like many Radicals in the early 1950s, Alfonsín condemned what he believed were the fascistic tendencies of Peronism and its persecution of political rivals.[6] Though his view of Peronism shifted over the coming decades, out of both necessity and his own changing political beliefs, Alfonsín never waivered in his disdain for Peronism's more corporatist elements, which he blamed for endemic political instability. Alfonsín recalled feeling a sense of "liberation" when Perón was finally overthrown in September 1955.[7]

Alfonsín's political star rose in the turbulent decade of civilian and military governments that followed Perón's overthrow. In 1958, after four years in municipal politics, he was elected to the Buenos Aires provincial congress; he was then elected to the national congress in 1963. In 1965, he became the head of the UCR–Buenos Aires party committee. Throughout these years, Alfonsín negotiated the schisms that divided the UCR during the presidencies of fellow Radicals Arturo Frondizi (1958–1962) and Arturo Illia, whose own government was deposed by another military coup in 1966. The Radical Party split over how and to what extent it should work with Peronism.[8] Alfonsín aligned with the most anti-Peronist wing of the party. For several years, he remained loyal to its leader, party boss Ricardo Balbín, who once famously declared that he would rather "lose 1,000 governments" than negotiate with the Peronists.[9] Eventually, Alfonsín broke with Balbín and ran for his party's nomination for the presidential election of 1973. Though he lost to Balbín, out of that defeat emerged Renovación y Cambio (Renovation and Change), a party faction led by Alfonsín that solidified his growing influence within the UCR and brought together a coalition of collaborators and advisers who formed part of Alfonsín's administration a decade later.

Raúl Alfonsín may be best remembered for his anti-dictatorial stance during the 1970s and 1980s, but many of his political positions were forged in the context of the military regime that preceded the Dirty War. The 1966 overthrow of Arturo Illia left a deep imprint on Alfonsín and the evolution of his antiauthoritarian beliefs. In the polarized climate of the late 1960s and early 1970s, when across the political spectrum a growing number of Argentines rejected the premise of a liberal party system that many believed had expired, Alfonsín and his cohort called for a defense of institutions and representative democracy. The Alfonsín-led wing of the party promoted a platform that placed it squarely within the ranks of social democracy and avoided the language of revolutionary upheaval.[10] Yet Alfonsín's Renovation and Change movement also couched its platform in many of the same terms as left-wing movements of the day—in favor of "national liberation" and "anti-imperialist" in nature—a political future that Alfonsín believed could only be realized through the ballot box. This stance also rejected the secondary position of the Radical Party in political life. In making their arguments, Alfonsín and his supporters believed that the UCR could reclaim the political clout and constituents that had been lost to Peronism.[11]

By the early 1970s, Alfonsín's collaborators included law school peers and congressional colleagues. This close-knit circle worked with Alfonsín over the course of the next decade, becoming key advisers and cabinet members during his presidency. He also began to enjoy the support of a younger generation of new party affiliates, who sought to rebuild the ranks of the Radical Party in universities. In 1968, these young party hopefuls created an organization called the Junta Coordinadora Nacional (JCR), or the Coordinadora, as it became known, which aligned with Alfonsín. As revolutionary movements gained momentum in universities and student centers, the Radical Party activists of the Coordinadora represented a curious anomaly. One observer noted, "During a period of generational conflicts, they followed the footsteps of their fathers into the ranks of the Radical Party."[12] This description rightly reflected the profile of the youngest members of the nation's oldest political party, who were staid, traditional, and more conservative in aspect and mores than their New Left counterparts. The new party hopefuls were not immune, however, to the markers of youth culture, donning long hair or taking part in sexual experimentation. Keen observers of the changes in the world around them, they were sympathetic to African liberation movements and celebrated the triumph of the Cuban Revolution and the election of Salvador Allende in Chile.[13] Like Alfonsín, they differed most notably from their contemporaries because they wanted to salvage the party system and revive the Radical Party as part of a project for "Argentine liberation."[14] This particular political ethos of young Radicals located them on the margins of the revolutionary era. It also uniquely positioned them to survive the next decade of political terror and to gradually rise through the ranks of the Radical Party. Throughout the dictatorship in the 1970s, the organizational strategies they had incorporated during the days of their student activism helped maintain and extend Radical Party bases in the midst of widespread repression, forming the basis of their growing allegiance to Alfonsín and their eventual participation in his campaign and government.

Despite the formal suspension of political life after the dictatorship began in 1976, Raúl Alfonsín, like many politicians, remained active. He maintained a public presence throughout the late 1970s, publishing when he could. He returned to his law practice and used his influence to defend a handful of political prisoners, even meeting with his old schoolmate, Albano Harguindeguy, interior minister during the military regime, to secure the safety of leaders of the Coordinadora. Critically, he participated in the growing human rights movement as a member of the Permanent Assembly of Human Rights (APDH), founded in 1975, and maintained Radical Party networks with the support of the Coordinadora and his most trusted colleagues.[15] By the early 1980s, when the regime began to show signs of decay, Alfonsín and his cohort formed part of a heterogeneous oppositional front of political parties, unions, and human rights organizations that began to play a vocal role in calling for a democratic return.

In their later recollections of Argentina's descent into terror, Alfonsín and his collaborators would flaunt their calls for temperance, implying that they had foreseen the extremes that state violence would reach following the 1976 coup.[16] It would be a mistake, however, to construe this position as political prescience. Alfonsín and his growing cadre of advisers and supporters caused more of a stir within the Radical Party than within a political climate hurtling toward violent confrontation. The limited reach of Alfonsín's reformist message—not its originality or foresight—spared his cohort the worst forms of repression following the March 1976 coup. As formal political life began to resume after the Malvinas War, Alfonsín took full advantage of the shift in public mood in favor of democratic institutions.

In June 1982, as the Malvinas War came to an end, Alfonsín was known as one of the few outspoken critics of the conflict, which he labeled a reckless and doomed endeavor. Even before the end of the fighting, he called for "the immediate creation of a civilian transitional government."[17] Though the plan did not materialize, Alfonsín's objections to the war set him apart from other political elites, the majority of whom lent their support to the military adventure. When plans were put in motion for the return to constitutional governance, Alfonsín's opposition to the war afforded him a legitimacy that his counterparts lacked, and this allowed him to confront the armed forces, Peronism, and internal Radical Party rivals all at once.[18] Over the course of the sixteen-month period encompassing the junta's announcement of its inglorious withdrawal from power, the onset of presidential campaigning, and the elections of October 1983, the Alfonsín-led wing of the Radical Party designed a democratic future—and a winning electoral platform—that promised a break with Argentina's authoritarian past, as well as a broadly defined notion of rights that responded to expectations for individual liberties as well as social well-being.

THE EMERGENCE OF *ALFONSINISMO*

But as preparations for constitutional return got under way following the Malvinas War, few would have predicted that Raúl Alfonsín would ever win the presidency. A mid-career politician and prominent member of the Radical Party, in mid-1982 he was still better known within his party than outside of it. Nonetheless, Alfonsín took an early lead in channeling the popular expectations and anxieties of the coming transition. On July 16, 1982, shortly after the military regime lifted a ban on political gatherings, Alfonsín organized a rally at the Argentine Boxing Federation in the center of Buenos Aires. According to some estimates, up to four thousand people crowded into the venue to hear him speak. Another three thousand gathered outside in the wintry night air next to speakers set up at the last minute to blast the event into the streets. Behind the elevated stage, a banner announced the rallying cry of the evening, and mimeographed pamphlets floated from the rafters; "Let's Take Back the Nation with Democracy and Participation!" they declared.[19] Earlier in the day, event organizers had scrambled to finalize the preparations, spacing chairs throughout the vast hall. Many worried they would not attract enough people to fill the space.[20]

Alfonsín's fifty-minute speech reflected the frustrations of many Argentines in the aftermath of the Malvinas War. Every day, new details emerged about the mistreatment and neglect of soldiers returning from the South Atlantic, the mass graves of disappeared victims of state terror, and the contested timeline for the restoration of constitutional government. The situation facing Argentina was not "an ideological problem," Alfonsín proclaimed; it was "life or death" itself.[21] Seated in the balcony, members of the human rights organization Mothers of the Plaza de Mayo, the evening's most prominent attendees, listened as Alfonsín called for a "moral response" to the disappeared and as he addressed all Argentine mothers who had "suffered the on-going pain of seeing [their] children recruited by the guerrillas, punished by state repression, or driven to war and the humiliation of defeat."[22] Turning finally to the military junta, he condemned the unjust economic policies that had plunged "workers and young people into poverty" and warned, "there will not be democracy without democratic armed forces."[23] Amid the rising tide of chants and songs, the rally foreshadowed the tenor of the months leading up to the October 1983 presidential election with a vocal demand to remake a political system based on "morality" and "ethics."

The Boxing Federation rally was not the first, and certainly not the largest, demonstration in and around Buenos Aires at the time. Just a few weeks before, thousands of demonstrators had met with violent repression during a protest following Argentina's surrender to Great Britain. Despite its small size compared to the growing mobilizations sweeping the country, the Boxing Federation rally marked an important turning point in the long struggle against the dictatorship. It was the first semisanctioned political meeting since the official lifting of a ban on political gatherings. As such, the rally was also a projection for the immediate future, an opening—real and symbolic—of Argentine political life following six years of military rule, and the unofficial launch of the presidential campaign that would culminate in Alfonsín's inauguration in December 1983.

From the night of the Boxing Federation rally, Alfonsín gradually began to build momentum, not only besting internal Radical Party rivals but also upending—if only briefly and in ways that would condition the trajectory of his government—the historic dominance of the armed forces and Peronism in Argentine politics. Radical memories of the Boxing Federation rally play on party mythology of the UCR as the erstwhile defender of democratic institutions. Alfonsín drew upon this historical memory, capitalizing on renewed popular demands for institutional democracy following the violent suspension of public life.[24] By the end of 1982, Alfonsín's public appearances and rallies, which attracted ever-larger crowds and attention, followed a familiar pattern. The starting premise of his stump speeches evoked Argentina's decade-long political crisis, dating to the chaotic presidency of Isabel Perón and the military coup of March 1976. Alfonsín drew stark contrasts between this recent civil strife and its foil—a restored republic guided by adherence to the constitution. This "democratic commitment," as he termed it, depended on each individual of the body politic rejecting the extremes of both right-wing authoritarianism and left-wing militancy. One hallmark of his rallies was a collective reading of the preamble to the constitution. The theatrical gesture moved crowds, as it also underscored a guiding principle of Alfonsín's message that from constitutionalism all else would follow to put an end to Argentina's endemic breach of institutions.

Upon first glance, Alfonsín's rising popularity took root in a standard platform of political liberalism, grounded in a notion of ethics and decency, with Alfonsín at its symbolic center. In 1983, however, the promise of restored democratic institutions was inextricably tied up with the response to the economic and social suffering caused by the dictatorship. As 1983 began, the economic situation continued to deteriorate, with the ongoing effects of the regional economic crisis now being fully felt. The seventh anniversary of the military coup on March 24, 1983, came and went with no official message or fanfare as had been the case in years past, the day overshadowed by news of the rising cost of living—13 percent in February 1983 alone—and alarming stories about the debt incurred over the course of the military regime.[25] These realities shaped the message of Alfonsín's candidacy, which placed great emphasis on the social well-being that would result from the restoration of the rule of law. Alfonsín frequently regaled his supporters with lists of the concrete ways that life would improve under a democracy with him at the helm. One flyer encouraging voters to affiliate with the Radical Party in March 1983 listed ten concrete changes that would follow the election, which are worth quoting at length:

1. Rule of law and effective civil control to subordinate the military and security forces. Dismantling the repressive apparatus.
2. Defense of salaries and jobs.
3. Curbing inflation and promoting economic development.
4. Recovery of national industries.
5. Affirmation of the rights to health, education, and housing.
6. Protection of social legislation and the pension system.
7. Defense of the rights of women and young people in society.
8. Protection of the family, children, and senior citizens.
9. Human rights, justice, and administrative honesty.
10. Affirmation of economic and territorial sovereignty.[26]

This ranking, and others like it, emphasized a type of popular republicanism anchored by the twin pillars of civilian rule and sovereignty. Its baseline message conveyed an expansive notion of rights that placed social welfare front and center. While the systematic terror of state violence captured public attention, human rights—defined as protection of the physical body from torture and violence—were often subsumed as part of the promise of a broader rights-based regime. As a candidate, Alfonsín described how all Argentines had "lived through an era of the denigration of their fundamental rights," identified as health care, food, and shelter, among others.[27] The insidious violence of the regime was manifested in the steady degradation of daily life. "Human rights" in this sense meant more than protection from torture; it represented guarantees of social justice as well.

To that end, Alfonsín reserved special attention for the economic crisis and its most visible effects. On May 1, 1983, International Workers' Day, he issued a bleak assessment of national life in the wake of seven years of military rule:

The nation's soul is saddened by the cruel spectacle of malnourished children. . . . They are the poorest people of the poorest provinces. But we are hypocritically hiding the true geographic limits of hunger: This misery, this malnourishment, this precarious housing, is located on the doorstep of Buenos Aires and in Buenos Aires itself. I vow before the people and the Republic to take back the Argentina that has been robbed from us. No child will go hungry in Argentina ever again. We will apply economic policies that lead to full employment. . . . We will deal with health care and popular education. There will be democratic unions. And let us be clear: There can never be long-term welfare without political liberties.[28]

In this speech, Alfonsín introduced hunger—and the economic policies that had caused it—as one of the many cruel legacies of the dictatorship. As demonstrated in the previous chapter, the discovery of hunger had already played a role in the breakdown of the regime, and it continued to surface as presidential campaigning got under way. In April 1983, the minister of social action declared that "nobody went hungry in Argentina," adding that the soup kitchens that proliferated throughout the outskirts of Greater Buenos Aires "were a political ploy."[29] Photos of hungry children from the northern province of Tucumán that surfaced in the press, and the ongoing solidarity campaigns of churches in places such as Quilmes, home of the 1981 Hunger March, exposed a vastly different reality. As the economic situation continued to deteriorate, the minister's cynical statement belied the palpable effects of economic suffering. Hunger was real, and it was encroaching on the center of the nation.

Alfonsín's concerns about hunger built on an idea that was already in circulation, one that he used to differentiate himself from the cruelty of the military authorities and to lay claim to an irreproachable moral and social issue. From that International Workers' Day on, the promise to end hunger occupied a prominent place in his campaign. Alfonsín frequently boasted that eradicating hunger was the only pledge he would make as a candidate. Along the campaign trail, he announced that his government would create an emergency food program—the Programa Alimentario Nacional (PAN)—to reverse the nutritional emergency created by the dictatorship, and as if to emphasize the urgency of the matter, he declared, "We will not pay the national debt with the hunger of the people."[30]

Expectations for socially attuned democracy came together in Alfonsín's most well-known campaign slogan; "With democracy, one eats, one is educated, one is cured" quickly became one of the hallmark messages of his candidacy. If state violence killed and disappeared, democracy had the ability to heal and to reverse the most detrimental effects of military rule. Democracy was thus anthropomorphized in the wake of terror. It was living and breathing, and for a brief time, its messenger became Raúl Alfonsín. Argentines projected hopes for their personal and collective futures onto Alfonsín's broad message, leading one observer to remark at the start of 1983 that Alfonsín "represented the best interpreter of this particular historical moment."[31] As a candidate, Alfonsín painted stark contrasts between military rule and constitutionalism, while his attention to social well-being took direct aim at his main challengers in the Peronist party. According to Alfonsín's definition of democracy, political and social rights could be achieved without sacrificing one for the other. Yet realizing this vision meant confronting Peronism and its historic claim to be the main agent of social change in Argentina.

CAMPAIGNING BETWEEN THE LIVING
AND THE DEAD

The campaign for the presidency began in earnest in the early months of 1983. Despite a crowded political field that eventually included twelve contenders for the presidency, for most Argentines the race came down to a contest between the nation's two major political forces—Peronism and radicalism. At the start of 1983, however, Peronism faced a dilemma. The movement had long balanced various internal factions and differences between the party and its union base. Throughout the early 1970s, left- and right-wing sectors battled, first for Juan Perón's allegiance upon his return from exile, and then for the soul of the movement in the wake of his death. With the onset of the dictatorship in 1976, left-wing militants and industrial workers felt the wrath of state terror and economic liberalization as the junta drew a straight line between what it saw as the revulsive changes wrought by Peronism and political and social subversion. Argentines had to look no further than the shuttered factories in the industrial zones of major cities, falling union rosters, or pink slips to grasp the economic effects of the regime. Of course, the policies that contributed to manufacturing's decline did not reside with Peronism. Yet for many members of Peronism's base, the reverberations of abuse and economic retrenchment linked directly back to the persecution of workers over the course of the dictatorship, a type of violence that union bosses had been unable to halt and, in some cases, actively promoted.[32]

Early on in the political race, Alfonsín tapped into widespread disgust with the most conservative Peronist leaders, whom many Argentines linked to the breakdown of institutional rule. Alfonsín exploited those perceptions through a rhetorical strategy that emphasized military and right-wing Peronist collusion. In April 1983, he publicly denounced a "pact" between upper-echelon military and union leaders. The pact allegedly stipulated that if a Peronist government assumed office, it would guarantee a military amnesty. Though Alfonsín admitted that he did not have technical proof of such an agreement, that was hardly the point.[33] In equating Peronism with the nation's darkest period of repression, the charge fueled fears that a Peronist victory would perpetuate a pattern of violence and impunity that many were anxious to leave behind.

As the opening salvo of Alfonsín's campaign, the strategy worked on a few fronts. It first consolidated Alfonsín's power within his own party. In July 1983, Alfonsín beat his contender, Fernando de la Rúa, in the Radical Party primary, securing for himself the UCR nomination for the presidency. For their part, some of the most orthodox Peronist leaders only seemed to confirm Alfonsín's charges of union-military collusion. Following the release of the military junta's "Final Document," the armed forces' attempt to justify state terror and to secure exemption from possible prosecution, Ítalo Lúder, who would in a few months gain the Peronist nomination for president, declared: "[Responding to] these excesses is not the responsibility of the constitutional government, rather of those who committed them."[34] Such comments did not allay anxieties about Peronism's illicit dealings with the armed forces or the prospect of an amnesty for military leaders. By contrast, Alfonsín presented himself as the alternative to a future of impunity, with a promise of transparency to break a pattern of authoritarian repression.

As has been well documented, the human rights abuses of the dictatorship presented some of the most pressing concerns in the waning months of the military regime.[35] On a daily basis, the revelation of crimes committed by the armed forces wrenched open the viciousness of the junta and fueled the ongoing mobilization of human rights organizations, which led the charge to make the prosecution of the military a principal responsibility of any future government.[36] Yet in the uncertain period between the end of the Malvinas War and the October 1983 election, there was no societal consensus around human rights or overnight adhesion to its values. Despite evidence of the regime's crimes, no agreement existed about how and to what extent the military's abuses should be addressed, save the powerful (and often diffuse) notion that the crimes committed by the armed forces should not be allowed to happen ever again. As campaigning picked up during the first half of 1983, Raúl Alfonsín emerged as the candidate with the clearest plan for prosecuting the armed forces. His proposal for prosecution evolved in conversation with jurists from the University of Buenos Aires's Society for Philosophical Analysis (SADAF, Sociedad Argentina de Análisis Filosófico) and identified three levels of responsibility.[37] It distinguished between officials who gave orders, subordinates who followed orders, and those who "had committed excesses" in fulfillment of their duties.[38] Like the major human rights organizations at the time, this proposal stood firmly against any type of amnesty for military officials. Writing later about the plans to prosecute the armed forces and the eventual trial of the military juntas in 1985, Alfonsín emphasized what he saw as their ultimate purpose: "We needed to leave a mark on the collective conscience that there was no group, however powerful, that was above the law, and that could sacrifice human beings in the service of supposedly valuable undertakings."[39]

More so than his Peronist contenders, Alfonsín began to gain notice as the mainstream politician who best articulated a clear break between an era of impunity and a new age defined by the rule of law.[40] Despite a robust oppositional labor movement that emerged as a powerful voice against the regime, Peronist leaders with closer ties to the armed forces remained the public face of Peronism. The general picture of the movement in the months leading up to the elections was of chaotic, often violent, power struggles.[41] Several rallies erupted in brawls and gunfire, scenes that evoked raw memories of the breakdown of civilian rule. The vacuum left in the wake of Juan Perón's death in 1974 had intensified bitter contests between conservative hardliners, moderates, regional factions, and union leaders. While most parties had confirmed their candidates by July 1983, the Peronist candidate for the presidency was not selected until early September, less than eight weeks before the October 30 election. Eventually, Ítalo Lúder secured the nomination. A longtime party leader, Lúder had served for a time as president of the senate, then as interim president of the nation for thirty-four days in 1975. Despite his reputation as a moderate, during his brief tenure he had signed off on some of the most contentious decrees of the period immediately preceding the dictatorship, which authorized state repression and the "annihilation" of subversion nationwide.[42]

But in many ways, it was still Peronism's election to lose. In the months before the election, political parties scrambled to affiliate voters according to new election rules and timelines. By April 1983, 2,966,472 people had reaffiliated with a party. While a record number of those affiliations went to the Radical Party, the majority of new voters formally identified as Peronist. Polls throughout 1983 revealed that while many Argentines supported Alfonsín's growing momentum, a large segment of the population believed that the Peronist candidate, Ítalo Lúder, would ultimately win.[43] Lúder himself boasted that "being the Peronist candidate for president is equal to being the future president of Argentina." After all, the Peronist party had never lost in open presidential elections during its forty-year history. In the last free elections in 1973, the party had swept 61 percent of the vote. Peronist campaign materials in 1983 relied on this precedent and proclaimed, "the memory of the people will be enough for us."

The Peronist and Radical Party candidates thus presented Argentines with a striking choice between adherence to rebuilding institutions and the continued specter of political crisis. A closer look at campaign materials illustrates this point. Some of Alfonsín's earliest pronouncements as a candidate emphasized the history of the Radical Party as the political force most dedicated to the defense of democratic institutions in Argentina. Campaign flyers and literature frequently cited Leandro Alem, the founder of the UCR, who in 1890 laid the groundwork for the nation's first mass political party. With even more fervor, Alfonsín drew inspiration from Hipólito Yrigoyen, whose second presidency was deposed by a military coup in 1930, inaugurating a cycle of military dictatorship that would endure for the next fifty years. Since Alfonsín's first attempts to gain control of the Radical Party in the early 1970s through his Renovation and Change movement, he had presented himself as following in the footsteps of Yrigoyen and his commitments to popular democracy, morality, and ethics, which Alfonsín actively cultivated. Through this reading of his party's history, Alfonsín connected his campaign for a new and just Argentina to the nation's first experiments with democracy. Likewise,

Alfonsín placed great emphasis on the impact that the 1966 military overthrow of Arturo Illia had had on the evolution of his anti-dictatorial beliefs. Illia's downfall, which had initiated a decade-long descent into state terror, provided further proof of the UCR's steadfast moral compass against the antidemocratic impulses of the nation's economic and military elite. Though this interpretation overlooked a conservative cadre of Radical Party luminaries who frequently threw their support behind nondemocratic rule, Alfonsín's message emphasized over a century of steadfast party enthusiasm for constitutionalism. He made the case that the UCR "was ready to govern" in line with the most progressive of Radical Party traditions.[44] To that end, Alfonsín rarely missed the opportunity to remind Argentines that the Radical Party had defended "the rule of law and full democracy" during the many years that it had held power during the twentieth century.[45]

While Alfonsín highlighted the democratic bona fides of the Radical Party, the most forceful message of his candidacy centered on the immediate legacies of the outgoing regime. Campaign propaganda insisted that Argentines faced a clear-cut choice between life and death, between dictatorship and democracy. One iconic poster depicted Alfonsín clasping his hands together in an embrace to symbolize the imminent resolution of the antagonisms of Argentine political life. Another popular slogan of his campaign was *somos la vida* (we are life). Highly produced television spots played on this theme. One ad begins in a darkened room, with smoke swirling in ominous ribbons against a door as a voiceover declares that a vote for Alfonsín is "more than an election. It's an open door to life." The scene then cuts to an Alfonsín speech juxtaposed against a light-filled image of the Plaza de Mayo packed with thousands.[46] Alfonsín outdid his opponents, pioneering the use of television ads, image consultants, and polling, which helped to enhance his standing as the representative of a new political generation in the service of a democratic and politically modern Argentina.[47] The overall message of his campaign emphasized a historic rupture, with Alfonsín as a bridge between a violent past and a more just future.

This message of a brave new political age also reached across the political spectrum. The Christian Democrats, who had several prominent human rights activists among their leaders, declared that casting a vote for their party would be "for the right to life!"[48] Oscar Alende, the candidate of the center-left Partido Intransigente (PI), encouraged Argentines to "vote for change!"[49] Even Álvaro Alsogaray of the conservative Unión del Centro Democrático (UCeDé) utilized the key words of the day in his ads: "Until now, you knew he was right. Now show him through your votes."[50] Despite important ideological differences, the major political parties and their candidates celebrated the return of electoral politics and free elections as the first steps toward a future of stable institutional life.

By contrast, the look and tone of the Peronist campaign seemed to offer a promise to go back in time. To that end, the central figure of the campaign was Juan

Perón, who had died nine years earlier in 1974. Ítalo Lúder frequently declared that his victory would signify "the Triumph of Perón!" Campaign materials, emblazoned with an image of Perón from the 1940s, displayed the initials "PV" for *Perón vuelve* (Perón will return). Images like these heightened the sense that the presidential race would come down to a contest between Perón and Alfonsín, between the dead and the living. Peronist rallies and campaign ephemera placed emphasis on the iconography of the first Peronist period from 1945 to 1955, an era marked by dramatic social changes and the extension of welfare. This focus was sound in at least one important respect. In the midst of the worst economic crisis facing the nation since the 1930s, many individuals yearned for a return to an era of prosperity and social justice. Indeed, as discussed previously, the rights-based discourse that contributed to Alfonsín's growing popularity harkened back to an earlier period of well-being that had emerged at midcentury. Lúder promised a "revolution of peace" and "social revolution," using many of the same slogans and recipes from thirty years before. At the end of the dictatorship, however, this program was darkened by the shadow of recent violence. The most recent memories of Peronism conjured up the pandemonium of the period leading up to the dictatorship. The more orthodox leaders at the helm of the race were unable to acknowledge the extent to which political culture had shifted. That misreading began to alienate even the most loyal supporters in one of the geographic hearts of Peronism.

Alfonsín represented an increasingly viable alternative throughout the Peronist strongholds in the industrial suburbs of Greater Buenos Aires. The story of Jorge Cobos illustrates this trend. Cobos grew up in the working-class neighborhoods of Quilmes, one of the largest townships of Greater Buenos Aires and the site of the 1981 Hunger March and land takeovers that contributed to the breakdown of authoritarian rule. At age fourteen, he was forced to leave school and go to work at a printing press nearby to help support his family. Though he came from a Peronist household, Cobos had never been active in politics. As mobilizations against the dictatorship gained momentum around him throughout 1981 and 1982, he stayed home, describing himself later as part of a generation that had been "asleep" during the dictatorship. Sometime toward the end of 1982, a friend invited him to a book presentation at which Alfonsín spoke. From that point on, he recalled, "I was totally hooked. . . . We got caught up in the fury of politics, coming out of the dark night, and we believed in so many things."[51] Cobos's recollections of his burgeoning support for Alfonsín call to mind the carefully crafted messages of the Alfonsín campaign, with their emphasis on the dichotomies of dictatorship versus democracy, past versus present, and darkness versus light. Cobos described his growing engagement in political life almost as an awakening, also indicating that he was not the only one of his generation to share his sentiment.

Jorge Cobos was twenty years old in 1983. Young, inspired by the candidate and the coming end of the regime, he immersed himself in municipal politics, helping to support Alfonsín's candidacy and that of other local Radical Party candidates as well. Even as enthusiasm for Alfonsín grew, Cobos remained skeptical of his chances to win nationwide, especially in historically Peronist districts such as Quilmes and other parts of Greater Buenos Aires. In his words, "I thought that we would have a strong turn out and nothing more." But he witnessed on an intimate level how the political landscape began to shift. Cobos firmly believed, "Alfonsín won because of the Peronist vote. . . . I don't mean the upper-level leaders or the party hierarchy, but people saw in Alfonsín what Peronism had once offered them." He volunteered an example from his own home:

> My father [was] a Peronist, and he had a photo of Perón hanging by the door. When you walked into my house, the first thing you saw was the photo of Perón. And then I put up a photo of Alfonsín, and [my father] never got upset because it was true: [in 1983] he felt more represented by the way that Alfonsín expressed himself politically than by his own candidate. And I am convinced that he voted for [Alfonsín], pretty convinced.[52]

Through this glimpse into the intimate politics of family life, we see the ways that the return to democracy raised expectations that an Alfonsín government might fulfill the historic promises for well-being that had animated the earlier democratic opening of Peronism. Jorge Cobos's story is just one example of how Alfonsín attracted the support of a traditionally Peronist base and new generation of political actors. But this story was not at all exceptional. With his message of an era of a rights-based and prosperous future, Alfonsín successfully channeled popular expectations for the coming democratic restoration. Nowhere did those hopes surface more sharply than in Greater Buenos Aires, where the dictatorship had taken a devastating toll. The magazine *Humor* described Alfonsín as "the only non-Peronist politician who has any real chance to obtain the highest office in the land. He is quickly becoming the leader of a growing coalition that includes. . . . Peronists disillusioned by the behavior of leaders of the movement."[53]

If Jorge Cobos's story was not totally unique, neither was his support for Alfonsín necessarily the spontaneous awakening he described. It was also the result of several years of deliberate political work on the part of Radical Party brokers to build and maintain party bases, even in the midst of the dictatorship. Leopoldo Moreau, a leading member of the Coordinadora, the youth wing of the Radical Party that lent its support to Alfonsín beginning in the early 1970s, described the efforts of Radical Party activists to sustain political engagement over the course of the regime. "When the [dictatorship] began," Moreau recalled, "the political cadres—meaning us—took a step back from the riskiest work, which was university organizing. . . . And we ended up going back to neighborhood organizations, and the local party networks that we were more or less able to keep up."[54]

By the end of the dictatorship, the Radical Party counted among its members a significant cohort that had survived the dictatorship and that had remained politically active within the confines of authoritarian rule. Moreau highlighted the professional and university background of the young party activists, drawing on a familiar description of Radicals as mostly "middle class." But that group also included popular and working-class party hopefuls such as Jorge Cobos, who entered political life as the dictatorship drew to a close. Cobos did indeed belong to a generation that grew up during the dictatorship, one that was too young to have been directly involved in militancy in the early 1970s. That generation politically engaged for the first time in 1983. And unlike a decade before, when radicalism had conjured up the stale exhaustion of liberal democratic process, the message at the heart of the party at the end of the dictatorship reflected a vision for a future grounded in institutional life that drew in increasing numbers of people.

As official campaigning came to a close in October 1983, Alfonsín convened his largest gathering yet under the shadow of the obelisk in the Plaza de la República, in the heart of Buenos Aires. He issued a final call for national unity: "There will no longer be Radicals or anti-Radicals, nor Peronists or anti-Peronists when it comes time to prevent the insanity of any future military coup."[55] That image, even of exaggerated national unity, could not have contrasted more sharply with the UCR's most powerful political contenders. During the closing night of the Peronist campaign, the candidate for governor of Buenos Aires province burned a coffin with the initials "U.C.R." and "Alfonsín, R.I.P" emblazoned on the side. In popular memory, the image of the coffin in flames and the explicit violence of the act cemented the Peronists' fate in the elections. By 1983, this was precisely the political scenario that most Argentines wanted to move beyond. Voters overwhelmingly chose the living over the dead.

Early in the evening on October 30, 1983, when it seemed clear that Raúl Alfonsín would be the next president of Argentina, there was euphoria in the streets. A few miles from the center of Buenos Aires, Jorge Cobos wept with joy along with the celebrating crowds. Raúl Alfonsín won the election with just over half of the popular vote—51 percent nationwide—more than ten points ahead of Italo Luder, who received approximately 40 percent of the votes. In the legislative elections, the Radical Party gained majority control of the lower chamber, though it lost control of the Senate to the Peronist party by two seats.[56] Given past Peronist victories and the certainty with which many commentators had counted on a Peronist win, these results astounded many. Even more surprising, Alfonsín swept a majority of the nineteen municipalities that then constituted Greater Buenos Aires, Quilmes included.

As this chapter has shown, one result of the devastating toll of the dictatorship had been the creation of a space for the emergence of an *alfonsinista* project and the historic Radical Party win in places where no political affinity may have otherwise existed. Seven years of state-sponsored terror led to reevaluations of not only armed struggle, but also institutional democracy, which by the early 1980s was widely connected to a promise of physical and material security. Alfonsín fit into and defined this political space better than any of his rivals. He championed institutional democracy as the remedy for political violence. But he combined his message of republicanism with a vision of rights that fused political freedom with social welfare.

This ideological shift coincided with widespread recriminations against Peronism. By the end of the dictatorship, many Argentines linked Peronism to a legacy of instability and military repression, a belief that Alfonsín strategically exploited throughout his campaign. While he capitalized on the memory of the Radical Party as historically democratic, Alfonsín's popularity took root in an expansive and malleable vision of a democratic future that many Argentines—from the neighborhoods of Buenos Aires's struggling industrial suburbs, middle-class enclaves in the capital, and beyond—transferred onto their personal and collective aspirations for a definitive break with an authoritarian past. In addition to pledging to prosecute the military and address the fate of the disappeared, Alfonsín gained legitimacy by proposing a broadly conceived notion of rights, which distinguished him from his main political contenders at the time. Alfonsín presented his proposals as the democratic antidote to decades of political and economic crisis through specific pledges about food, education, employment, and welfare. This platform helped Raúl Alfonsín win the election. Fulfilling it would prove a more difficult challenge.

"With Democracy One Eats"

The Programa Alimentario Nacional

When Raúl Alfonsín assumed the presidency on December 10, 1983, he repeated a by then familiar campaign promise, vowing that no child would go hungry in Argentina ever again. The specter of hunger was one more disquieting legacy of the dictatorship. During the military regime's extended exit from power following the Malvinas War, stories of childhood malnutrition, rising food prices, and soup kitchens unsettled beliefs about Argentina as a food-secure nation. Regime officials repeatedly denied the existence of hunger and described soup kitchens as a "political ploy."[1] Yet hunger rose to prominence during the 1983 elections, proof of the widespread violations of life and livelihoods wrought by seven years of military rule. The right to eat galvanized Alfonsín's platform and formed part of his concise definition of democracy. Hunger symbolized the imprint of military rule, and its eradication reflected a promise of the newly restored democratic state. Food, and access to it, became a measure of the constitutional return.

This chapter examines the flagship social program of Argentina's constitutional restoration. The PAN (Programa Alimentario Nacional), as the program was known, was an attempt to curb widespread hunger caused by the policies of the military regime through monthly deliveries of nonperishable goods to families in need. At its height in 1986, the PAN produced 1.3 million food boxes per month.[2] Though no official figures exist regarding the exact number of recipients, approximately 5.6 million Argentines—up to 17 percent of the population—were receiving the PAN food aid every month by the second half of the decade.[3] It was the largest food program in Argentine history and the first time a national government was compelled to rely on massive food distribution to feed its citizens.

The significance of the PAN went far beyond food distribution, however. As a metaphor and tangible reality, hunger animated a particular vision of human rights, upon which the transition was based. The government's pledge to eradicate the hunger caused by the military regime formed part of a comprehensive rights agenda that aimed to protect citizens from physical harm and to secure their material welfare. In the extensive literature on Argentina's "transition to democracy," military trials and bitter reversals of justice have received the most attention. Yet the Alfonsín government sought to distinguish itself from the dictatorship not just by restoring political institutions and civil liberties, but also by guaranteeing certain minimal social rights, the right to eat being foremost among them. In turn, individuals judged the Alfonsín government on the basis of not only its attempts to prosecute the crimes of the armed forces but also its ability to fulfill demands for well-being.

The PAN took root in the refoundational impulse of the new democracy. But within a few years of its inauguration, the food program had transformed into a symbol of the limitations of the Alfonsín administration's social agenda and the changing fortunes of the welfare state at the end of the twentieth century. Long-standing interpretations of the Radical Party have emphasized its transformation into a vehicle of middle-class interests following the rise of Peronism at midcentury, lacking a robust social agenda with the ability to compete with the Peronist movement.[4] The history of the PAN complicates this narrative, even if it does not totally reverse its conclusions. With the momentum of electoral victory spurring them on, Radical power brokers saw the PAN as a chance to usurp the moral authority of Peronism in the realm of social justice. Overall, the Alfonsín government failed in this endeavor. The PAN, the most ambitious welfare program of its day, promoted social citizenship, consumption, and participation as its core goals. Yet in its design and in its day-to-day operations, the PAN began to separate welfare in Argentina from its historic association with a politically mobilized working class. Eventually, a reformist sector of the Peronist party used the perceived shortcomings of the PAN to revive the movement and to reclaim Peronism's role as the standard bearer of social justice for post-dictatorship Argentina.

Reconstructing family life also formed a critical part of the PAN's objectives. During its six years in operation (1984–1990), the program relied on the support of women aid recipients to implement this state-led policy in their homes and neighborhoods. Policy makers described food aid as an emergency reparation to strengthen popular diets and to in turn help construct democracy beyond the family table. In Greater Buenos Aires, a region that received the most food aid over the course of the decade, PAN networks organized communal purchases, coordinated disaster relief efforts, and convened meetings in churches and schools to facilitate food delivery. It was in these remade political spaces that ideas of rights and democracy were reinterpreted in ways that often challenged the Alfonsín government's welfare platform. Though the PAN was initially designed as a temporary program, over the course of the 1980s the need for food aid grew more acute in the face of creeping inflation and fiscal crisis. As stalled economic reforms and debt hampered the government, the continual need for a national food program accentuated the limits of the Alfonsín administration's ability to attend to citizen well-being and economic recovery. For an increasingly vocal sector of conservative and promarket political forces, the PAN bolstered arguments against the very need for an interventionist, welfare state.

A DEMOCRATIC SPRING: THE FIRST ONE HUNDRED DAYS OF DEMOCRACY

The first one hundred days of the Alfonsín government (December 10, 1983–March 23, 1984) was an ambitious period aimed at restoring political life and institutions. Members of the newly appointed government argued that at stake were the consolidation of the democratic state and the reconstruction of institutions that had been decimated, not only by the most recent dictatorship, but also by fifty years of alternating civilian and military rule. Upon assuming office, the administration set overlapping priorities: it sought to legislate the rule of law via the newly restored congress to diminish the historical grip of both the armed forces and Peronist trade unions on public life. As a candidate, Alfonsín had successfully tapped into perceptions of the antidemocratic impulses of both institutions through his announcement of a "pact" between military and union officials. Radical Party officials interpreted their electoral victory as proof of a collective desire to transform political culture.[5]

Prosecuting the crimes of the military lay at the center of many Argentines' expectations for justice following the end of the dictatorship. The new administration got off to a swift and encouraging start. On December 13, 1983, three days after his inauguration, Alfonsín signed decrees ordering the prosecution of the three juntas that had ruled during the military dictatorship, as well as leaders of the left-wing organizations ERP (People's Revolutionary Army) and Montoneros. He repealed a "Law of Pacification"—a self-amnesty issued by the military regime, which would have protected junta members from being tried—and ordered the arrest of top military brass. He also authorized the creation of the CONADEP (National Commission on the Disappearance of Persons), the investigative efforts of which resulted in the publication of the *Nunca Más* report a year later.[6] These measures boosted the moral authority of the new government and were among the most prominent early steps taken by the administration.

In addition to reining in the military through investigations and prosecution, Alfonsín also attempted to make good on another electoral promise: to dilute Peronist control of trade unions. As with the military trials, the moment seemed opportune. Peronism had been weakened by perceptions of collusion with the dictatorship, while the upper echelons of orthodox leaders had been discredited by electoral defeat. The project to reform the unions, known as the Mucci Law after then labor secretary Antonio Mucci, included provisions for open and public control of union elections, bureaucratic decentralization, and minority representation. In short, the law sought to "democratize" the unions, as many Radical Party officials characterized the initiative.[7]

Human rights and union reform set the tone for this initial period, but they were accompanied by other sweeping measures meant to overturn authoritarianism. In early 1984, Alfonsín sent a bill to Congress seeking to restore academic freedom and university autonomy. The Supreme Court judges who had served during the dictatorship were forced to resign. The Senate passed a law easing film censorship, repealing statutes that had been in place for over thirty years.[8] Along with military prosecutions and union reorganization, these measures aimed at establishing political freedoms and civil liberties in the name of the democratic rule of law.[9]

The PAN also formed part of the ambitious policy agenda of Argentina's newly restored democracy. Concretely, the PAN was a monthly food subsidy of roughly thirty pounds of nonperishable goods, including: powdered milk, cooking oil, noodles, polenta, flour, corned beef, lard, and sugar. It was delivered in a box known as the Caja PAN, or breadbox, using the program's acronym. The program's main objective was to provide 30 percent of the monthly calorie requirements for a family of four. Beneficiaries were signed up by program workers, known as PAN agents, and every month the female head of household was required to attend a meeting, along with about thirty other women, to pick up the box at a distribution center, such as schools, churches, neighborhood clubs, and municipal buildings. The meeting was an important part of the program design, geared toward ancillary community development and "social solidarity" projects, which ranged from public health and nutrition workshops to the creation of community gardens.

Food purchases for the program were administered by the state regulatory agency, the National Grain Board (Junta Nacional de Granos, JNG), which solicited public bids from national firms for the purchase of all products. The food was sent via railroad and truck to two packaging plants, located in Buenos Aires and Entre Rios. In Buenos Aires, production could reach 50,000–55,000 boxes per day at the bustling Central Market, located just over the capital limits (see figure 1). In Entre Rios, which was responsible for all of the PAN deliveries in the northeast, production averaged 20,000–22,000 boxes per day.[10] Before even reaching program beneficiaries, the PAN passed through channels of national and provincial government and private business, touching hundreds of lives.

Evidence of the program was difficult to miss even for those whose lives the PAN did not immediately touch. The food came packaged in a large cardboard

FIGURE 1. Workers prepare PAN boxes in the Mercado Central, Buenos Aires. Photo by Enrique Rosito.

box, with an unmistakable blue PAN logo emblazoned on all sides (see figure 2). In addition to the National Grain Board's posting bidding requests in newspapers and magazines, the program enjoyed the backing of a state-sponsored publicity campaign. Print ads declared, "Now it is time to break bread," signaling that the PAN was part of a moment of national altruism and collective duty.[11] Television commercials included a children's nursery rhyme and a voice-over announcing, "Solidarity will overcome solitude."[12] Very quickly, the PAN emerged as a prominent, visible, and material symbol of the democratic return.

FOOD AID AND WELFARE: THE PASSAGE OF THE PAN

Radical Party government officials often boasted throughout the 1980s that the PAN was an unprecedented welfare initiative. While the program did marshal resources, food, and personnel on a scale rarely seen in Argentina, declarations about the PAN's novelty belied a much longer tradition of food distribution dating back to the late nineteenth century. Italian, Eastern European, and German mutual aid societies had secured food for their fellow countrymen as part of their initiation to a new land.[13] The Catholic Church, Jewish organizations, and women's philanthropic groups had regularly provided food aid as part of their charity works. In

FIGURE 2. Stacks of PAN boxes ready to be shipped from the Mercado Central in Buenos Aires. Photo by Enrique Rosito.

the twentieth century, municipalities and provinces experimented with food subsidies beginning in the 1910s. During this same period, Radical Party committees also built patronage networks through the distribution of the so-called *pan radical*, cheap food dispersed to would-be voters in anticipation of elections.[14] These initiatives emerged in tandem with some of the first national social protection laws for workers, children, and the impoverished, and laid the foundations for the modern welfare state.

The rise of Peronism in the 1940s solidified the link between food aid and state-led welfare. During this era, food provision played a key role in the emergence of a type of socially grounded citizenship that connected individual prosperity and consumption to national industrial and economic advancement.[15] The Eva Perón Foundation provided food through its orphanages, old age homes, and tourism sites. The Argentine Institute for Promotion of Trade (Instituto Argentino de Promoción del Intercambio, IAPI) concentrated on guaranteeing low food costs for consumers through subsidies to agricultural producers.[16] Price controls and government-sponsored food markets also helped to expand working-class diets, and meat consumption rose to an average of ninety-three kilograms per person by 1950.[17] Food security during the first Peronist era (1945–1955) was premised on the abundance of resources and generative models of economic development. These policies, according to one well-known assessment, led to the widespread "democ-ratization of well-being."[18] By the second half of the twentieth century, the welfare state in Argentina was inextricably associated with the experience of the Peronist years through the validation of the cultural life of the industrial working class and overlapping notions of social mobility and consumption.

The PAN drew upon the foundations of midcentury welfare programs, but it also marked a shift in the ways that policy makers conceived of aid in the aftermath of military rule. Radical Party government officials saw the PAN as a chance to seize the moral authority of Peronism in the sphere of social justice. Though government officials did not explicitly reference the Radical Party's early-twentieth-century food welfare initiatives, the PAN formed part of a larger project to reclaim what Alfonsín and his advisers argued was the popular democratic legacy of their party. During congressional deliberations for the passage of the PAN in February 1984, Peronist lawmakers voiced some of the loudest concerns along these very lines. Juan Carlos Barbeito, a Peronist congressman, summarized his party's objections. In addition to claims that the PAN did not go far enough in addressing the root causes of hunger, he was most upset by the Radical Party's incursion into what he saw as a Peronist issue. Barbeito exclaimed: "Evita used to say that where there is a need there is a right. We [Peronists] believe in this as a pillar of our doctrine of social justice. And we want to rescue this social cause for ourselves." Though Bar-beito supported the PAN and urged quick approval of the program, he concluded, "When we Peronists were in power . . . we would have done things differently. . . . With just one phone call we could have had an emergency program up and running within 48 hours. That is the Peronist way!"[19] The Peronist block broke into applause when he finished speaking.

Barbeito was touching on a sensitive point: The Peronists were not in power. The 1980s was a decade of upheaval for the Peronist movement. First, the party had lost in the presidential elections of 1983. Second, the traditional working-class base of Peronism had been attacked through the military's systematic gutting of the manufacturing economy. Finally, Peronism itself was associated with collusion with the armed forces, an issue that Raúl Alfonsín had successfully exploited dur-ing the presidential campaign. The PAN threatened to encroach even further on Peronism's claims to social rights. And that was precisely the point. The Radical Party sought to take full advantage of the new scenario, while Peronism embarked on a period of regrouping and renovation.

The stakes involved in approving the PAN also transcended Radical versus Per-onist rivalries. Many lawmakers saw the food program and the resources that it would mobilize as vital to rebuilding trust in constitutional authorities after years of military rule. Miguel Monserrat of the center-left Partido Intransigente, a mem-ber of the congressional commission that wrote up the PAN law, described the food program's place in Argentina's nascent democracy as "the duty and inescapable responsibility of the State."[20] Monserrat expressed a generally shared vision of the PAN and the necessity of a welfare-granting state. There was, however, one vocal exception to this commonly held view. Álvaro Alsogaray, the congressional representative of the conservative Unión del Centro Democrático (UCeDé), voiced the strongest critique of the PAN. Alsogaray made it clear that his party was "not prepared to give the [PAN] a blank check without any idea about how much it will cost, no matter how well intentioned the motives."[21] Alsogaray concluded with a general commentary about what he believed were the real causes of Argentina's social emergency: "These problems . . . tend to appear in countries where state planning, state intervention, and inflation reign. In countries where the social economy of the market reigns, there are no problems of hunger. Someday, Argentina will be the same."[22]

Though the voice for promarket, state retrenchment grew louder as the decade proceeded, in early 1984 Alsogaray and the protestations of the UCeDé were still outliers. Nonetheless, while lawmakers generally agreed that the PAN was an essential program, they did not necessarily like it. Some recoiled at the idea of the program as mere charity. For others, the PAN's existence forced an uncomfortable acknowledgment of the problem of poverty and food scarcity in Argentina. Miguel Monserrat of the Partido Intransigente expressed shock that "in a country that has an abundance of food and is an exporter of proteins, we find ourselves at the end of the twentieth century with food deficits that contribute to the decline of Argentines' living conditions."[23] Another congressman voiced a deeper anxiety surrounding the existence of hunger: "Today more children die from hunger in Argentina than in Ecuador, Chile, Peru and Costa Rica—nations notoriously poorer than ours."[24] According to these assessments, Argentina's historic ability to feed its citizens had acted as a bulwark against underdevelopment and preserved its standing in the region. Through dictatorship, debt, and industrial breakdown, however, Argentina was a decidedly less food secure nation in 1984 than it had been a decade earlier.

Responding quickly to what officials described as a "food crisis" was thus one of the top priorities of the Alfonsín government. Accordingly, the PAN was designed as temporary, palliative relief. Government officials presented the program as an extraordinary measure that would be eliminated as soon as the economic difficulties left behind by the military regime were solved by government reforms. As short-term, palliative aid, the PAN was not connected to generative economic programs or long-term recovery efforts. The reasons for this divergence from midcentury welfare models reflected the urgency of the social emergency, but they also had their roots in the exuberance of the return to democracy. The PAN emerged in the midst of a widespread belief that crossed party lines and that permeated public life: many individuals had confidence that the economic and social problems facing the newly restored constitutional government would be reversed swiftly.[25] In

February 1984, lawmakers optimistically approved the PAN for two years—enough time, they believed, to reverse the hunger left behind by the dictatorship.[26]

THE RIGHT TO EAT

Despite the unease surrounding the existence of hunger, policy makers in charge of the PAN at the Ministry of Health and Social Action designed the food program in the absence of any substantial evidence regarding the severity of the social emergency facing Argentina.[27] When the first PAN boxes were distributed in 1984, the most recent precedents for state-sponsored food programs were targeted deliveries of powdered milk to pregnant women and infants up to one year old. There was also a school lunch program, instituted in 1972, which had languished during the dictatorship. The records for these programs are difficult to access, and it is doubtful that they included information about food recipients or other data.[28] At the start of the Alfonsín presidency, the anecdotal snapshots of suffering that circulated in the press and in public debate, though alarming, were not based on concrete data about hunger or its victims. The PAN, then, formed part of a larger effort to restore Argentina's statistical base, rebuild government institutions, and measure the impact of military rule.[29]

In 1984, the publication of the report *La Pobreza en la Argentina* revealed that 22.3 percent of the entire population suffered from "unsatisfied basic needs" in terms of housing, access to food, hygiene and sanitary facilities, and employment opportunities.[30] PAN officials also helped lead the charge of tracking hunger and determining need. From census data and door-to-door surveys, PAN officials created a "Map of Social Emergency" for the entire country. And what they discovered was a vast panorama of need. According to María del Carmen Banzas de Moreau, the technical director of the PAN, "We didn't just have a census, we had a census of poverty."[31] A decade's worth of systematic state violence, economic liberalization, and deindustrialization had directly contributed to a decline in living standards for wide swaths of individuals. The military regime had accelerated a new form of impoverishment that was encroaching on the outskirts of industrial and urban centers, leaving in its wake a legacy of material deprivation and insecurity. In this context, PAN aid underscored the emergence of a new social subject defined primarily by destitution. The program's preoccupation with eradicating hunger also began to revise ideas about the goals of state-led welfare, which were no longer necessarily geared toward promoting the social ascension of employed workers, but rather toward providing palliative, emergency aid to "poor people."

Throughout the 1980s, debates regarding food and the growing visibility of poverty overlapped with debates regarding human rights and the military's crimes. In his official presentation of the food program, Raúl Alfonsín described the PAN as fitting neatly within the framework of his government's political platform:

"Food is a fundamental human right. . . . Ensuring that right for all Argentines is one of the commitments that we make as a people."[32] Food aid, he continued, constituted a necessary emergency measure to reverse the "immoral policies of the dictatorship," which had used men and women as "pawns of economic adjustment."[33] In his presentation, Alfonsín associated food relief with the consolidation of democracy and the creation of democratic subjects, concluding: "[D]emocracy will be a fiction for any child, man, or woman, whose bodies and minds are dulled due to lack of food. In order to transform people into protagonists of their lives and country, society owes them social reparations. This food program is a reparation that must not be delayed."[34] Argentina, according to the program's mandate, faced a material and ethical crisis. Palliative food relief aimed to provide compensation for the wrongs of the dictatorship and to forge a new social pact.

At the onset of the new democracy, government officials saw poverty relief, eliminating hunger, and exposing human rights abuses as overlapping forms of redress. Their attempts to measure and address poverty correlated with attempts to investigate the dictatorship's systematic violation of human rights. The inauguration of the PAN in 1984 coincided with the CONADEP's twelve-month, nationwide probe of the military's crimes. Though the CONADEP is primarily known for its investigations of gross human rights violations and the publication of *Nunca Más*, the commission also conducted its own surveys of the basic needs of the regime's most impoverished victims. Evidence gathered from Greater Buenos Aires and the provinces of Tucumán and Mendoza confirmed the widespread deprivation revealed in PAN officials' surveys of hunger. Yet the CONADEP's inquiry more starkly emphasized the dramatic decline in living standards or fall into poverty of hundreds of families following the disappearance of a loved one and family breadwinner.[35] Their material needs included furniture, housing, food, clothes, school supplies, medicine, and other health services.

These concerns were already clearly in the minds of those directly touched by state repression. For example, Néstor, a twenty-nine-year old former political prisoner who was in captivity from 1975 until early 1984, wrote to the CONADEP and described the reality faced by others in his situation. In his letter he demanded the "most basic human rights required by individuals," which "fall under the direct and indirect control of the Constitutional Government. These are: work, housing, social program coverage, and educational scholarships."[36] Another survey, typical of many conducted by the CONADEP, described a single mother whose husband had been disappeared in Mendoza. She lived in a dilapidated dwelling, "without sanitary services, proper flooring, gas, or plumbing. The roof is in bad condition, which means that every time that it rains the house becomes uninhabitable."[37] Though many individuals indicated that they struggled to put food on the table, the most pressing concern facing families of the disappeared, according to the CONADEP investigation, was decent housing. Food aid through the PAN did come as welcome relief to many, but the CONADEP investigation also highlighted the extended family and community networks that helped to feed individuals and to keep extreme hunger at bay.

Nonetheless, social workers affiliated with the CONADEP relied on the PAN to provide immediate support to the family members of the disappeared. They made concerted efforts to ensure that the PAN and other government housing and pension programs reached the individuals most affected by political violence.[38] Of particular concern for the CONADEP were female-headed households and the children of the disappeared being raised by grandparents. Throughout 1984, regional chapters of the human rights organization Movimiento Ecuménico por los Derechos Humanos (Ecumenical Movement for Human Rights, MEDH) also acted as intermediaries between the poorest victims of state terror and their access to state services. The organization frequently lobbied both CONADEP and PAN officials to ensure the widest possible reach of the food program. The message of "food as a human right" increasingly inspired the efforts of religious activists and human rights organizations. The PAN, with its promises to eradicate the hunger created by the dictatorship, formed a lynchpin of this effort.

THE PAN IN GREATER BUENOS AIRES

The PAN was officially launched in May 1984 in Greater Buenos Aires. On its first day, some fifteen thousand families passed through the distribution centers set up by the municipality of Quilmes, the inaugural site of the program. The local press was on hand to snap photos of mothers and their children exiting the centers, carrying large cardboard boxes containing several pounds of nonperishable goods. One resident, who accompanied his wife, declared, "This food is going to be a big help. If my wife and I organize ourselves, we'll be able to make it last for about 15 days. . . . [I]t will allow me the chance to look for work."[39] Another community leader, more cautiously optimistic, put the significance of the program in larger perspective: "We are placing our hopes on the new authorities, now that we live in a democratic country. We are still suffering the consequences of the military dictatorship, and we do not want to fall back into the trap of poverty. . . . We do not want hunger knocking on our doors any longer."[40]

The selection of Quilmes for the inauguration of the PAN made sense for a number of reasons. For one, there was obvious social need throughout the municipality and the surrounding areas in the midst of unemployment and factory closings. Several townships, Quilmes most especially, had also gained prominence because of the 1981 Hunger March and the soup kitchens set up by the local archdiocese. The soup kitchens were transformed into a moral symbol of the injustices of the regime and highlighted for the first time the problem of hunger in Greater Buenos Aires. Quilmes was also a politically important site. The Radical Party had swept the district during the 1983 elections. Eduardo Vides, the Radical Party mayor, had soundly beaten the Peronist candidate, Roberto Morguen. As Vides was fond of boasting, "Proportionally, I gained more votes for mayor of Quilmes than Alfonsín did in the district."[41] With Quilmes being one of the biggest, and historically Peronist, townships of Greater Buenos Aires, launching the PAN there was part of the strategic effort to build on the Radical Party's momentum deep in the heart of Peronist territory.

While the PAN's highly centralized design linked it directly to the executive, the program also took on a life of its own in the places where it functioned. In day-to-day operations, the PAN depended primarily on program workers, known as PAN agents, who were responsible for signing up beneficiaries and for ensuring food distribution during meetings. PAN agents were the public face of the food program on a local level, and their labor often determined the outcomes of the program in a given municipality. There were approximately thirty-two hundred agents throughout the country, the majority of whom worked on a volunteer basis.[42] Greater Buenos Aires was the only area that employed full-time, salaried PAN workers. On the one hand, this signaled the critical need for food aid in the area. In Greater Buenos Aires, field agents were often responsible for delivering food to between six and eight hundred families per month.[43] On the other hand, the full-time field agents also evinced the high stakes of ensuring that the PAN achieved success in the politically contentious outskirts of Buenos Aires, where Radical Party leaders hoped to make inroads.

Many field agents working in Greater Buenos Aires recall the PAN as a trans-formative personal and political experience. Selected by municipal program coordinators, field agents typically came from in or around the communities where the PAN functioned. The agents were young, most of them in their early twenties. Almost all had links to local Radical Party politics, which could range from loose affiliation via family connections to direct campaigning for Radical Party candidates during the 1983 elections. For some, the PAN was a starting point for a career in politics. For others, it was a chance to put university careers into practice for the first time.

One PAN agent, named Catalina Vera, was in her early twenties when a local member of the Radical Party recommended her for the PAN. A native of Quilmes, she was assigned to work in a shantytown located a few blocks from where she grew up. Over the course of the dictatorship, as she had completed her studies in psychology, married, and had a child, she had witnessed changes to the town. "It was quite a sight," she said, "to turn the corner and see a new *villa miseria* [shanty-town]." For Catalina, the PAN was less an opportunity to advance politically than her first chance to put her psychology degree to good use. Catalina also felt inspired by the chance to participate in the political moment. As she described it, "I was a total fan of Alfonsín. . . . My father had already passed away by then, and I identi-fied Alfonsín with that father figure. . . . I considered myself a Radical, but I wasn't one of those who wanted to move up the [party] ladder." "For me," she concluded, "I didn't want to politicize. I was more interested in the social questions."[44]

Another PAN agent, Jorge Cobos, was in his early twenties when he was recruited to work with the PAN in Quilmes. As discussed in the previous chapter, Jorge had become involved in politics for the first time during the 1983 elections, even convincing his father, a lifelong Peronist, to allow a portrait of Alfonsín to hang in the entrance to their family home.[45] For both Jorge and Catalina, the PAN transferred onto very personal aspirations. In Jorge's case, the PAN was his initiation into municipal politics and the beginning of a lifelong involvement in local and provincial Radical Party dealings. As PAN agents, Jorge and Catalina felt a deep sense of pride in their work that went beyond food delivery. Catalina described her role as "a public health worker, not just a coordinator of merchandise. . . . The PAN was a way for us to help one another, after the individualism of the military [regime]. . . . As a PAN Agent, I raised consciousness that together we could actually do better."[46]

While many PAN agents recalled their time working with the food program as a transformative personal experience, the reactions of those on the receiving end of the aid were more ambiguous. On the one hand, the food was critical aid, which provided an important supplement and temporary relief from hunger. One man remembers receiving the PAN box as a child, saying that it "saved" him and his four siblings while his parents were out of work. "It was food," he said, "not clientelism."[47] Other recipients were pleased that corned beef was included in the food package.[48] Corned beef was primarily a product made for export, and the inclusion of the canned meat signified a new type of national belonging through consumption. On the other hand, for some the contents of the box were completely antithetical to their social practices. In the central pampa regions of Argentina, many boxes came with dried black beans. PAN officials received reports of beans being used to stuff children's toys or thrown into the streets, because according to food recipients, "beans were what Indians ate."[49] For others, the experience sparked intense feelings of humiliation. Many women would take the food out of the prominent box with its big logo and place it in plastic bags to take home. Others were skeptical of government incursion into their neighborhoods and refused to come out to get the food at all. In one area of Quilmes, home to a large Bolivian community, PAN meetings were brief affairs. The women only spoke Quechua and were reluctant to participate in the ancillary activities.[50] Many women went to the meetings and did not think much about them until the next month. The PAN, they said, was one more of a series of aid programs.

In structure and design, family was at the heart of the PAN's vision of civic life. The PAN, according to a description of the program in training manuals, sought to help parents, "not replace them." The manual continued, "We respect [parents'] situation as citizens and as part of a social reality, in a country that has not been able to ensure them the right to work, housing, and education, and that has not helped feed their children."[51] If restoring the integrity of family life was an aim of the PAN, women were responsible for guaranteeing its success. Female heads of households were the only individuals allowed to accept food. Mothers were required to attend monthly community meetings to receive the food box. PAN officials believed women would be more open to receiving aid than their male counterparts. They also assumed that women would be less inclined to squander the goods, and that as women, they "would know what to do with the food," rationing it for their families over the course of the month.

The PAN's women-centered focus took cues from social programs dating to the mid-twentieth century. As Carolina Barry has explored, during the first Peronism, female activists of the Partido Peronista Femenino (Peronist Feminine Party) frequently used community meetings for literacy instruction, cooking classes, and political formation. The gatherings were attempts to "Peronize" families and to gain movement followers through outreach to women. The PAN's monthly meetings recalled these encounters and constituted deliberate efforts to build support for the Radical Party. Direct contact with female heads of households was also an opportunity to outflank male breadwinners and Peronist unions and to thereby challenge Peronist dominance, especially in the outskirts of Buenos Aires.[52] In this way, the PAN mirrored Peronist social programs of the past, even as PAN agents described their work as part of a new era in national life.

Official descriptions of the PAN cast food, family, and the critical role of mothers as building blocks of a new, rights-based democracy. In his presentation of the PAN, Raúl Alfonsín emphasized that food aid would "strengthen family relations and the mother-child bond as an expression of Argentine solidarity."[53] Along the campaign trail, Alfonsín had made special appeals to Argentine women, and to mothers in particular. His campaign propaganda characterized mothers as "the main protagonists of [Argentina's] march towards greatness" and "responsible for the social reparations" that awaited the nation following the end of the dictatorship.[54] Maternal references like these called to mind the Mothers and Grandmothers of the Plaza de Mayo, whose denunciations of state terror had exposed the regime's violent dismantling of domestic family life. Often, however, Alfonsín's message to Argentine mothers did not explicitly mention political violence, but rather a more encompassing notion of social injustice that they would help to overcome. "Cast your votes against malnutrition!" exclaimed a campaign flyer directed at women. "You maintain the family, balance the budgets . . . and you know that infant mortality and malnutrition are not just statistics."[55] The daily struggles to provide for family needs reflected a national emergency that many women could relate to—and voice indignation about—even if their lives had not been directly impacted by state violence or acute hardship. While families had been broken during the dictatorship through a combination of political and economic violence, the PAN sought to rebuild them, with mothers guiding the state-led process in the home.

In theory, the PAN positioned women as bearers of democratic practice and knowledge. In practice, the PAN did not set out to challenge traditional notions of motherhood or family life. The ideal family that emerged from the PAN envisioned a nuclear family, with a male breadwinner at the helm and a female dedicated to child-rearing and domestic management. In the three PAN training manuals published between 1984 and 1988, no mention was made of women working outside of the home or raising families on their own. Yet the PAN could often offer women rich and surprising spaces for exchange. The monthly food distribution meetings were an integral part of the program, geared toward complementary public health, literacy, and education programs. Throughout the 1980s, this aspect of the PAN attracted the attention of social scientists and food specialists throughout Latin America. In 1986, a Brazilian anthropologist conducted fieldwork in Greater Buenos Aires. His field notes provide a rich window into a PAN meeting and are worth quoting at length:

> The PAN Agent began by asking all of those present what the word "woman" meant to them, and they had a "brain storm" session as a group. . . . The Agent began by opening up the question of personal health in a very simple manner. She drew a picture of a body and asked each woman to affix a body part to the drawing. . . . Finally, she asked each woman to say something nice about themselves. I thought the dynamic of the group worked very well, and that the PAN agent in charge of the meeting was trying to introduce the idea that the women were valuable, and that they mattered as individuals. All of this was geared toward transmitting the basic public health message of the meeting, which was that they all commit to scheduling a gynecological exam over the course of the next month. . . . [L]et me make clear that the women had a very difficult time talking openly about sexuality and believing that they were important. I was also very impressed that the PAN agent was herself an ex-recipient of the PAN. She was able to transmit the message of the meeting in a very clear way because she was a lot like them.[56]

This description is evidence of a particularly dynamic PAN meeting, illuminating what scholars have described as the gendered realms of transitional politics in Latin America.[57] The PAN was not explicitly geared toward democratizing gender relations, but many women used PAN meetings to articulate a range of gender-based political demands. Catalina Vera recalled that during the meetings she coordinated, a class on food preparation could morph into a discussion about the ill-functioning sewage systems in Quilmes or the dirt roads that became impassable when it rained. During a meeting in which municipal officials provided information for getting national identity cards, women opened up with frank stories about the discrimination they repeatedly faced at the municipal offices. One woman told of being humiliated when she went to the municipality to seek a subsidy. In confusion she said she had come for the "suicidio," as opposed to the "subsidio." As she recalled the embarrassment she felt as the municipal workers laughed at her, other women opened up about their travails in the face of the local authorities. PAN meetings were at once direct contact with the state and forums safely removed from it. At the same time, the issues women discussed in meetings did not necessarily include the PAN agent present or local government officials. Women opened up about domestic violence and about their children. For others, the monthly meeting was a rare occasion to visit with neighbors, to exchange gossip and neighborhood news. Some used the meeting as a chance to exchange recipes for the PAN goods or to coordinate communal food purchases and childcare duties. "The food," as Catalina remembered, "was just an excuse."[58]

Over the course of the PAN in Greater Buenos Aires, this communal aspect of the program also raised alarms. For the Buenos Aires federal police force, the PAN represented a potential threat. Throughout the program's six years in operation, the police took great interest in the progress of the PAN, especially its dealings with local, progressive churches. For the police, the PAN structure reeked of a leftist menace. In classified memos, security agents took great care to file detailed descriptions of the participation of priests and residents of *villas miserias*. The sense from these communications was that the PAN meetings represented the coordinated mobilization and organization of poor people, and with it echoes of the upheavals of the armed revolutionary movements of the 1970s.[59]

This reading was somewhat off base, however. The PAN mixed paternalistic poor relief with the political impetus and rhetoric of democratic openings. While evidence suggests that the PAN could be a mobilizing experience for many PAN recipients and agents, the idea was not to redefine family or to bring democracy into the home in any radically transformative way. The fact that women were the main recipients of aid, while grounded in a practical logic, coded poverty as a primarily female issue, while reinforcing the program's charitable nature. The PAN also failed to gain new adherents to the Radical Party or to replace the territorial and cultural dominance of Peronism in Greater Buenos Aires. More often than not, critics of the PAN cited the program as a form of propaganda—"food in exchange for votes"—often linking the program to local corruption, clientelism, and nepotism. Going forward, critiques of the food program on a national stage also began to harmonize with growing calls for state downsizing and an overall belief in the exhaustion of welfare programs, based on negative judgments of the worthiness of demobilized, poor, and unemployed citizens and their families.

THE PAN ON A NATIONAL STAGE

The PAN had a concrete history in the provinces and municipalities where it functioned, but it also occupied a place in larger political debates, especially as the

Alfonsín government faltered in the fiscal realm. As originally conceived by law-makers, the PAN was an emergency measure approved for two years that would be eliminated as soon as government policies remedied the economic crisis left behind by the military regime. It emerged at a time of great optimism at the start of the democratic return and of overall support for the Alfonsín government. When the PAN was extended for the first time in 1986, however, it coincided with the beginning of severe economic woes and waning enthusiasm for the Radical administration. By then, the early gains of the Plan Austral, the economic plan that had eradicated inflation seemingly overnight, began to stall. In the face of rising food costs caused by inflation, more individuals joined the rosters of the PAN. The ongoing need for food aid unleashed a range of criticisms from across the political spectrum.

For members of the Peronist party, the PAN was proof of their movement's claims to social justice and welfare. Following the Peronists' defeat in the 1983 presidential election, the party entered a period of dramatic flux and steady trans-formation.[60] The Alfonsín administration assumed office with hopes that its elec-toral victory would continue to sway Peronist loyalties during a moment when it seemed as though Peronist allegiances were up for grabs as never before. But those aspirations faded quickly. Members of the Radical administration underestimated the Peronist labor movement's ongoing ability to adapt and regroup, a fact that had been soundly proven over decades of proscription, leadership changes, and the recent de-fanging of the movement through state terror. The Alfonsín govern-ment's early plans to reform the trade unions led almost immediately to the reuni-fication of the CGT, which had been divided during the military dictatorship. In early 1984, the administration's most ambitious project to reorganize the Peronist trade unions, the Mucci Law, failed to pass in the senate by one vote.[61] The failure of the Mucci Law constituted a costly legislative defeat for the new administration. It set the stage for a renewed Peronist block in Congress, where Peronists con-trolled the Senate, and increasingly tense relations between the administration and the labor movement, which virtually paralyzed the government several times between 1983 and 1989 with thirteen general strikes.[62] Increasingly, the Alfonsín administration's goal became the maintenance of "social peace" to avoid the public fallout from general strikes. The demise of the union reform law suggested that the democratic restoration constituted less a break with the past than a profound reworking and adaptation of political identities and institutions.

Almost immediately following their loss in the 1983 presidential election, Per-onist leaders set out to understand the causes of their defeat, embarking on a short-lived, though profound, remaking of party structures. Peronist reformers sidelined the more "orthodox" union bosses associated with the military regime, whom they blamed for their electoral defeat. Jettisoning union hierarchies, local Peronist activists created new patronage networks among the urban poor on the neighborhood and municipal levels.[63] The reformers also set out to challenge the Radical Party by adapting the language of republicanism espoused by Alfonsín and his supporters and began to institutionalize and modernize the Peronist party. These efforts paid off. Between 1985 and 1987, leaders of the Peronist Renovation, as the Peronist reform movement was known, not only gained ground within their party but also reasserted Peronist dominance in regions where the Radical Party had bested them in 1983, the province of Buenos Aires foremost among them.[64]

For leaders of the Peronist Renovation, the PAN provided a perfect foil for their efforts. In 1987, Antonio Cafiero, recently elected governor of Buenos Aires on the Renovating ticket, took aim at the PAN: "It gives me a good laugh when I see Radical committees creating organizations for communal purchases, as if that were 'participation.' Let's talk about participation in power, let's talk about participation in wealth, let's talk about participation in salaries. Not these small and peripheral models of communal purchases, these PAN handouts, or anything else that spoils [enturbiar] the minds of Argentines."[65] Cafiero's depiction of the PAN emphasized the demobilizing instrument of food aid as charity. He contrasted the robust and galvanizing force of Peronism with an image of the Radical Party that relied on unambitious gestures such as communal purchases and the staid procedure of political committees that ignored the structural causes of economic and social disenfranchisement. With the government making more concessions to international lenders and forming plans to privatize select national industries, and the growing discontent in Greater Buenos Aires and other urban centers, Peronist renovators highlighted the ways that the Alfonsín government had fallen short of its social agenda—and argued that the scenario would look quite different if they were in power.

While the reform-minded sector of Peronism used the PAN to support its transformation, the food program also sparked debates about the very necessity of a welfare-granting state. For a vocal sector along the center-right of the political spectrum, the PAN was evidence of a bloated and dysfunctional public sector. The newspaper La Nación summarized this position succinctly in a 1988 editorial, shortly after the PAN was extended for the second time: "Given the state of the nation, in light of the current economic crisis, the distributive works of the paternalistic benefactor state will never be solved by such measures." The solution, the editorial argued, was to "divest the state of such bureaucracy."[66] This sentiment was echoed by members of the conservative UCeDé, which grew steadily over the course of the decade as the main advocate for neoliberal reforms in Argentina. María Julia Alsogaray, the daughter of UCeDé founder Álvaro Alsogaray and herself a rising force in Congress, argued that the PAN was "creating a generation of children of the State. . . . By receiving food from the hands of the State and not from their parents their psychological structure is changed fundamentally, and we cannot expect them to have the necessary dose of energy and individual activity that is essential in order to propel this country forward."[67] To conservative critics, food distribution represented a potential danger, and their commentary linked the PAN to accusations of government overreach and the possible disintegration of family life. For supporters of the UCeDé, the PAN reinforced arguments in favor of promarket prescriptions. These claims rested on an assertion that the market would be more efficient at meeting human needs than the state, a proposal that gained strength at the precise moment that state-based projects such as the PAN began to falter.

Though critics pointed to the PAN as proof of the spendthrift ways of an antiquated state apparatus, in reality the PAN encompassed a small percentage of expenditures.[68] Over the course of its six years in operation, food prices fluctuated due to inflation; however, the average PAN box cost the state approximately US$12.[69] Purchases made directly through the National Grain Board also streamlined costs. Foodstuffs included in the PAN box often fell 40 percent below their retail value.[70] Evidence also suggests that the PAN frequently propped up faltering regional enterprises. In 1987, the Mar del Plata Chamber of Fishing Industries signed a contract for the production of eighty-five hundred tons of hake (*merluza*) to be canned and included in the PAN boxes. According to one estimate, the purchase accounted for a "20% increase in local [production], a significant boon to local businesses, and the maintenance of jobs for employees who work directly or indirectly within the fishing industry."[71] Purchases for the PAN also supported the sunflower oil industry and led to increased consumption of corned beef, a product primarily geared for export.[72]

The PAN was decidedly less costly and inefficient than its detractors claimed. Yet the image of the program that emerged in public life tended to confirm negative impressions. Stories circulated denouncing food recipients who sold their boxes, exchanged food for alcohol, or stole merchandise from distribution centers. In 1988, twenty thousand PAN boxes were found, seemingly left to rot, in a warehouse in the province of Corrientes.[73] In Berisso, located in the province of Buenos Aires, PAN boxes regularly disappeared at night from a technical school that functioned as a PAN distribution center.[74] In Mar del Plata, along the Atlantic coast, PAN agents denounced the local director of the program for laziness and for failing to do his job.[75] These stories illustrated snapshots of the PAN from around the country. They appeared frequently in local and national media, then just as quickly vanished. Remnants of the PAN lingered in the public eye, however, and they formed a general picture of a program hampered by unaccountable public servants or scheming beneficiaries. Rumors and innuendo surrounding state welfare programs and the moral rectitude of welfare recipients were hardly new.[76] But the PAN also had a special charge in the context of democratic restoration. According to its mandate, the PAN sought to form new citizens while feeding them and encouraging participation. Mainstream impressions of the program directly contradicted these aims. Despite the varied trajectories of the PAN in the locales where it functioned, the PAN that emerged in public opinion squandered goods on the least worthy individuals.

There was some truth to reports of PAN breakdowns. Each time the program was extended (in 1986 and 1987), that extension coincided with a decline in operations. Delivery times for food aid grew longer as the program wore on. Instead of thirty days between deliveries, wait times could extend past forty. And though the intervals between deliveries became longer, the amount of food in the PAN box remained the same. That meant that food recipients struggled to stretch the goods over a longer period of time. In addition, the contents of the box were rarely consistent. Corned beef, one of the most popular foods, only appeared in the boxes until 1986. Other staple goods were often left out completely. Oil was substituted for lard; polenta and flour varied from month to month. One program worker calculated three hundred variations of the contents of the boxes over the course of five years.[77] Not surprisingly, PAN recipients complained about these fluctuations and protested that they did not have any say in determining the contents of the boxes. There were attempts to survey the popularity of items, but that information was never applied in any concerted way to make changes according to the requests of welfare recipients.[78]

While PAN beneficiaries objected to being left out of decisions regarding the box contents, other families and individuals who fit the official criteria for food aid were left out of the program altogether. A 1988 report found that 12 percent of households—approximately 230,000 families—received the PAN in the nineteen townships that then made up Greater Buenos Aires.[79] The PAN did reach intended beneficiaries, but it did not help all families in growing need of assistance. The report concluded: "Almost 100,000 structurally poor households and 350,000 pauperized households have never received the PAN."[80] The same report charted a 12.7 percent increase in poverty throughout Greater Buenos Aires between 1980 and 1987.[81] According to the report's findings, the PAN had good coverage, but it did not address the food security of all of the people who increasingly required aid.[82]

Against widely circulated images of a bloated state or unworthy aid recipients, the PAN instead confirmed a picture of government institutions and citizens struggling in the absence of resources. As more individuals required assistance, the state food program was less equipped to provide for them. The PAN stumbled at the very top of its administration as the inflationary economy put limits on individual as well as government purchasing power. The National Grain Board continued regular purchases of food, but the currency was not worth as much, nor could it buy as many goods as prices crept higher. Enthusiasm for the PAN waned even among the program's most enthusiastic boosters. Jorge Cobos acknowledged, "There was a decline in the program. I would say that the PAN Agents were tired.

The pay was nothing, and after three years, two or three years, of working day and night against I don't know how many problems. . . . [W]ell, there was a bit of a decline even among the agents in terms of their momentum to want to do things."[83]

Despite the decline in PAN operations, critics of the program could not feasibly call for its outright elimination. As financial woes deepened, the need for aid also increased. From mid-1987 onward, many officials lobbied for the transfer of the program to the provinces. For the UCeDé, arguments about federalizing the PAN supported their proposals for decentralization and dismantling the welfare apparatus. For members of the Peronist party, transfer of the PAN to the Peronist-controlled provinces supported their arguments that the administration of welfare and poverty reduction were their domains. The Buenos Aires minister for social action, Alberto Cormillot, argued that the PAN was "indefensible," citing figures of approximately 400,000 children who went to bed hungry each night in the province as proof that the PAN had failed.[84] During a 1988 visit to Quilmes, the site of the PAN launch just four years before, and with the next presidential elections already in sight, Cormillot confidently declared that "the grave problem of malnourished children in marginalized neighborhoods will be solved definitively with the victory of Peronism in 1989."[85]

Throughout its six years in operation (1984–1990), the PAN reflected the promise and limitations of the Alfonsín government's social agenda. The pledge to eradicate the hunger caused by military rule formed part of the administration's initial goals to rebuild a rights-based democracy. Over time, however, advocates and detractors wielded food relief and talk of hunger to expose the fissures at the center of constitutional return and the transformation of the welfare state at the end of the twentieth century. Actors of varied political positions—from Peronist reformers, to food recipient families, to the conservative politicians of the UCeDé—voiced understandings of the Alfonsín administration as an impediment to economic development and social justice. Seen from across the political spectrum, the PAN seemed to herald the exhaustion of a particular type of welfare, at least as conceived by the Alfonsín government.

The history of the PAN illuminates the changing politics of need in the aftermath of military rule. The dictatorship shifted the geographies of extreme hunger to include urban centers such as Greater Buenos Aires. Faced with this emergency, policy makers experimented with new ways of measuring and responding to poverty. In seeking to quickly alleviate the most acute forms of suffering, the PAN divorced aid from other avenues of economic advancement and social mobility, ultimately breaking with forms of welfare provision that had emerged during the first era of Peronism at midcentury. And though the Radical Party's 1983 electoral victory sparked hopes among Alfonsín's supporters that they could capture Peronism's social base, the PAN eventually helped shore up the Peronist Renovation, allowing its leaders to reaffirm the movement's commitment to social justice and to remake its identity into the "party of the poor" in Argentina.

The Alfonsín government did not preside over the end of state-led welfare in Argentina, however. The more accelerated dismantling of social programs would come over the course of the 1990s, and paradoxically under the leadership of a Peronist government working in concert with the forces of the UCeDé. However, the ideological groundwork for the retrenchment of welfare programs found fertile ground in the context of the democratic return. The PAN did provide critical relief to many in the name of "fundamental human rights." Yet a closer look at the PAN also reveals a more restricted vision of social welfare and family life, a vision that addressed the most pressing but most elemental need and by means that had little capacity for fulfilling other demands.

The narrow designs of the PAN, which emphasized the charitable and palliative nature of food distribution, ultimately reinforced arguments that programs such as the PAN were wasteful, unnecessary, and futile. "What is the PAN good for?" asked a 1986 article on the program shortly after it was extended for the first time. How would the "nutritional deficits of several million Argentines" ever be solved if the PAN did not "generate enough work to solve economic problems?" And how, the article concluded, could the food, "which barely covers a third of the monthly needs of a typical family," ever hope to "combat the poverty of tomorrow?"[86] As time wore on, realizing the promise of the "right to eat" would continue to test the foundations of the democratic return.

4

"Chernobyl Chickens"

Economic Planning and the Caso Mazzorín

For several weeks in the winter of 1988, Argentines closely followed the story of several thousand tons of chicken purchased by the government. According to the rumors, mysterious trucks began moving foul-smelling cargo through the outskirts of Buenos Aires, hauling loads of putrefying, state-bought poultry. The fleets, it was said, roamed the streets in the dead of night, towing ashen and fetid birds in search of dumping grounds and leaving a rancid stench in their wake. These whispers gained momentum over the coming days and weeks. Evening news programs shocked viewers with images of decaying chickens dumped into the Buenos Aires Ecological Reserve, seemingly left to rot, symbols of government waste and inefficiency. The most damning rumors claimed that the poultry, much of which had been imported from Hungary and Yugoslavia, was contaminated by radiation from the recent Chernobyl nuclear disaster. Comedians dedicated entire routines to the "radioactive" birds, lambasting public officials, whom they portrayed as distant and corrupt with little regard for public welfare. Eventually, congressional hearings on the matter drew overflowing crowds and a media frenzy to the Ministry of Domestic Trade (Secretaría de Comercio Interior, SCI) and led to the resignation of its embattled secretary. Governors across the country issued warnings against eating chicken. Poultry consumption, steadily on the rise over the previous decade, plummeted nationwide. Domestic chicken producers, consumer groups, and opposition politicians cried foul. What eventually became known as the "Caso Mazzorín"—named after the official who had overseen the poultry purchases—coincided with the beginning of a severe economic emergency that ended in a crisis of hyperinflation. It began, however, with little to no fanfare a few years before, at a moment of widespread faith in government efforts to restore fiscal stability.

This chapter examines the scandal of the government-purchased chicken in relation to the Alfonsín administration's attempts to deal with a complex economic crisis following the dictatorship. At its outset, the Alfonsín government inspired confidence that civic openings would pave the way for swift economic recovery, and with it a level of material comfort for all Argentines. Throughout 1984, the first full year of the constitutional return, the legacies of state terror were still coming into focus. "Democracy," the ubiquitous expression of the day, animated public confidence in the ability of the new administration to confront post-dictatorship realities and the aftershocks of the regional debt crisis. Informal polls signaled high levels of support for the president and the course of the transition. Food provision was one vehicle through which the Alfonsín government sought to fulfill the promises of restored democracy. Programs such as the PAN (discussed in chapter 3) were designed as necessary, though temporary, relief measures as recovery took effect. Yet individuals continued to feel the weight of economic constraints. As state planners moved between tense negotiations with Argentina's international lenders and fraught domestic debates about the end of state-led development, government planners gradually relinquished decades-old Keynesian policies in favor of heterodox "shock" programs. By 1985, the exigencies of what the Alfonsín administration termed a "wartime economy," which called for individual sacrifice and financial austerity, had altered the terms of the transition and the Alfonsín coalition's vision for a rights-based, democratic future.

Scholars have investigated how the military dictatorship began to reorient the Argentine economy toward neoliberalism, a process that began in the 1970s and came to fruition in the 1990s.[1] Less attention has been paid to how this transformation was experienced during the decade in between. The Caso Mazzorín, as this chapter shows, illustrates how consumption and everyday economic activity connected individuals most intimately to fiscal planning and a changing economic order. Throughout the 1980s, the realms of daily life—from the butcher shop to the local vegetable stand—emerged as battlegrounds of democratic restoration. In 1988, when rumors of rotting chickens exploded in the media with accusations of government corruption and illegal procurement of contaminated foodstuffs, they marked the end of a popular belief that associated constitutional return with stability and material well-being.

Beyond the raucous media spectacle, what followed the discovery of the chickens also revealed much more about the accommodation of powerful economic actors in the new democratic system and the inability of the Alfonsín government to manage the fiscal situation and public unrest. Industrial food producers insisted that the chickens represented material proof of the antiquated interventionist policies of the mid-twentieth century. As the scandal dragged on, public fallout from the case also reflected cultural sentiments that associated chicken, a far less popular dish than beef in a predominantly meat-eating nation, with economic malaise and scarcity, just as the country teetered on the edge of hyperinflation.[2] Though tabloid journalists and opposition politicians fabricated many features of the story, this understudied, though infamous, food scandal convinced many of the irredeemable crisis of the regulatory state shortly before the full-scale implementation of neoliberal policies in the 1990s.

"CAUGHT BETWEEN TWO WORLDS:" ECONOMIC PLANNING, 1983–1985

In the final days of 1983, the noted economist Raúl Prebisch delivered a sobering assessment of Argentina's financial prognosis. "We cannot expect miracles," he said to an audience in his native province of Tucumán. "We must have faith, and above all, patience."[3] Prebisch, whose work had influenced a generation of theorists and state planners with his ideas about development and the fundamental inequalities that resulted from Latin America's role as a producer of raw materials for foreign markets, had recently been named an economic adviser to the newly inaugurated Alfonsín administration.[4] His appointment reflected the government's initial economic strategy, which embraced the fiscal recipes of the postwar period. Whereas the dictatorship had attempted to steer Argentina's economy away from its manufacturing base, many government officials believed that economic recovery depended on a return to the cornerstones of ISI and Keynesianism. Even as economic experts such as Prebisch wrung their hands at the fiscal panorama, and as columnists warned of a "ticking economic time bomb," officials harbored great hopes for a quick recovery.[5]

The Alfonsín administration's first economic team adopted a developmentalist agenda. The top officials at the Ministry of Economy and the Central Bank were longtime Radical Party collaborators. They had cut their teeth as young economists under the tutelage of Prebisch and in government posts during the 1950s and 1960s.[6] Bernardo Grinspun, the irascible minister of economy, began his career with the Illia government (1963–1966), later forming part of Alfonsín's inner circle of trusted associates. The echo of mid-1960s fiscal policy shaped the economic approach of the administration's first year in office.[7] As Grinspun described it, his top priority upon assuming his post was to "raise the factory curtains once again." The reactivation of the industrial economy, the restoration of real wages, and putting an end to unemployment aimed to reverse the economic policies of the dictatorship while modernizing the Argentine economy. Almost immediately, however, debt and the burden of inflation got in the way of Grinspun's intentions.

By 1984, Argentina's debt had reached approximately $45 billion, with interest payments hovering between 6 and 8 percent of GDP.[8] Alfonsín proclaimed repeatedly that only the "legitimate" debt would be paid, and he authorized a congressional committee to investigate its origins.[9] Argentine economists also played a prominent role in the creation of the Cartagena Consensus, which brought together several Latin American nations in search of common solutions to the growing problem of debt and the ascendance of financial institutions such as the International Monetary Fund (IMF) in the region.[10] Combined with this initiative, administration officials initially assumed that the IMF and the US Federal Reserve, which set global interest rates, would look favorably upon Argentina as it democratized and emerged from its long night of violence.[11] Argentine officials encountered no such goodwill. Rumors circulated in the international financial press that Argentina's debts would be classified as "problem loans," since the country had fallen behind on interest payments.[12] Added to these perceptions of economic insolvency, Bernardo Grinspun did not make a good impression on Argentina's lenders. In one infamous encounter, he was rumored to have dropped his pants during a meeting at the IMF. Post-dictatorship economic realities only meant the deepening of debt; crippling interest rates led to reluctant requests for more loans by the end of 1984.[13]

Though debt and inflation ultimately derailed many of Grinspun's original plans, there were some positive signs of recovery throughout 1984. Industrial and agricultural production expanded by 3.8 percent and 3.1 percent, respectively.[14] Increased spending on education and the extension of social programs such as the PAN food program also alleviated some of the more harmful effects of the economic emergency. But these alone could not offset the lingering crisis. During the first year of the Alfonsín administration, consumer prices rose by more than 600 percent. Despite faith in a swift economic turnaround, fiscal woes threatened to eclipse the euphoria of democratic return. The result was a growing sense of economic emergency that permeated daily life at the dawn of the democratic era.

In March 1984, as the Alfonsín administration approached its first one hundred days in office, the government announced a one-week restriction on consumer sales of red meat in butcher shops, restaurants, and supermarkets. According to the domestic trade secretary, who announced the measure, the sales restrictions were an emergency provision, geared toward reigning in agricultural producers, whom the administration blamed for spurious activities resulting in rising food prices. Government officials hoped that a one-week suspension of meat sales would ultimately lower consumer prices by providing a brief respite from inflation, while also boosting reserve stocks of meat. According to the conservative journalist Joaquín Morales Solá, however, the measure only exacerbated a stubborn problem. "The scarcity of many food products and their rising prices produced an unusual event," he wrote. "The government opened up a conflict in the streets, in daily life, whereas before these conflicts were limited to the bell towers of political power. The fights over the union law, or the first clashes with the military do not affect the stomachs of Argentines."[15] Morales Solá tapped into popular understandings about the relationship between wages and prices, their ability to shape daily experience, and by implication, the fortunes of political leaders.[16] His editorial fanned the flames of public outcry against the measure, which strained faith in the government's ability to quell economic anxieties at the onset of the democratic return. As Morales Solá was well aware, governments had experimented with consumer sales restrictions dating to the second Peronist administration, which limited purchases of red meat in the early 1950s in order to build reserve stocks. The 1984 sales restrictions, while geared toward a similar goal, raised fundamental questions about the new limits of state regulation of domestic markets.

From the start, the sales restrictions failed to achieve their intended results. Anxious shoppers emptied supermarkets in Buenos Aires and the surrounding suburbs in the days leading up to the imposition of the measure. Consumers reported price hikes of over 50 percent on goods ranging from eggs to parsley. By the second day of the weeklong sales suspensions, the newspaper *Clarín* announced shortages of substitute foods such as chicken and fish. The president of the House Wives Association issued a statement in protest: "The consumer doesn't have any of these economic ideas in mind [when they shop]. . . . When housewives go into the butcher shop, we want good quality meat at good prices!"[17] Addressing his critics in the days following the end of the sales suspensions, Ricardo Campero, the domestic trade secretary, stood by the measure: "When people say that I threaten the freedom to buy and sell, I say that the freedom to eat is threatened when the ability to buy and sell under monopoly conditions, under usurious conditions, eliminates the freedom to consume that all Argentines deserve."[18] As he denounced the ability of food producers and distributors to inflate prices, Campero defended a government promise to ensure the basic right to food through state regulation of markets.

Despite efforts to restore a measure of economic stability, by the one-year anniversary of the Alfonsín administration, the panorama looked bleak. Consumer prices continued to rise, and in 1984, annual inflation peaked at 688 percent, up from 433 percent the previous year.[19] Runaway price increases undermined the purchasing power of real wages and cut into modest salary increases. Loan restructuring with the IMF essentially meant that Argentina would get new loans in order to pay interest on old loans. The administration's early attempts to create a Latin American "debtors club" had also begun to fizzle. At the same time, the overall burden of the debt continued to grow.[20] Often the official response from the government did little to reassure citizens. While Alfonsín decried the pressures of global lending institutions and repudiated the economic philosophy of the military regime, his pronouncements could also sound vague and imprecise: "We are going to combat inflation, and at the same time we are going to make real wages grow, and at the same time we will expand the Argentine economy. . . . The technocrats of failure, the technocrats of Argentine misfortune are afraid. They say [our goals] are incompatible. To them, we say no."[21]

Part of the haziness of Alfonsín's language stemmed from the fact that he, along with his economic team, did not always grasp the global and domestic economic scenarios they were describing. The early 1980s marked the final death throes of the postwar economic consensus. For close to forty years, states around the world had taken the lead as guarantors of welfare, jobs, and economic growth. By the 1980s, the common sense of that approach was in full crisis. Advocates for a new world order argued that the path to economic and personal freedom lay in divesting the state from market controls. The separation of the fiscal from the governmental realm formed the essence of a burgeoning neoliberal worldview. Policy makers at the IMF, World Bank, and US Federal Reserve stood at the center of these transformations.[22] In the United States, the recessionary dip and inflationary fears of the late 1970s coincided with the emergence of a conservative block, which helped shore up support for formulas "to curb the power of labor, deregulate industry, agriculture, resource extraction, and liberate the powers of finance both internally and on the world stage."[23] It was "morning again in America," as Ronald Reagan broadcasted. Yet Reagan's domestic vision was completely bound up in the global arena, in particular with the fate of the debtor nations of the developing world, whose debt came due in US dollars.

Argentina's fiscal planners recognized these challenges, even if they could not foresee their resolution. During a March 1985 visit to Washington, D.C., Alfonsín spoke stridently about the economic realities that were conspiring against Latin America's new democracies. During a Rose Garden address, with Reagan by his side, he painted a clear picture of the problem of debt in the region. "Our democracies have inherited very heavy burdens," he began. "That is why, Mr. President, in Latin America, we are ready to govern with the austerity that our times are demanding. We are making the necessary adjustments to overcome. But we cannot make adjustments that will actually impose sacrifices on those that have less. . . . And to ask from our peoples . . . a bigger effort, is no doubt to condemn them to marginality, to extreme poverty, to misery."[24] Alfonsín's remarks came in the midst of a new round of tense negotiations with the IMF for a $500 million "bridge loan," which the IMF refused to grant if Argentina did not adopt austerity measures such as inflationary controls and reductions in public spending.[25] While Alfonsín conceded that some austerity was needed, he delivered a firm rebuttal to the prescriptions of the IMF and its proponents in the Reagan administration with a warning about the looming threat of rising debt for the democratic future of the region and the well-being of its citizens.

As the legacies of the dictatorship came into sharper focus throughout 1984–1985, it was not just external financial difficulties that concerned economic officials. The regime had also radically transformed the workings of the Argentine economy. The move away from manufacturing toward finance produced several simultaneous consequences: While small and medium-sized businesses, industrial workers, and other popular sectors bore the hardships of the new economic model, oligopolistic producers with ties to transnational markets and capital gained greater sway over the domestic economy.[26] This became most apparent in the realm of food prices. While Bernardo Grinspun revived the use of regulatory agencies such as the National Grain Board (JNG) and the Junta Nacional de Carne (National Meat Board, JNC) to control food prices and to keep at bay economic monopolies, large agricultural producers were able to flout those controls relatively easily.[27] As with the growing realization of the problem of debt, it quickly became clear that the dictatorship had reshaped Argentina's domestic economy by fortifying the links between international conglomerates and local firms, which leveraged those connections to pressure the government in various ways.

From rising food prices to factory closings, these new economic realities visibly marked Argentina. However, the full-scale implications of the shifting global order were nebulous at best. As mentioned previously, the first cohort at the helm of the Ministry of Economy had come of age professionally decades before. In the intervening years, the world had changed profoundly. Much like the public perceptions of the economy, state actors also approached the fiscal realm with a sense of the unknown. The embrace of full-scale privatization and deregulation was not yet part of the common sense of government practice and lived experience—not globally, and certainly not within Argentina. The effects of the dictatorship prompted widespread calls to oppose neoliberalism's advocates. However, the path of mid-twentieth-century state planning was not only increasingly untenable on a global stage, it was also not working on the ground. "We were caught between two worlds," as one administration official characterized the dilemma.[28] The tension between the encroaching reality of a changing global economy and the constraints of fast-expiring methods of economic planning began to alter the Alfonsín administration's fiscal course from 1985 on.

WARTIME ECONOMY, 1985–1987

In early 1985, Bernardo Grinspun resigned. The appointment of his successor, former planning secretary Juan Vital Sourrouille, marked a dual shift within the administration, generationally and in terms of economic philosophy. Unlike Grinspun, Sourrouille had no formal affiliation with the Radical Party. The cohort of younger technocrats that made up his team had built their careers regionally and abroad in think tanks and academic institutions.[29] Like Grinspun, the functionaries under Sourrouille had also been trained in *cepalista* theories of development and dependency. However, the new group at the head of the ministry disagreed with Grinspun's approach to economic recovery, which had looked to expand industrial production and consumption. Instead, they argued that economic stability lay in inflationary controls. The recently installed planners feared an inflationary spiral along the lines of the 1975 Rodrigazo, the economic crisis that had accelerated the demise of Isabel Perón's fragile government.[30] That recent memory, plus the growing pressures of Argentina's lenders to tackle inflation in order to obtain new loans and refinance existing debts, fortified their convictions: Controlling inflation and the growing deficit overshadowed all other economic concerns in order to maintain debt payments and to safeguard domestic peace.

Alfonsín introduced the changes in economic planning to the public in April 1985. The trial to convict the juntas had recently begun, and rumors circulated of a possible military revolt. With apprehension in the air, Alfonsín issued a call for an assembly in the "name of democracy." Thousands converged on the Plaza de Mayo. The Radical Party faithful joined columns from the Peronist Party, the Partido Intransigente, human rights group, and unions, among many others, to defend the integrity of Argentina's fledgling constitutional government. Representatives from fifteen political parties warmed up the crowds by reading a joint statement repudiating the military threat. The chants, signs, and slogans of the gathering proclaimed widespread popular support for democratic institutions and the diminished power of the armed forces. To cheers, Alfonsín began his speech from the balcony of the government house with a tally of the achievements of the young democracy and a firm commitment to continue the trials. "Compatriots," he declared, "Your presence shows the strength, not of a single government, but of a democracy and a society that is . . . ready to fight to preserve its rights."[31]

Minutes into the speech, however, the president veered dramatically from the subject of the military to the economy. "But that is not what has brought you here tonight," he began. "I want to talk about the extreme difficulties that we will face. . . . We have inherited an economy off the rails and a devastated state." Continuing, he identified three challenges ahead:

> First, there is the legitimate voice of popular sectors who are expressing just demands. There is, at the same time, the need to put the economy in order, and this will be achieved through an adjustment, which will be hard and which will demand all of our strength. Finally, there is a third pressure, which is the need for economic growth. Recessions, when they persist over time, demoralize people and impede the realization of democracy. In this difficult situation, when faced with a hemorrhaging economy, we must address popular demands, and at the same time we have to order the economy and we have to grow. Compatriots, this is called a *wartime economy*, and we all need to draw conclusions.[32]

As Alfonsín braced the public for hard times going forward, he highlighted the popular mandate of his government, according to which social justice and economic growth were compatible and mutually reinforcing goals. The announcement of a "wartime economy," however, ran counter to the delicate balance of social and economic forces required to consolidate democracy. Alfonsín's pronouncement inverted the relationship between civic openings and economic health originally promoted by his government. "Wartime economy" implied that without economic stability there would be no political democracy. From the vantage point of the government house balcony, it was difficult to distinguish the cheers from the jeers as Alfonsín spoke. But it was not hard to imagine that for the crowds assembled in the plaza, the vision outlined by the president smacked of a radical departure in thought and action.

Alfonsín went on to compare Argentina's situation with the devastation of postwar Europe and Japan, nations, he affirmed, that were "now among the wealthiest in the world."[33] The path forward called for collective sacrifice. Argentina, a wartorn nation, required drastic new measures. Combating inflation was at the top of that list. Though he did not mention specifics, the president described a new approach to the economy, which would prioritize reducing the fiscal deficit through cutbacks in public spending. The other component, he added, would be privatization of select state enterprises. Inflation controls, reductions in public spending, and privatizations made up the baseline reforms advocated by Argentina's international lenders. Turning inward, Alfonsín also addressed industrial, agricultural, and labor leaders. He called for their cooperation and the creation of a new social pact to combat inflation. The president described these adjustments as the necessary sacrifices of a people committed to safeguarding democracy. The economic emergency constituted a state of exception. As such, the crisis justified a change of course to salvage democracy via the same recipes the president had so often decried. Riffing on his most popular campaign slogan, Alfonsín warned of the consequences of inaction, concluding, "[D]emocracy will not permit it, because democracy means voting, but it also means eating."[34]

Though few doubted the diagnosis that something needed to be done to improve the economy, Alfonsín's depiction of a wartime crisis akin to those of postwar Europe and Japan struck many as disingenuous. For one, even as Argentina blazed a path of democratization in the region, there was no Marshall Plan for South America. International support and investment demanded austerity measures that hampered economic reconstruction and domestic expansion. The United States, far from supporting Argentina, was ideologically and economically engaged in "democracy promotion" of a far different sort in Central America.[35] "Wartime economy" was also an infelicitous choice of words. While Alfonsín sought to rouse patriotic fervor through calls for individual sacrifice and collective will, the regime had also galvanized support for the sacrifices of a justified "dirty war." Finally, there was the ruse of the speech itself. Alfonsín issued a call for a national gathering to repudiate the military. But when people arrived at the plaza, they learned that inflation, not the armed forces, was the true enemy of democracy. Alfonsín's announcement of a wartime economy shifted the terms of the democratic transition. That switch, plus the announcement of a drastic change in economic planning via recipes associated with the military regime, alienated the crowd. Supporters and members of oppositional parties filed out of the plaza in dismay.

Though critics charged that Alfonsín was readying the nation for full-scale structural readjustment, the resulting plan proved much more heterodox. In June 1985, the administration launched the Austral Plan, a "shock" program aimed at halting inflation and promoting economic growth and employment. Its core consisted of a monetary reform and the creation of a new currency, the Austral, which cut three zeros off the peso, dramatically reducing inflation almost immediately. The plan also included other promarket recipes. The Central Bank committed to curbing bill printing, while overall state expenditures were reduced from approximately 35 percent of GDP in 1983 to 28.8 percent in 1986.[36] Other aspects of the plan, however, remained grounded in Bernardo Grinspun's early intentions via a system of price controls and salary and tariff freezes.[37]

Once announced, the Austral Plan required weeks of preparing Argentines for changes. Banks closed to stock up on the new currency; updated maximum price listings appeared in newspapers; grocery stores recalculated merchandise; and conversion lists were posted on city billboards to help people adjust to new exchange rates and timetables, from rental properties to business contracts. The success of the wartime economy depended on public adherence to the plan. It counted on the daily economic actions of individuals to keep the economy solvent, whether via maintaining bank deposits or adhering to price controls. On the day the plan launched, an official from the Ministry of Economy passed a bank with a line stretching for two blocks. "We're screwed," he thought, assuming that people were anxious to take their money out of the banks in order to buy US dollars. But as he cautiously approached people in line, he learned that they were there to renew their deposits. Thrilled, he ordered coffee for the entire crowd.[38] Government officials were genuinely surprised that the Austral seemed to meet with acceptance. At the same time, they counted on the fact that the economic plan left individuals very little room to divest from the national economy, to which they were intimately connected and on which their well-being depended.

The administration staked its legitimacy on the success of the Austral Plan. Almost immediately, the gamble worked. Inflation dwindled, dropping drastically from month to month. Between 1984 and 1985, annual inflation went from 688 percent to 385 percent.[39] Though this was still high, individuals felt the positive effects straightaway. The Austral Plan initiated the greatest period of social peace during the Alfonsín presidency. Despite a general strike in early spring 1985, tense relations with labor were offset by the successful completion of the military trials and the sentencing of nine of the main junta leaders. In the November 1985 legislative elections, the Radical Party received approximately 43 percent of overall votes, maintaining its majority in the Lower House. Economic peace also gave the administration the chance to move forward on two of its boldest initiatives, a proposed constitutional reform and the transfer of the capital from Buenos Aires to the Patagonian city of Viedma. By mid-1986, inflation had reached its lowest point since 1974.[40] Government propaganda declared the success of the wartime economy: "We are all fighting inflation. All Argentines. . . . [Our] only loss will be inflation."[41]

While the Austral Plan inched Argentina closer to the free-market formulas of the nation's lenders, another of its goals sought to regulate and stabilize internal markets via well-tested price controls on basic foodstuffs. These policies, which were designed to stave off inflation by creating equilibrium between wages and consumer prices, fell under the purview of the domestic trade secretary and directly connected citizens to economic planning via their everyday consumption. Following an initial period of strict freezes, by mid-1986 the maximum prices for goods ranging from milk and yerba mate, to household cleaning supplies, to beef and chicken began to shift from month to month. Satirists and pundits played on the dizzying task of keeping up with changing controls. At first, firms and food distributors adhered to the pricing guidelines, which helped maintain overall public confidence in the measures. Nonetheless, a growing gap between official prices and actual consumer costs produced a resurgence of inflationary fears. In July 1986, for example, the domestic trade secretary authorized an 8.4 percent increase on staple goods contained in the "family basket." Following the announcement, however, disgruntled shoppers reported increases of up to 20 percent on various products.[42] A butcher in the Flores neighborhood of Buenos Aires described the scenario in stark terms: "If you copy the prices on the board they won't reflect what really happens. I sell at higher prices, as we all do, than the ones we receive."[43] The tension between government-administered prices and the actual cost of goods fueled anxieties about black market speculation and possible shortages, setting off increasingly tense standoffs between agricultural and industrial food producers and state regulatory agencies. In this context, the events involving state-bought chickens and rumors of their possible contamination exploded the wartime economy and upset the ideal that economic well-being was possible within the new democracy.

PRICE CONTROLS AND MARKET REGULATIONS

Beginning in April 1986, the domestic trade secretary authorized the import of several thousand tons of gutted whole chickens. The JNG, the regulatory agency that also administered purchases for the PAN food program, oversaw the operation. Between August 1986 and April 1987, approximately thirty-eight thousand tons of government-purchased chicken arrived from France, Brazil, Venezuela, Uruguay,

Yugoslavia, and Hungary.[44] The purchases aimed to expand the low domestic supply and consumption of chicken and to offset the cyclical price variations of red
meat—an abiding staple of Argentine diets—especially during the winter months,
when meat supplies in domestic markets typically declined and the price of both
chicken and red meat spiked. Officials at the Ministry of Domestic Trade hoped
that the purchases would stabilize internal markets by lowering poultry prices and
by preventing domestic chicken producers from engaging in further price speculation. The measure, a well-established method of government regulation, had also
recently been applied in the case of potatoes imported from Poland and pork purchased from the United States. In all three cases, the operation functioned in much
the same way: the state made purchases through the JNG and paid the storage costs.
Then, when the domestic trade secretary determined that domestic markets needed
an infusion of certain goods, the products would be sold at a cost lower than the
original purchase price and released into domestic markets for sale. Presumably the
savings transferred to consumers in the form of a subsidy and lower food prices. In
turn, these policies would help to fulfill a government promise to ensure the basic
right to eat through state intervention in domestic markets.

Despite the precedent of similar interventions in food markets having been
implemented dating back to the 1930s, the poultry imports intensified already
strained relations between the state and agricultural and industrial food producers.[45] Following several decades of sustained growth and industrialization, heavily
subsidized by the state, by the 1980s production and international commodity
prices for a variety of agricultural staples dropped.[46] With the return to constitutional rule, several agricultural sectors, including the poultry industry, declared
themselves in crisis. Bitter clashes with the Alfonsín government over export taxes,
tariffs, and price controls escalated throughout the decade.[47] In 1985, the head of
CEPA (Centro de Empresas Procesadoras Avícolas), the lobbying group representing industrial poultry producers, wrote to the Ministry of Domestic Trade stating
that the controls limiting the maximum sale price of chicken were weakening an
already debilitated industry and "threatening the imminent paralysis of several
production facilities, and the jobs that they support."[48] The governor of Entre Ríos
province, home to 40 percent of chicken production nationwide, sent an urgent
letter warning of the "imminent" demise of the industry. Though he reiterated his
support for the recently announced Austral Plan and its system of price controls,
he argued that an exception should be made to adjust prices to be more favorable
to the poultry industry.[49] A similar telegram from the Restaurant, Hotel, and Bak-
ery Association warned of growing shortages of food such as chicken, fish, and
seafood, and urged speedy government intervention.[50]

Though it was still considered a secondary substitute for red meat, poultry
consumption had been steadily rising in Argentina since the late 1970s. In 1978,
Argentines ate five kilograms of chicken per person each year.[51] Those numbers

had been slowly on the rise ever since. Unlike the robust beef, wheat, and growing soy industries, which were oriented toward export, chicken produced in Argentina served mainly domestic markets. In the face of high levels of beef consumption—registering a whopping 75 kilograms per person in 1984—and concerns that those levels were not sustainable going forward, government officials saw an opportunity to make chicken more of a staple of Argentine diets. One way to do this was to urge national industries to increase production and to provide incentives such as state subsidies to do so. Proposals to reactivate the poultry industry did not get very far, however. In 1985, shortly after the announcement of the Austral Plan, Cargill, the multinational agribusiness giant and one of the two largest chicken producers in Argentina, informed the Ministry of Economy that it would halt its chicken production in protest against the recently announced price controls.[52] In the face of the Cargill "lockout," chicken supply in domestic markets dropped, and prices soared by over 121 percent. The Ministry of Domestic Trade, which had already floated proposals for poultry imports, authorized the measure by the end of 1985.

Plans to expand domestic poultry consumption were already in motion when Ricardo Mazzorín assumed the post of domestic trade secretary in April 1986.[53] An economist by training with ties to Alfonsín and his cohort dating to the late 1970s, Mazzorín was now in a prominent position charged with administering prices, regulating the supply of basic goods, protecting consumers, and negotiating with agricultural producers and food distributors. These tasks often worked at cross-purposes. Two previous secretaries had held the position since the end of the dictatorship, including Ricardo Campero, the official who authorized the 1984 restriction of red meat sales and endured the subsequent public fallout. Like his predecessors, Mazzorín quickly came into conflict with agricultural producers. In June 1986, just a few months after he assumed his post, the Argentine Rural Society (SRA), Argentina's oldest and most powerful lobbying group, representing the interests of the nation's landowning elite, and the Argentine Rural Confederation (CRA), which brought together medium-sized agricultural producers, organized a seventy-two-hour strike.[54] Their grievances included routine demands for tax breaks, an end to export tariffs on wheat and other agricultural products, and "the suspension of any and all *dirigiste* and interventionist policies that block production."[55] Following the end of the strike, Mazzorín issued a response to the producers: "Expect from me my sympathy, understanding, psychoanalytic therapy, anything but price liberations."[56]

Despite clashes like these and the ongoing protestations of domestic chicken producers, the poultry imports proceeded without much incident.[57] Brief mentions appeared in the press noting the first arrival of chicken from Brazil, ready for sale in June 1986. A total of 38,103 tons of government-purchased chicken arrived over the following year. By August 1987, 10,175 tons had been sold to 120 domestic distributors, including four of the biggest supermarket chains and providers: Santiago Domingo, Carnicerías Coto, Disco, and Hogar Obrero.[58] Another 3,000-plus tons were sold to Cuba as part of bilateral agreements between the two nations. That left a remaining reserve supply of approximately 24,000 tons of chicken, which were stored in ten refrigeration facilities paid for by the state. And there they sat, undisturbed, until mid-1988, when stories of rotten poultry electrified the public consciousness.

Why did this story, involving a well-established government regulatory measure and based mostly on hearsay and misinformation, cause such a public uproar, two years after the original poultry imports? Part of the answer lies in the broader context of the case, which unfolded against the collapse of the Austral Plan.

"CHERNOBYL CHICKENS" AND THE DECLINE OF THE AUSTRAL

The extended period of relative economic stability inaugurated by the Austral Plan abruptly came to an end in early 1988. Price controls, which for close to two years had maintained a tenuous peace between the government, business, and labor, faltered as inflation reared its head again. The year 1988 began with inflation hovering around 175 percent, more than double that of the previous year.[59] Critics of the administration busied themselves with debates over who or what was to blame for the inflationary spike, settling squarely on monetary policy and government regulatory measures. One financial consultant, who at first insisted that the records of the domestic trade secretary should be burned in the public square, called for a complete shutdown of the office. At the very least, he stated, the government would demonstrate its "willingness to accept market prices." As fantastical as such proposals sounded, remarked one journalist, they spoke to the realities of an economy "bordering on the absurd."[60] Under increased pressure, in April 1988 the government removed the price controls on all but a select number of goods contained in the family basket. The price liberations compounded the problems of an already weakened administration and ultimately did little to halt the steady rise in prices. Ricardo Mazzorín, who just a few years before had vowed to defend the system of price controls, publicly blamed rising consumer costs on food producers and accused the press of distorting the economic panorama.[61]

While the media manufactured a certain level of economic anxiety, individuals felt inflation most acutely in their kitchens and around the family table. "Eating is inflationary!" ran one headline.[62] Prices and inflation may have dominated the news, but that was because the urban middle classes felt their access to consumption rapidly changing. "The image of the petite-bourgeoisie with a car, apartment, and summer getaway belongs to the past," lamented one article.[63] Gone, it also seemed, were the days of the large supermarket purchase, which could sustain families for the entire month. Indeed, budgeting for the coming month, let alone the coming week, proved futile, as salaries did not keep pace with the rising costs of living. Shoppers complained of the exhausting task of bargain hunting as they ventured far beyond their neighborhood vendors in search of lower prices. Economic tightening even seemed to be having an impact on diets. One butcher observed: "Some people have stopped eating meat and they are becoming, what do you call them? Vegetarians," a scandalous proposition, he suggested, in a largely meat-eating nation.[64] In 1987, Argentines consumed 74.6 kilos of red meat per person each year. That figure represented a drop from a previous peak of 81.5 kilos in 1986.[65] Though it still had one of the highest levels of meat consumption in the world, ranking Argentina as one of the most food-secure nations in Latin America, statistics like these only heightened the sense that a bygone era of prosperity was slipping away.

It was against this background that an enterprising television reporter shocked viewers with a live broadcast from the Buenos Aires Ecological Reserve. In the glow of the early evening, the camera zoomed in on piles of discarded chicken, which when held up for closer inspection appeared covered in dirt and grime. These, the reporter claimed, were the remnants of approximately one hundred tons of rotten poultry that had been dumped after the cooling systems shut down at a government-paid refrigeration facility. The primetime display of alleged government waste in the midst of a wartime economy and collective thrift had an immediate, visceral impact. The gears of the Buenos Aires political scandal machine sprang into action. Never mind that the journalist who uncovered the story had been tipped off by a longtime business associate, the same politician who then led the subsequent congressional investigation into the case. Or that the reporter, finding no evidence of the chicken at the Ecological Reserve, had followed the frantic instructions of his producer to "get me some chickens in time for the 8 o'clock broadcast!"[66] The notorious "pollos de Mazzorín" (Mazzorín's chickens) became synecdoche for government corruption and malfeasance at a moment of creeping economic unease.

For several weeks, the story captivated national attention. Congressional hearings, the forced resignation of Mazzorín, and court battles that lasted through the next decade quickly followed. Opposition to the government-purchased chicken brought together lawmakers from poultry-producing regions and promarket politicians with ties to agribusiness. Their criticisms of the measure varied, but one overarching theme stressed the presumed misuse of public funds at a time of economic belt-tightening. Alberto Pierri, a Peronist congressman and the head of the congressional domestic trade commission, summed up the sentiment: "It doesn't seem logical that while the state finds money to buy chickens it can't find the cash to pay pensioners!"[67] Elected officials from chicken-producing regions such as the Entre Ríos province claimed that the imports damaged an already struggling national industry.[68] For many, the case came down to disregard of the general welfare—of citizens, consumers, and small producers—on the part of state officials. Arguments such as these ran through all subsequent public conversations about the case. Ultimately, it was the state's ability to regulate and intervene in domestic markets that was up for debate.

The charge was led by Alberto Albamonte, a congressman from the conservative Unión del Centro Democrático (UCeDé), whose leader, Álvaro Alsogaray, had refused to give the PAN food program a "blank check" in 1984.[69] Since then, the UCeDé had achieved some significant victories. Following legislative elections in 1987, the party became the third political force behind Peronism and the Radical Party and the main advocate for neoliberal reforms in Argentina. The party's platform listed among its goals the restoration of Argentina to its former status as one of the world's wealthiest nations by "replacing the current inflationary and *dirigiste* system" with the "free play of market forces."[70] As a relatively unknown UCeDé congressman with a penchant for publicity, Albamonte had gained notice for previous media stunts. In one instance, he rented an elephant from a traveling circus and rode it along the avenue of a well-heeled neighborhood of Buenos Aires. Draped in the names of select public enterprises, the animal represented the lumbering unproductivity of a heavy-footed state.[71] Shortly afterward, in protest against the government chicken, Albamonte paraded a giant Styrofoam bird in front of the Ministry of Domestic Trade to force a congressional investigation into the matter.[72]

At a time when attempts to stabilize the economy through the Austral Plan had begun to flounder, Albamonte and other members of his party fueled public ire. According to UCeDé leader Álvaro Alsogaray, the economic crisis "was not fleeting," but rather proof of "the exhaustion of an economic system," adding, "there is broad agreement on this point, from the Communists to our party."[73] Despite different critiques of the socioeconomic order, Alsogaray could more and more rightly claim that across the political spectrum there existed a belief that a type of developmental capitalism had run its course in Argentina. The uproar surrounding the government chicken illustrated this notion concretely at the level of daily experience. During the congressional hearings, which drew several hundred members of the press to an overflowing congressional annex, Albamonte denounced the chicken as "an event, which merited the unanimous revulsion of the citizenry."[74] He followed with an interpretation of the case and what he saw as its broader significance: "This occurred because all of the sudden a Domestic Trade Secretary became an entrepreneur and used the government to make a lousy deal for us all."[75] In his estimation, the world of business and the business of the state should have no business whatsoever. Reflecting years later on the specific law that had enabled government regulation of markets, he concluded, "Not even Stalin had such a powerful tool at his disposal."[76] As overwrought as these descriptions may have been, they spoke to a mounting concern that government efforts to regulate the economy only harmed citizens, if all that came of them was rotten chicken.

For their part, lawmakers and government officials defended the legitimacy of the measures. During his congressional testimony, Mazzorín emphasized Argentina's "long tradition" of food market regulations to protect consumers, declaring, "I uphold the regulatory state and the administration of prices to attend to popular needs."[77] Despite media attention and public reprobation, he argued, the government chickens were not at all exceptional.[78] To his critics in agriculture and industrial food production, he conceded that their concerns about the fate of their industries "were legitimate," but asserted that "I do not subordinate my decisions to them, rather to the consumer."[79] Addressing the charge that the poultry imports from abroad hurt national producers, Mazzorín cited statistics that showed a 17.5 percent uptake in chicken consumption, from 11 to 13 kilos per person between 1986 and 1988—an increase that presumably benefited the industry.[80] During that same period, the price of chicken had risen by 320 percent, a figure that while high, was still less than the cost of red meat, which had risen by 458 percent. Mazzorín concluded, "I know what the numbers tell me: the domestic supply increased and with that consumption as well." "Where," he asked, "is the damage?"[81]

Mazzorín cast the state in the role of consumer protector. Though grounded in the legal authority and historical precedent granted by his position in the Ministry of Domestic Trade, that reasoning did not come through in the public debates that followed. Instead, the image transmitted by the media—and of Mazzorín in particular—alternated between an aloof technocrat wedded to mathematical calculations that did not reflect reality and a rouge government official skirting the limits of the legally permissible. On this point, it did not help that the president and other high-ranking Radical Party officials remained silent on the matter. Mazzorín's arguments were sound, but they did not win the debate. Most Argentines believed that the chickens were rotten, and with them something much bigger.

The "pollos de Mazzorín" quickly assumed a place in popular culture. Comic in their goosey flesh, the birds became the subject of cartoons, variety-show sketches, and political gossip columns that played on the porous borders between government corruption and public safety. One comic strip riffed on the Alfred Hitchcock film *The Birds* and depicted Alfonsín tormented by squawking chicks that would not let him sleep.[82] In this and other caricatures, government officials were portrayed as feckless and bumbling with nary a care for the public. At issue as well were the excessive amounts of poultry that the state had seemingly let go to waste during a time of constraint. Despite the fact that the head of the National Food and Agricultural Safety Service (SENASA) testified that the remaining chickens in storage were fit for sale and human consumption, the damage was done. According to one observer, "No one would dare try to sell [the chickens] domestically. Public insanity prevents it."[83]

The most sensational stories claimed that several thousand tons of chicken purchased from Hungary and Yugoslavia were contaminated with radiation from Chernobyl. The satirical magazine *Humor* featured recipes especially crafted for these particular birds. Among the culinary suggestions were "Chicken a la Nagasaki," made with "hydrogen mushrooms" and guaranteed with a stamp of approval from the Argentine Atomic Commission.[84] References to the nuclear disaster in Eastern Europe were not necessarily accidental. They echoed the conservative critics of the Alfonsín administration—the campaign led by Alberto Albamonte, for example—who associated state intervention in domestic markets with the socialist bloc's failed command economies. Allusions to Chernobyl and Nagasaki also contained a morbid fascination with the destruction of both the environment and humanity that reflected the deep cynicism and despair of the political moment. The association with epic forms of human degradation made the chickens seem like something more sinister and destructive than just a minor public health problem or ill-conceived government scheme. These depictions also drew upon cultural notions of chicken as less hygienic and more prone to disease and rot than red meat. The turn to chicken—still a far less popular dish than beef despite rising consumption rates—encapsulated the national malaise.

Denunciations of the "pollos de Mazzorín" tended to highlight government corruption and indictments of the regulatory state. However, criticisms of the episode were not necessarily monolithic in their implications or political positions. For some, the chickens were a clear example of the negative influence of oligopolistic producers in the democratic era. One journalist, commenting on the results of the episode, noted how both Cargill and San Sebastián, the two main poultry producers in Argentina, with interests in other food markets, kept small producers and consumers at their mercy because of their ability to set prices across the chain of production.[85] The journalist did not exempt government officials from culpability, however. The real scandal in his estimation was the Alfonsín administration's inability to rein in the economic monopolies and the limited reach of its economic programs. "It's no wonder the air smells rotten these days," he concluded.[86]

During the weeks that the chickens captured national headlines, the value of the austral continued to fall sharply against the dollar, and the dismal news circulated that in May 1988 alone the cost of living rose by 15 percent. With the collapse of the Austral Plan imminent, ongoing negotiations with the IMF came to an abrupt halt as the fund declared Argentina noncompliant with a previous agreement and cut off all access to further payments. In an eleventh-hour effort to salvage the plan, Juan Sourrouille's team introduced the Plan Primavera, or "Spring Plan," which did little to stop the fiscal spiral and earned the almost immediate ire of agricultural producers over a rise in export taxes, and of unions over the program's limited wage policies. Columnists wrote of the "suffocated middle class" and noted the great distance between government declarations about the economy and the everyday struggle to remain solvent. One editorial noted, "What the computers and government technocracy cannot capture is the exasperation felt amongst those who believed in the miracle of a healthy and stable currency created by the Austral Plan."[87] Read against the demise of the Alfonsín administration's attempts to revive the Argentine economy, the government chickens were more than an isolated skirmish between distant state officials and business elites; they reflected the macroeconomic disarray that impacted individuals' lives via consumption and the most basic of human needs.

When the Plan Primavera was first announced in August 1988, leaders of Argentina's major business and industrial associations spoke in reserved support of the anti-inflationary measures. During a press conference held at the presidential residence, Carlos de la Vega, head of the Chamber of Commerce, acknowledged his organization's past disagreements with the Alfonsín administration, though he reiterated his organization's endorsement on the condition that the government commit to "structural changes, especially those related to public spending and state reforms."[88] Alfonsín then took the stage. Describing the new accords as an alliance between the forces of "production and democracy," his comments had the tone of a somber rebuttal: "Our commitment is simple. We will agree to continue on this path of fiscal discipline through the reform of the state, [a commitment] which also depends on you. . . . These times require solidarity above all."[89] Alfonsín's remarks stood in stark contrast to the call for thrift made three years earlier during the announcement of the "wartime economy" in the Plaza de Mayo. This time there was no public invitation to collaborate with the economic measures to come. The fortunes of the government now rested in the hands of a small group of economic actors, not on the popular bases of support that had buoyed the administration at its onset. With virtually no mechanisms in place to ensure that businesses and financial firms would comply with the price agreements, and with little incentive for them to do so, the final attempts at stabilization seemed less like an alliance than a hostage situation.

The Alfonsín administration was operating in increasingly constricted global and domestic terrains. Yet more and more, its ideals of a complementary world of economic well-being and political liberties rang hollow and detached from the course of events.

In August 1988, in the wake of the recent collapse of the Austral Plan and with the government chickens barely out of the headlines, Alfonsín was booed during a speech at the annual gathering of the Rural Society of Argentina. In response, he accused the nation's agricultural producers and landowning elite of sabotaging his government and of working on behalf of the same economic institutions that had supported the military dictatorship.[90] His face-off against some of the nation's most powerful economic actors was widely applauded. Yet as with his defense of the debtor nations of Latin America in his White House address several years before, those convincing rebuttals did not always translate into complementary government policy. The constrained political and economic climate in which the Alfonsín government operated after the dictatorship often compelled it to adopt positions that increasingly undermined its social agenda and legitimacy. In 1985, the announcement of the wartime economy asked Argentines to live with less and to brace for austerity. But while Alfonsín could boldly denounce the prescriptions of Argentina's lenders and the domestic economic establishment, his government's policies often seemed to favor them, even as they booed him and cut off international credits.

The scandal over the chickens marked the death knell of the government's attempts to revive the national economy in keeping with past forms of state intervention and regulatory tools. The initial measure sought to deliver on a promise to provide basic necessities for all in the wake of the military dictatorship. The uproar that ensued, which coincided with the Alfonsín government's concessions to international creditors, eroded that aim and ultimately emboldened the most free-market voices in Argentina. Over the short term, fears of contaminated poultry led to a rapid, 25 percent drop in sales and consumption. Those losses were offset by a more significant victory for large poultry producers such as Cargill and San Sebastián, whose ongoing refusal to adhere to price controls ended in their favor. A journalist from *Humor* summed up the broader implications of the episode: "In the future it will be near impossible for officials to put their signature on any measures intended to regulate markets and to impede monopolistic manipulations. Meanwhile, the chickens from multinationals like Cargill and San Sebastian are on display with ribbons. Aren't we Argentines crafty!"[91] The case of the government chickens demonstrated the ability of powerful food producers to censure and circumvent well-tested regulatory policies. Those aligned with agribusinesses—from the UCeDé, to chicken producers, to sectors of the media—helped manufacture a scandal where none existed. Even if the blunt free-market liberalism of the UCeDé was not yet palatable to most Argentines, the episode convinced many that state meddling in markets was untenable and that few other alternatives existed. Years later, long after the remaining chickens had been sold to Russia for a fraction of their original price, the pollos de Mazzorín were still recalled as a defining scandal of the Alfonsín presidency and a paradigmatic case of government overreach. Throughout the early 1990s and beyond, as the full force of structural readjustment policies began to take effect, the chickens surfaced from time to time, a memory of bygone forms of state intervention—warning specters of scarcity and the battle scars of a wartime economy.[92]

5

"Dear Mr. President"

The Transition in Letters

In February 1988, an accountant from Buenos Aires named Daniel wrote a letter to the president. He did so, he believed, "on behalf of a great number of Argentine citizens . . . the people journalists refer to as 'undecided voters,' not tied to any party or absolute ideological theories." Daniel described himself as one of many, "tired of what the country had lived through up until 1983, who gave his support, who believed in you entirely, and in all of the measures the country needed. Only courage was necessary to assume the responsibility that 52% of the citizenry had given you." He recalled the early days of the Austral Plan and boasted, "It was the first time in my life that I lived with acceptable levels of inflation, and it did not matter what had to be done to maintain that stability. I felt proud to be Argentine and of what people could achieve with their efforts." But Daniel's tone soured abruptly in the following paragraph, "It was a shame, Mr. President. The only one who didn't follow through on its word was your government." He went on to decry how the early successes of the administration had been eclipsed by political infighting and the scramble for votes. How, he asked, could Alfonsín have gone astray, given such overwhelming initial support? "What a disappointment!" he exclaimed as he concluded with the point of his message: "Mr. President, you have cheated the people and have damaged the sectors that you theoretically claim to defend, the lower and lower-middle class. That is why the people—and I include myself in this group—have lost their faith and hope in you. Mr. President, I am asking you to move up the elections as soon as possible. We have already lost four years. I beg you, let us not lose two more."[1]

Daniel's letter offers a personal glimpse into the lived experience of Argentina's transition to democracy. It narrates intimate details of personal history and embeds them as part of the broader social expectations that accompanied constitutional restoration. For many individuals, Alfonsín's election was the first in their lifetimes free from violence and exclusions, and over the course of the 1980s, thousands of Argentines saw the democratic opening as the opportunity to write unsolicited letters to the president. Their messages inspire reevaluation of the history of Argentina's democratic return. Until recently, investigations of this period have been dominated by studies that analyze Latin America's democratic transitions as guided by government elites, electoral politics, and military trials. The personal letters to Alfonsín took place in between the headlines of the most dramatic institutional moments. As such, the letters complicate the very notion of a "democratic transition" by grounding political transformation in the quotidian realms of family, neighborhood, and marketplace, among others. Though writers filled their letters with details of the changes that accompanied the end of military rule in Argentina, they did so in dialogue with past political frameworks and with an eye toward future uncertainties.

What compelled individuals to write to the president? Who wrote? What did they hope to achieve? And what are the meanings of the correspondence?[2] This chapter analyzes public letter writing as a political act, in which the boundaries between supplicant and leader are blurred and the dynamics of citizenship and state making are at their most vivid. It argues for the ongoing importance of letter writing as a popular cultural and political practice that endured through the end of the twentieth century, a period that has received relatively little attention compared to earlier epistolary histories.[3] Citizen petitions from the 1980s open a window onto an evolving moral economy of democracy, which positioned individuals as both participants in and architects of constitutional return.[4] The messages reflect a prolonged moment of political change, distilled through personal lives and emotions, which reveals the shifting social meanings of the transition to democracy itself.

There was no official call to correspondence with the restoration of democracy, and the majority of letters to Alfonsín never received any response. Yet thousands of Argentines from across the country viewed the constitutional return as the chance to write to the president with their advice, complaints, and hopes for the new era.[5] Argentines of all ages and walks of life wrote to the president. Alfonsín received letters from members of the middle and working classes, from elites and impoverished individuals, and from political supporters and opponents alike. Despite their diffuse range of concerns and subject matter, the epistolary archive of the Argentine transition must be read as more than the observations of random, atomized individuals. The letters from the 1980s evidence the exuberance of renewed democratic participation. They also reveal the historical questions at stake during a period that saw both government officials and citizens grappling with the consequences of simultaneous political opportunity and economic uncertainty. The correspondence analyzed here reflects the diversity of petitioners and their concerns, with attention paid to the ways that writers addressed the meaning of the democratic return in their lives.[6]

The chapter first explores the democratic expectations of letter writers during the first two years of the Alfonsín presidency (1983–1985), a period of widespread support for the government. It then turns to an examination of the limits of national political openings through a discussion of concepts of rights and citizenship that emerge through the correspondence. Writers relied on familiar tropes of self-presentation and political posturing reminiscent of other correspondence to twentieth-century leaders, most notably Juan and Eva Perón. However, the workers, housewives, business owners, and unemployed individuals, among others, who wrote to Alfonsín often took pains to emphasize that they represented, above all, "apolitical," "disinterested" citizens. In their letters, writers expressed a notion of citizenship rooted in the language of human rights, the legitimating principle of Argentina's constitutional restoration. As citizens faced the realities of encroaching economic reorganization, they framed their rights claims in reference to earlier definitions of a democratic, benefactor state that became less viable as the decade proceeded. Thus, while the letters to Raúl Alfonsín harkened back to frameworks of "populist" patronage forged during the first Peronist period, there were critical differences as well. The tension at the heart of many of the letters to Alfonsín saw petitioners celebrating the democratic return while attempting to come to terms with a state much less materially equipped or able to respond to demands for social rights and redress. By the final months of the Alfonsín presidency in 1989, letter writers made explicit the vast undoing and refashioning of their democratic expectations.

DEMOCRATIC HORIZONS

Following seven years of brutal military rule, which left behind legacies of torture, disappearance, and economic turmoil, Argentines celebrated the return to democracy in 1983 with euphoric expressions of hope for an era of justice and peace. Christmas cards, photos, newspaper clippings, and hastily written messages scrawled on carbon paper began arriving at the government palace immediately following Raúl Alfonsín's inauguration on December 10, 1983. In addition to congratulations and well wishes for the new president, authors acknowledged that they were witnessing an age of new beginnings. Jorge, a fifty-five-year old emergency room doctor, expressed the effervescence of the moment. "The hour of truth, justice, decency, and honesty has arrived," he began:

> Argentines are proud that a simple, human man full of great virtues will be able to
> rescue this sick Argentina from its stage four coma, as we say in medicine. You have

already begun by stepping firm and I can assure you that from October 30 1983, until today I have shed many tears of joy. We have had great Radicals, H. Yrigoyen, Alem, Balbín, Illia, and now you. What happiness for our beloved Argentina![7]

Jorge's letter conveyed a sense of historic renewal, with Alfonsín passing into the pantheon of national and Radical Party heroes. Many letter writers shared this sentiment. Small business owners, grade school children, housewives, and factory workers described in vivid detail the discussions they were having at home, work, and school in the wake of the elections. However, petitioners often paired their optimism with an awareness of the challenges that lay ahead. Jorge described Argentina as "sick" and Alfonsín as the doctor with the cure. Writers depicted Argentina as a nation in need of "healing" and expressed their faith in Alfonsín as possessing the antidote. A retiree named María recalled a conversation with her friend, who described Alfonsín as a "witch doctor" because "of all of the measures you have to take, and all the people and issues you need to attend to." María disagreed slightly with her friend. No magic potion was necessary, she explained, "I prefer to think of you as the right medical doctor to save this sick nation from the many serious illnesses we are suffering."[8] The repeated image of sickness in the body of the nation had its roots in the recent past. Some of the most enduring propaganda of the military regime had depicted Argentina as under attack from a corrosive cancer or invading parasites. For his part, Alfonsín evoked the idea of a nation in need of healing throughout his campaign, and government officials rehabilitated the metaphor, sometimes unwittingly, as a succinct diagnostic of the state of the nation during the administration's lowest moments. "Health versus sickness" also echoed one of the founding principles of the return to constitutional government, which positioned political democracy as the complete antithesis of authoritarianism.

Writers described the promise of 1983 as a decisive break with Argentina's political past. Yet the country's new democracy was forged amid the ruins of state terror, a legacy that encompassed not only the human rights abuses of the regime, but also a hobbled manufacturing economy and skyrocketing debt. In their depictions of daily life, writers outlined a picture of a nation emerging from dictatorship. A letter from Martha, a homemaker and mother of three, is emblematic of the growing difficulties described by many. After "much deliberation" she decided to write Alfonsín in the hopes that he could help her husband, Mario, recover his job. In 1979, he had been fired from the refinery where he had worked for almost a decade. Since then, she explained, her family had "experienced hard times, and we are still struggling." To make ends meet, Mario sold veterinary supplies, driving "between 300 to 400 kilometers a day" in the family's "run-down, 1971 Renault 6." After car and housing payments, "everyday more expensive," the family was barely able to cover the cost of food. Pregnant with her fourth child, Martha explained that her baby gave her the courage to write Alfonsín to ask him to reverse the "injustice committed against [Mario]" and by extension her family. Though she knew Alfonsín "faced many challenges," she believed he could help, concluding, "sometimes you need to push miracles a little to make them happen."[9]

Though "democracy" was not mentioned by name, the future that Martha envisioned echoed a broader expectation that the democratic era would improve her quality of life. Writers put forward a panorama of need. Mothers wrote on behalf of sons to enlist them in apprenticeship programs; families implored the president's help to pay bills and to schedule social worker visits; pensioners requested assistance to enroll in the government-sponsored housing program; and small-time entrepreneurs solicited loans to save their businesses, or to start new ones. These appeals may be typical of citizen petitions to leaders. However, read through the lens of restored constitutional government, the correspondence to Alfonsín takes on a specific meaning, one that connected the promise of the democratic era to ameliorating years of want through fortified public services and government outreach. A popular definition of democracy comes into focus through the correspondence, which combined political openings—enacted in letters through a personal relationship with the president—with a socially grounded vision of rights, collective welfare, and individual prosperity.

While many petitioners wrote the president asking for material assistance, throughout the 1980s authors also wrote with a variety of proposals for what they believed Alfonsín must do to set Argentina on a new course. The volume of these letters indicates how seriously Argentines engaged with and sought participation in the course of democratic return. Proposals range from one-line missives—"To reactivate the economy do the opposite of what the IMF tells you!"—to treatises on assembly line production in the northern province of Tucumán.[10] Proposals represent a rich genre of correspondence sent throughout the decade that is difficult to classify. However, over the course of Alfonsín's first two years in office (1983–1985), the period of greatest support for the government, citizen proposals emphasized economic recovery. Enrique, a retiree from the outskirts of Greater Buenos Aires, designed intricate formulas for the sale of fiscal lands, a deposit scheme to pay off public debt, and fixed-term bonds to "end the constant flight of capital abroad."[11] A man named Diego sent his sketches for a five-year plan to revive agricultural production, "without any additional cost to the state." He was so certain of his claims that he assured the president that if he came across as a bit "loco," he would be happy to send references to vouch for his credentials.[12] There were so many proposals of this sort that at one point in 1984, Alfonsín's longtime secretary, Margarita Ronco, drafted a form letter in response, thanking petitioners on behalf of the president and encouraging their ongoing support: "As [President Alfonsín] continues to face tremendous responsibilities, he will need the support of citizens like you who, with maturity and determination, secured the return of democracy."[13]

Economic recovery was on the minds of many in the early 1980s. When he took office, Alfonsín faced an unprecedented debt of US$43 billion.[14] Unlike inflation, which by the late 1970s had been incorporated into the everyday "survival strategies" of Argentines in ways that altered consumption patterns and economic decision making, foreign debt remained the purview of economists and technocrats until 1982, when the debt crisis sparked off in Mexico hastened the economic collapse of the military regime and thrust the issue into the public realm as never before.[15] Throughout 1984, the comings and goings of Bernardo Grinspun, the administration's first economic minister, and his epic negotiations with the IMF filled countless newspaper editorials and hours of evening talk shows.

Letters regarding the foreign debt poured in. Along with the specter of inflation, debt was one more legacy of authoritarianism that threatened to eclipse the return of democracy. However, unlike media coverage of debt, which chronicled high-level meetings of state officials and international lending organizations, citizens cast the social impact of debt in a different light. On the one hand, authors emphasized the newness of debt as a national concern, the burden of which was not yet fully known. On the other hand, unlike inflation, which writers commented on as a force beyond personal control, debt seemed a concrete problem many believed could be easily undone. Hilarina, writing from her one-room apartment in the south of Buenos Aires, declared that she and her fellow compatriots would be willing to "donate a paycheck or a month's rent" to help pay off the debt. In this way, she concluded, "We would feel what it really means to be Argentine. And we would fulfill our duty to the nation, just like Remedios de Escalada de San Martín!"[16] Patriotic fervor imbued many of the letters, and writers frequently signaled their participation in a project of nation rebuilding.

Schemes, proposals, and big ideas overwhelmed the early correspondence to the president. Many writers sensed this and acknowledged that their letters might be headed for bureaucratic oblivion, often commenting along the lines of, "I know this will probably never reach you." Indeed, the vast majority of letters never reached Alfonsín, and most did not receive a response, though all were stamped with a date of entry, assigned a file number, and, depending on their content, summarized by secretaries and sent on to the corresponding national, provincial, or municipal agency. The epistolary trail often ended there. One of the few letters to receive a personal response from the office of the president was from Gummi Industries, a car parts manufacturer, informing the president that the workers, "by spontaneous decision," had pledged one day's salary toward debt repayment. In addition, the letter continued, the company would donate an unstipulated amount every month "for as long as the country needed it." Attached was a check for 71,788 pesos made out to the Ministry of Economy for "Debt Payment." The workers justified their contribution "[as a] consequence of the spiritual state of the nation, unprecedented in the political history of our country and not seen since the days of National Organization." In response, the president's brother and personal secretary, Guillermo, thanked the workers and acknowledged the president was "deeply moved" by their gracious gesture.[17] The letter arrived at the presidential offices in May 1984. By then, Alfonsín may certainly have been moved, as labor relations were irrevocably strained following the failure of the Mucci Law, the government-sponsored union reform initiative, and escalating labor unrest, which would result in thirteen general strikes by the end of Alfonsín's term.[18] The Gummi letter also reflects a broader sentiment at the onset of the Alfonsín presidency, when national debt, which became so commonplace a burden on governability over the next two decades, was initially regarded as somehow manageable and disentangled from other realms of institutional life. "Pay and it will be resolved," the letters seem to suggest. References to independence and nation formation cast debt as imposed from the outside, an external constraint, which unlike the internally polarizing military trials or labor reforms could unite disparate camps in a common cause.

The return of democracy in 1983 represented a historic national turning point. Letter writers took seriously the promise of the new era and filled their messages with hopeful designs for the future. Citizens' letters sent during the first two years following the return to democracy reflected understandings of a symbiotic relationship between political openings and economic recovery. In their messages of counsel and appeal, these early letters recall one of the founding principles of the return of constitutional government, which positioned democratic rule as the complete antithesis of Argentina's authoritarian past. From the outset of the campaign, Alfonsín and his advisers presented democracy as the salve and panacea for the economic and political woes of military rule. They argued that if Argentina's economic and moral decline were the direct consequences of authoritarianism, it followed that political democracy would forge a new "social pact" to restore both financial and social stability.[19] While the dichotomy between dictatorship and democracy originated in broader theories of Latin American democratic transitions, it resonated throughout Argentine public life and had great implications for overall perceptions of the Alfonsín government, especially when it became clear that democratic restoration alone could not reverse all of the nation's fiscal woes. At the beginning of the administration, however, the tension between two seemingly antithetical political forms sustained widespread hope for the democratic horizons ahead.

THE LIMITS OF POLITICAL OPENINGS

Between late 1983 and early 1986, overall public approval granted the Alfonsín administration a wide margin for containing cleavages.[20] The UCR soundly won in midterm legislative elections in 1985, signaling confidence in the trajectory of the government. Yet there were noticeable cracks in the democratic euphoria, especially in the fiscal realm. By April 1985, when Alfonsín introduced the "wartime economy," which prioritized reducing the fiscal deficit through cutbacks in public spending, the privatization of select state enterprises, and inflation controls, important changes had emerged in the ways that individuals thought about the prospects for the democratic future and their place in it. Despite optimism about the future, letter writers frequently highlighted the limited impact of national political openings on their lives. For many, the democratic return had not ushered in the material changes that had fueled their expectations in 1983.

Petitioners often expressed their grievances in the form of complaints, a broad epistolary genre that spanned the decade and that highlighted overlapping concerns about state services and a changing economy. In 1987, a man named Eugenio seethed to the president as he recalled his quest to install and repair his home phone line. His letter included a dossier of bureaucratic travails, including attempts to contact the state phone company, politicians, even the federal police. "How can it be," he fumed, "that in full democracy <u>NOBODY</u> has responded to or even acknowledged receipt of my request!"[21] A similar letter from Velia described her attempts to contact the municipal authorities, though under more tragic circumstances. Her seventy-seven-year old father had recently been killed during a hit-and-run accident as he crossed a busy intersection in Buenos Aires. After her letters to city officials had gone unanswered, she decided to write to Alfonsín. "I am an Argentine citizen who awaited the triumph of democracy with much excitement," she began. "Thanks to Ex-Intendant Cacciatore"—the military mayor of Buenos Aires most notorious for razing entire neighborhoods and expelling thousands of residents to make way for a massive highway system—her street had become a "death trap," with car races day and night and drivers using the zone as a freeway. With an elementary school located nearby and no synchronized traffic lights, Velia feared another accident. Her petition campaign to make the intersection safer fell upon deaf ears, and in her mourning she endured a further setback, as the woman who had hit her father turned out to be the girlfriend of a police captain. Frustrated, she pleaded with the president to intervene locally, signing her letter, "*JUSTICIA!*"[22]

Velia was one of the few authors to allude to the policies of the military regime. For the most part writers did not cite recent history, though many of their grievances could be traced back to the deregulation set in motion during the dictatorship. Instead, blame for current injustices resided in the immediate present, in the institutions and public offices that citizens interacted with on a municipal and neighborhood level every day. Jorge and Velia employed "democracy" as a rhetorical flourish to bolster their claims and to ground them in the moral language of the day. In doing so, they and many others may have believed their petitions would be taken more seriously. It is impossible to say with certainty if writers only appealed to "democracy" because they thought that was what government leaders wanted to hear. Even allowing for that possibility, the urgency running through much of the correspondence reveals the ways that writers connected the democratic return to improving the material conditions of their daily lives. Concretely, democracy meant fixing traffic lights, installing phone lines, filling potholes, reopening factories in the industrial belt surrounding Buenos Aires, and fortifying sewage systems and water supplies. These were the tasks imposed by writers on the Alfonsín government and what it was ultimately judged upon.

In the case of contemporary Argentina, two instances of letter writing locate these petitions to Alfonsín within longer historical contests over rights and citizenship. Eva Perón received thousands of letters daily with requests for material assistance and financial support through her namesake foundation. Sending a petition to the Eva Perón Foundation was the way to obtain gifts, material support, and inclusion in the robust welfare state of the day.[23] Similarly, the public letter writing campaign "Perón Wants to Know," in the context of Perón's second Five-Year Plan, brought citizens closer to the centers of state planning.[24] In both cases, the letters to Perón and Evita evidenced expanding notions of citizenship and the redefinition of democracy along emancipatory and social lines by midcentury.[25]

In the 1980s, while many writers presented their demands as novel obstacles confronting the government, citizen concerns were also rooted in the memory of democratic traditions forged over the course of previous decades. State policies attuned to consumption and public service had first grounded democratic values and citizenship in the local and private sphere during the Peronist era (1945–1955).[26] Despite opposition to Peronism itself and the increasingly violent attempts by the armed forces to constrain political life, the social imprint of this period endured and influenced the democratic futures that citizens imagined for the rest of the century. The letters to Alfonsín concerning state services and infrastructure call to mind the letters sent to Juan and Eva Perón. Like that correspondence, the letters to Alfonsín not only positioned individuals as direct participants in a national political project, but also identified the state as the legitimate entity to secure citizen well-being. Writers during the 1980s did not generally frame their correspondence as explicit dialogues with the past; however, the ideal democratic government that emerged through their letters can be traced back to the midcentury expansion of an interventionist, benefactor state.

With this history in mind, the correspondence to Alfonsín is not unique or unprecedented. The letters often evoked the language and forms associated with clientelism, with writers frequently implying promises of their political support in exchange for material assistance.[27] Letter writers of the 1980s echoed the concerns of petitioners past—from emotional pleas for employment and economic support to commentary about the course of the nation. However, clientelism alone does not fully explain the letters to Alfonsín. In contrast to earlier archives of letters from the first Peronist period, those of the 1980s reflect a changing social contract between the government and its citizenry, framed by the new political constraints of economic crisis and neoliberal policy.

An increased frustration apparent in the letters to Alfonsín stems, in part, from a growing awareness of new limits on the state. Throughout the decade, streamlining the state hovered in public debate as one route to achieve fiscal solvency, keep inflation in check, and reduce the public deficit.[28] Writers may have agreed on the need for state reforms; however, no clear consensus emerged regarding how that should occur. To return to letters of complaint, petitioners painted a picture of a highly dysfunctional public sector in the midst of an economic tailspin. The long lines in government offices, paperwork, and recalcitrant officials, main tropes of the Argentine bureaucracy, were precisely what writers expected democracy to reverse. Yet the correspondence illustrates a state that was at once omnipresent, yet inaccessible; demanding, yet unaccountable; interventionist, yet ineffective. Some authors advocated privatization and outright dollarization of the economy. For many others, the state remained a source of jobs and security. From 1983 to 1989, thousands of employment requests were remitted to ENTeL, the state phone company, and SEGBA, the utility company of Greater Buenos Aires. Nor did letters break down easily along class lines, with the upper middle classes embracing structural readjustment, and lower-income sectors holding fast to the institutions and policies of the Peronist era. These ideas could exist together in seemingly contradictory ways.

A letter from Roberto, a father of four in Quilmes, the industrial town located on the southern outskirts of Buenos Aires where the PAN food program was launched, exemplifies how citizens' engagement with the state was in flux during this period. Roberto advocated *achicamiento del estado* (shrinking the state) as the solution to Argentina's economic difficulties, a surprising proposal given that several paragraphs into his letter he introduced himself as a municipal worker. "I have given 30 of the best years of my life to the public sector," he declared, not without a touch of pride. Several features of Roberto's letter deserve mention: For one, Roberto's use of the phrase *achicar el estado* echoes the dictatorship-era economy minister, José Martínez de Hoz, who infamously proclaimed that his policies would shrink the state in order to *agrandar la nación* ("shrink the state to enlarge the nation"). In one sense, Roberto was in line with mainstream center-right economists and commentators of the day, including many members of the Alfonsín government. Yet his solution to "shrink the state," far from purging the public sector, was special government-sponsored unemployment insurance and job-training programs to reposition municipal employees for work in state industries or the private sector. Roberto's letter hinted at a moment during the 1980s when associations of privatization were still somewhat up for grabs, when "shrinking" could imply reform and the maintenance of the state as benefactor and prime employer, not long before the massive application of neoliberal structural adjustment in the 1990s. Roberto concluded his three-page letter with a thoughtful commentary, connecting the declining industrial economy of Quilmes to Argentina's position in the global economy: "I ask myself what our role will be in the future if our industry is practically destroyed and we are not in any condition to compete with Japan, Germany, the USA, etc. etc."[29]

Like many writers, Roberto acknowledged Argentina's diminished economic position and the realities of the crumbling manufacturing economy. Authors repeatedly alluded to the fact that the dawn of the democratic era had coincided with a massive shift in national economic logics and identity, and they grappled with the interplay between internal and external constraints. A young man named Jorge wrote with a dilemma on December 10, 1984, the administration's one-year anniversary. At twenty-three, he had recently received his accounting certificate and hoped to marry and buy a house with his fiancée. "Like so many," he lamented, "we are unable to save money." Though they hesitated to write given "all of the problems facing the country," the young couple sought the president's counsel:

> [O]ur concern is this: our friends and acquaintances (people who call themselves honest!) advise us to invest in Dollars. We think this is detrimental to national interests, despite the benefits it could give us, and we systematically refuse to speculate with this kind of "investment." I would like to know your response as the representative of national popular interests.[30]

Upon first reading, Jorge's letter recalls national debt letters, acknowledging the interconnectedness of individual action and national economic well-being. But Jorge departed from the more positive implications of workers' donations and debt repayment. While debt might be imposed from outside, Jorge signaled two internal threats: dollars and the "dishonest" citizens with the will to use them. More critically, the letter highlighted a presumed incompatibility between "national popular" versus individual interests. Through polices of trade liberalization and repression, the military regime may have weakened the frameworks of state-led welfare and development—two cornerstones of what for decades constituted the "national popular"—however, the social recognition and articulation of that shift coincided directly with the return of constitutional government. Writers often expressed their dismay at the radical separation of national economic sovereignty from their individual security. "I did not speculate and look where it got me!" exclaimed an irate small business owner as he recounted the rise and fall of his furniture factory and subsequent bankruptcy.[31] Part of the Alfonsín government's mandate was to recuperate, recalibrate, and redefine the meanings of the "national popular." Throughout the 1980s, individuals struggled with their own definitions and repositioned themselves within altered political and economic landscapes. They did so as individuals and as citizens of a body politic. As the Alfonsín years wore on, however, the perceived antagonism of these spheres—between civic and private identities—became more rigid, to the extent that for many writers achieving a greater good would come at the expense of personal well-being, and vice versa.

CITIZENSHIP AND HUMAN RIGHTS

Though one of the enduring legacies of the Argentine transition to democracy is human rights policy and the efforts to end the impunity of the armed forces— from the much-lauded *Nunca Más* report, to the groundbreaking trials against the military regime, to the equally criticized limitations on legal proceedings—these events are strikingly absent in the correspondence to Alfonsín.[32] The democratic transition brought with it demands for accountability regarding the fate of thousands of disappeared. Human rights organizations and family members sought to position themselves for participation in the new system, seeking justice and information about loved ones. Initial measures taken by the government seemed to promise the realization of these goals. But in 1985, as the trial of the juntas began to expand inquiries into the actions of lower-ranking officers, sectors of the military threatened to boycott the proceedings, increasing fears of possible revolt. In response to escalating military unrest, in December 1986 Alfonsín persuaded Congress to pass the Full Stop Law, the first of two measures that would place limits on ongoing legal processes.[33]

Then during Holy Week in April 1987, the nation was put on high alert. A contingent of lower-ranking soldiers calling themselves the *carapintadas* (painted faces) occupied Campo de Mayo, the largest military garrison in Argentina, and demanded an end to the trials. As Alfonsín and his advisers debated how to handle the insubordinate officers, thousands gathered in the Plaza de Mayo and squares throughout the country to repudiate the military threat. Despite widespread popular support in defense of the new democracy, Alfonsín quickly lost approval. On Easter Sunday, after personally brokering the deal that ended the tense four-day standoff, Alfonsín spoke from the balcony of the government palace and declared, "La casa está en ordén [the house is in order] and there is no bloodshed in Argentina." He concluded with a demand for those gathered in the plaza to go home with their families to "celebrate Easter in the peace of Argentina." For many, the president's Easter pronouncement smacked of an illicit pact with the armed forces. But it was what followed that sparked widespread condemnation throughout the country. In June 1987, Alfonsín pushed forward the Due Obedience Law, which exempted from prosecution lower-ranking officers who had tortured or murdered while following orders, effectively putting an end to the trials.[34]

Of all the developments during the Alfonsín presidency, human rights policy has generated the most discussion and debate, with scholars generally agreeing that Holy Week marked a decisive turning point.[35] On Easter Sunday in 1987,

Argentines had been ready to defend the democracy. With the Full Stop and the subsequent Due Obedience Laws, hopes for justice were replaced by the sense that the government had backed down in its challenge against the military and reversed its stance on human rights, abandoning one of the main promises of the transition. The Holy Week episode revealed the ongoing power of the military to constrain newly restored democratic institutions (two more uprisings occurred before the end of Alfonsín's term). But Alfonsín's actions during and after the events also confirmed for many a lack of political will—whether in negotiations with foreign creditors, Peronist rivals, or the military insurgents—which the government was never able to recuperate or reverse.

While Alfonsín did receive letters and telegrams following military uprisings, as well as messages of moral outrage following the passage of laws to put an end to military trials, the overall epistolary silence is deafening compared to scholarly attention to the imprint of these events during the Alfonsín presidency and beyond. One important qualification is necessary on this point: with respect to human rights, individuals could mediate their concerns through activist networks and institutions, to the extent that a letter to Alfonsín was an unlikely, comparatively ineffectual, venue of protest or support. Petitioners often highlighted their inclusion as part of the "unaffiliated" masses, a status that not only justified unmediated contact with the president, but also distilled petitions to a pure state of need, opinion, or praise, seemingly impervious to outside political or ideological influences. This is not to argue that human rights were not a social concern of "ordinary" Argentines during the 1980s. On the contrary, the letters demonstrate a multivalent notion of human rights, transformed into ideals along the lines of Velia's call for "Justice!" following the death of her father. Taken as a whole, letter writers articulated a definition of citizenship grounded in a holistic notion of human rights that afforded all Argentines guarantees of material and physical security.

Rights language penetrated social life and was refitted to highly charged conceptions of home and national belonging, among others. The tensions between personal prosperity and democratic futures emerge forcefully in letters from individuals contemplating emigration or recently returned from abroad. Educated professionals with the training and means to look for work overseas began sending their descriptions of the difficult decision to leave Argentina as early as February 1984, two months into the administration. Susana was a young newlywed when she left Argentina in the early 1970s, "facing economic impossibility, and the uncertainty of those days, never knowing where another bomb was going to go off." Following several years in Venezuela and the United States, she and her family had settled in Italy, returning to Argentina following Alfonsín's election, happy at the prospect of doing "something for the country." Shortly after her return, however, she wrote of her difficulties in finding a job, lamenting that "little by little, we have begun to look abroad again . . . and I believe there are many of us in the same situation."[36]

Susana acknowledged membership in a wider community originally forced to go abroad by a combination of political violence and lack of opportunity. While the risk of "bombs going off" may have dissipated, Susana saw that threat as having been replaced by equally destabilizing economic forces conspiring to push her and her family out again. Silvia, a thirty-four-year old architect, wrote Alfonsín upon her return from six years in Italy with a similarly blunt assessment: "Mr. President, I have heard you say that the political exiles can come back with guarantees of work, security, and stability, but what about the economic exiles?"[37] Susana and Silvia's references to violence and exile, the latter a highly charged term with connotations of state terror and victimization, are striking. In their appropriation of the language of human rights, they identified themselves as casualties of the dictatorship and therefore entitled to guarantees of justice and redress.

Citizens framed demands for economic justice and social well-being as human rights at the heart of the democratic restoration. At the same time, the language of human rights afforded individuals new ways to talk about and assert much older struggles. Rights claims were particularly evident in messages from citizens outside of the middle class, who wrote of their ongoing fight against poverty. In 1986 Marta, a single mother of three, wrote about her six-year attempt to fight eviction and secure housing for her family in Córdoba and Buenos Aires. Toward the middle of her letter, she plainly declared, "I believe that if your heart has feeling enough to bring back all of the exiles, then you could also save us from the exile we were sent into by human insensibility. That would give us the chance to believe that Justice really does exist."[38] Marta described her own internal exile—an endless saga of canceled social worker visits and unscrupulous landlords—severed from the institutions meant to help her. That sentiment is echoed in a hastily written message from Zulema. Writing from "the entrance to the Tribunales court" in the center of Buenos Aires, where she was attempting to contest an eviction notice, the urgency of Zulema's letter is palpable: "Please, please we need 90, 60, even 30 days to find a new place to live." As she explained, the letter was her last-ditch effort to help her family: "Mr. President, I am turning to you because I know that you are a very Humane person, and that this is a Human Right. . . . Now that we live in democracy, how can our children live in the streets."[39] Human rights redefined citizenship during the 1980s, placing in greater relief the injustices against which the new democracy was measured. Yet individuals directed their demands for the human rights to a home, food, and employment, among others, to a state that was increasingly unable to follow through on the original promises of the democratic era.

REMAKING DEMOCRATIC EXPECTATIONS

Following the Holy Week uprising, the Alfonsín administration was embattled. The early gains of the Austral Plan, the economic plan instituted in 1985, which had dramatically reduced inflation, began to falter. As the price freezes originally implemented by the plan were gradually lifted, inflation rose steadily, cresting at 175 percent by the end of the year, more than double the rate in 1986. The turbulent year culminated politically in the midterm elections of September 6, 1987, which swept the Peronist party into congressional control and into the governorship of key provinces, Buenos Aires included. Following Peronism's defeat in the 1983 presidential elections, the party had entered a period of dramatic flux and begun a steady transformation from its traditional union base into a locally based "party of the poor." The 1987 electoral victory marked the movement's resurgence and its incipient overhaul.

In the wake of the midterm elections, the Peronist win emerged as a turning point with significant implications for the UCR government. Letters sent by self-proclaimed Alfonsín supporters and Radical Party members emphasized negative depictions of Peronism, imbued with contrasts of "corrupt" Peronists versus the stately and inherently "democratic" Radical Party. For example, a woman named Norma wrote a brief letter, in which she concluded, "as we all know, the Peronists are people of bad character [*mala calaña*]."[40] Others, like Elsa, framed the Peronist resurgence as proof of "a lack of civic maturity."[41] Yet even the president's most sympathetic admirers characterized the Peronist win in terms of a UCR failure in the economic sphere. Fiscal recovery, combined with an ambitious social agenda, was part of the administration's mandate from the beginning. The September 1987 elections reflected an overall perception that the administration was falling short on both fronts. Pedro, a lifelong Radical, sent his detailed analysis of the election results, including a vehement critique of internal UCR structures and tensions among party leaders. While these factors impacted the election results, Pedro believed the UCR loss was rooted more in "the gap between our basic needs [*canasta familiar*] and our salaries." "Mr. President," he reasoned, "you know that the flood of votes that went to Peronism was based in daily life [*pasa por lo cotidiano*]."[42]

Another message, from a pensioner named Eduardo, reflected the ire of one sector of the popular classes that had originally supported Alfonsín. Writing from the southern belt of Greater Buenos Aires, a region that experienced a wave of factory closings and capital flight throughout the 1980s, Eduardo blamed Alfonsín for abandoning the working class. As proof, he enclosed a series of articles from local newspapers chronicling the plight of pensioners from his area, including a graphic photo of an elderly man who had starved to death alone in his house. The photo's caption read, "Hunger: The Cruelest Battle!" Eduardo feared the same fate and vehemently analyzed the downturn of popular support for the government:

> You have forgotten about the workers and the pensioners! We are hungry! And that
> is the reason why we changed our position in the last election. We cast our *VOTO*

CASTIGO against the policies of your government, especially ECONOMIC AND SOCIAL policies.[43]

Despite the contrast in their tone, Pedro and Eduardo's letters shared opinions of government shortcomings and dashed hopes. Their messages, and others like them, are also signposts of the ultimate demise of the Alfonsín government's initial attempt to reconcile the "liberal republic" and the "popular republic," which had taken root in the democratic traditions of Hipólito Yrigoyen and Juan Perón. In the year and a half that remained of the Alfonsín administration, economic recovery would become the principal benchmark for measuring democratic solvency. Indeed, in the wake of the events of 1987, writers seemed to abandon the notion that the government could implement the social change that had fueled the hopes at the beginning of the administration. As daily life became more expensive and inflation rose, many argued that the future of the Alfonsín government depended solely on fiscal recovery; in their letters, economic stabilization tended to be equated with democracy itself.

As voters began to set their sights on the 1989 presidential elections, the year had a turbulent and bloody start. In late January, members of the leftist group Movimiento Todos por la Patria (MTP) stormed the La Tablada barracks on the outskirts of Buenos Aires amid growing rumors of another military uprising. By the time the confrontation ended the following day, twenty-nine MTP members were dead and thirteen more were in custody.[44] Not two weeks after La Tablada, the government's most recent economic stabilization plan collapsed following the World Bank's decision to cut off promised credits to Argentina. The bank's announcement sparked a prolonged bout of hyperinflation that did not let up fully until July. Between January and May 1989, the price of basic food goods increased, in some cases as much as 1,000 percent.[45] In late March, the governor of Buenos Aires declared the province in a state of emergency. He sent an urgent telegram to Alfonsín asking him to authorize the distribution of emergency food subsidies "in order to avoid the coming social chaos."[46] By the end of the year, inflation would reach 4,923.6 percent.[47]

Alfonsín addressed the opening session of Congress as president for the last time on May 1, 1989. As the economy continued its downward spiral, it seemed certain that the Peronist candidate, Carlos Menem, would easily beat the UCR candidate and governor of Córdoba, Eduardo Angeloz. From the congressional pulpit, Alfonsín could not ignore this fact or the social havoc wrought by months of hyperinflation. Recalling the milestones and setbacks of his presidency, Alfonsín emphasized that his greatest accomplishment was perhaps his very presence in Congress that day—no small feat, given that he was poised to transfer constitutional power to a democratically elected president for the first time in five decades. He concluded his speech by stating, "We have been so successful that the country seems to have forgotten what our main concern was in 1983. Today it seems natural that a government is able to fulfill its constitutional mandate."[48]

Letters flooded the presidential palace in the wake of the address. Echoing Alfonsín's assertion, writers commented on the ways that political democracy had indeed achieved a "commonplace" or "natural" status in their lives. However, that certainty had come at the expense of a radical redefinition of their expectations just six years earlier. One letter sent to Alfonsín during his final months in office was from María Luisa, who for the past six years had often been "tempted to write of the incredible hopes that I had for my country, my compatriots, and for my children." Though María Luisa wrote with pride that her children now lived in a "free country," her letter concluded with a bittersweet assessment: "But the years went by, and though I still think and believe that this is the best system of government, we have reached a desperate situation, Mr. President. How can you live if you cannot buy the necessities of life?"[49]

While María Luisa's doubts coincided with esteem for Alfonsín, other individuals were less sympathetic. Lucia wrote from Lomas de Zamora, from the south of Buenos Aires, shortly after the May 14 elections, in which Carlos Menem soundly defeated Eduardo Angeloz with close to 48 percent of the vote. Though Lucia was certain that "[democracy] was the best political system, [she noted that] our situation has become intolerable." Her letter vividly captured the impact of economic crisis in Greater Buenos Aires, from the empty shelves in her local supermarket, to the rising cost of medicines—"when they are available"—to the suspension of her mother's pension, to the general deterioration of her town center. As she looked around at her surroundings, she blamed public officials for the crisis and degradation of her town: "[E]very day we hear talk about public spending! So let's put public officials to work! Repairs, cleanups, just stop throwing money away!"[50]

Both Lucia and María Luisa recognized political democracy as a basic fact of their current reality. Yet in taking stock of their lives over the previous six years— María Luisa in resignation, Lucia in anger—the women let go of a belief that their material well-being could and would be safeguarded by the same democratic government that had been able to secure them other political freedoms. Read together, their letters lay bare the great transformation of democratic expectations from 1983 onward. At the start of the Alfonsín administration, the main tenets of liberal democracy and human rights were melded with a firm commitment to social justice and economic redistribution. Though not without its tensions and cracks, that vision encompassed both the hopes of letter writers and the promise of newly restored constitutional government. Endemic economic crisis and disenchantment with government policy, followed by the upheaval of hyperinflation, ultimately decoupled or unhinged the constituent parts of an inclusive and ambitious democratic agenda. Together, Lucia and María Luisa highlighted the uncomfortable distance between political democracy and social rights by May 1989 in the midst of an economic tailspin. That did not mean, however, that the aim of social justice had disappeared. On the contrary, social demands became even more acute, and letter writers placed in relief faltering welfare programs and a state ill-equipped and unwilling, in their eyes, to address growing critical needs.

Lucia wrote her letter on May 29, 1989. The next day she may have awoken to news that in the neighboring town of Quilmes supermarkets were being ransacked by "roving bands" of looters—alternately identified by the local newspaper, *El Sol*, as mothers trying to feed their hungry children or leftist agitators—holding defenseless owners hostage and emptying store shelves in the process.[51] For the past five days, similar reports had been pouring in from the outskirts of Rosario, Córdoba, and other parts of Greater Buenos Aires, accompanied by rumors of escalating street violence, food shortages, and supermarkets in flames, which placed entire communities on edge. In response to the social unrest, Alfonsín declared a state of siege for thirty days. The lootings, which were most widespread in Rosario, resulted in between fifteen and nineteen deaths over the course of nine days. In light of the chaos and an economic situation that had become untenable, Alfonsín, who for several days had firmly denied reports that he would step down, ultimately announced his decision to transfer power to Carlos Menem six months earlier than anticipated.

The letters to Alfonsín sent over the course of these tumultuous years traced the challenges of constitutional restoration. As writers inscribed themselves as part of a new national project, they tested revived public languages of democracy, human rights, and justice while laying bare the growing distance between their expectations and their daily lives. Military trials and labor reforms have received the most attention in the literature as the source of greatest achievement and chaos over the course of those six dramatic years, during which the survival of the Alfonsín government was in doubt more than once, beset by general strikes, armed insurrections, and disappointing reversals of justice. The letters to Alfonsín are embedded in these events, but the latter were often not at the center of writers' immediate concerns as they sat down to fire off a message. In the midst of overlapping political openings and economic retreats, Argentines' hopes for constitutional restoration were doubly rooted in calls for justice following the end of a brutal period of military repression and in the promises of state-led welfare, originally forged at midcentury. The main historical reference point for letter writers was not necessarily the immediate authoritarian past, but rather the memory of the benefactor state, which had emerged during the Peronist period. Despite the violence of military rule, which attempted to undo the foundations of state-led welfare, the legacy of previous democratic struggles remained intact and formed the basis of social expectations for the transition to democracy.

The letters to Alfonsín inspire new interpretations of Latin America's constitutional restorations by grounding letter writers' concerns in much longer contests over the meanings of democracy and citizenship that marked the twentieth century. During the 1980s, human rights redefined citizenship. Writers framed their demands as human rights for social well-being, which they attached to claims for home, employment, food, and national belonging, among other things. Through their messages to the president, citizens expressed the ways that the constituent parts of an initial, holistic definition of democracy had come undone through years of economic crisis, military unrest, and growing social inequality. Letter writers gradually relinquished their belief in a state that could guarantee both political rights and their material well-being. Taken together, the letters to Raúl Alfonsín narrate a history of diminished hopes and the narrowing of options over the decade. Yet the popular record of the social life of Argentina's democratic transition also restores a sense of possibility to the political debates of the 1980s, as writers struggled to make sense of the extent to which 1983 signaled the end of, a mere interlude in, or the radical redefinition of entrenched cultural conflicts.

One of the letters written to the president during his final days in office was from Graciela, a teacher in Greater Buenos Aires, who perhaps best expressed the arc of the Alfonsín years: "I agree when people say, because it hits close to home, that 'liberty won't feed you.' But freedom still tastes pretty good." As Graciela wrote "from her kitchen table before heading off to class" in late May 1989, she wove her personal history and her hopes and desires for Argentina with a forceful and prescient glimpse of the nation's future: "I would prefer to not wake up every morning to hear about rising prices, the exchange rate, and shortages. I want economic stability, security, and national progress, but I don't want to achieve that by paying the social costs of those great powers people consider 'Promised Lands'. . . . I want PEACE above all, in all its significance."[52]

Democratic Pasts, Neoliberal Futures

Hyperinflation and the Road to Austerity

The first reports came from Córdoba and Rosario. Small groups of women and children described by their "humble condition" quietly entered supermarkets beginning in the afternoon on May 24, 1989, and filled their bags and shopping carts with yerba mate, sugar, pasta, and cooking oil. They left calmly without paying, leaving cash registers untouched, to the amazement of shop owners. Similar scenes were repeated through the early evening in nine additional supermarkets, drawing crowds of up to five hundred people and taking store managers and employees by surprise. By nightfall, violent skirmishes with the police broke out in parts of Rosario, where would-be looters hurled rocks at supermarket windows and security forces. Police responded with tear gas as the crowd shouted "thieves!" and demanded that the store owners "lower prices" because "we are hungry!"[1] These uprisings marked the first of hundreds of food riots that swept Argentina's major urban centers during the final week of May 1989, capping off an already chaotic year of bloodshed, hyperinflation, and political upheaval.

If eliminating hunger formed part of a democratic promise at the start of the Alfonsín presidency, food was also at the center of the events that marked its end. Though estimates vary, up to 282 stores were looted in twenty-one cities and towns between May 24 and June 1, 1989.[2] Rioting began in the popular neighborhoods on the outskirts of Rosario and Córdoba and then spread to Greater Buenos Aires, where the most intense uprisings occurred May 29–31. The majority of the lootings took place in these three industrial centers, not in the nation's most impoverished rural regions. There had been other large-scale riots in Argentina in the twentieth century, but none on such a national scale, and none that galvanized such a collective response to extreme need and economic emergency.[3] The main protagonists were the urban poor, a sector that had grown over the decade in the struggling manufacturing regions of the country. Some uprisings proceeded in an almost orderly fashion and defied conventional notions of looting. There were repeated reports of women and children entering supermarkets and then being found seated in the aisles quietly eating food. "They left with their pockets empty, but their bellies full," remarked one store owner.[4] As the days passed, however, many of the uprisings turned violent. Police used tear gas and rubber bullets to repel crowds. In the township of San Miguel, the site of the most deadly uprisings in Greater Buenos Aires, one bus driver was killed, and residents accused security forces of fueling rumors that led to dangerous clashes between neighborhoods.[5] Throughout the country, hundreds of looters were arrested, and between fifteen and nineteen people were killed. By the time the riots finally subsided, the nation was under a thirty-day state of siege, and Raúl Alfonsín had announced his early resignation.

The events of 1989 produce a dizzying sense of whiplash. The year began with an attack by left-wing militants on the Tablada military barracks, which prompted a state response reminiscent of the darkest moments of Latin America's Cold War regimes. Before the flames had even been extinguished, the government's final economic stabilization plan collapsed. Widespread financial speculation ensued, which enriched Argentina's most powerful firms and sent the value of the Argentine austral and the dollar reserves of Central Bank plummeting. The dam finally burst on the fragile measures holding back an inflationary crisis. From February onward, prices began an upward ascent into full-blown hyperinflation. By the time the food riots broke out in May, the cost of living had risen by almost 2,000 percent.[6] "Economic terror" was how one author described daily life during hyperinflation, which plunged individuals into poverty in a matter of weeks.[7] All of this unfolded in the midst of a new presidential election cycle. The first transfer of constitutional power in six decades not marred by military intervention saw the return of a Peronist, Carlos Menem, to the presidency. Upon assuming office in July 1989, six months before his scheduled inauguration, he quickly pushed through a series of emergency economic laws, initiating a decade of austerity and the sweeping remaking of his party and the nation.

The year 1989 is alternatively analyzed as a break, turning point, or culmination in recent Argentine history. Depending on where and how intensely the spotlight aims, the year takes on all of these dimensions at once. Accordingly, the events at La Tablada marked the "final act of the Cold War" and the revolutionary Left on the national stage.[8] A few months later, the food riots put an end to Argentina's first post-dictatorship government. Carlos Menem, upon taking office, capitalized on the revulsive finale of the Alfonsín presidency and used the lingering specter of scarcity and social emergency to legitimate the beginning of Argentina's neoliberal turn, thus bringing to fruition an economic blueprint first envisioned by the military dictatorship. All this may be so. But to analyze 1989 means to take into full account the years immediately preceding it and the fate of a democratic project initiated in 1983. Food riots, as E. P. Thompson and others remind us, are a "highly complex form of direct popular action" and the expression of emergency in an existing social order.[9] Hunger and rising food prices in the context of runaway hyperinflation motivated looters, but those factors alone cannot explain the massive wave of rioting that swept Argentina in May and June 1989. The uprisings tested notions of common good and moral economy as understood until that point. Ultimately, they generated a new kind of politics and established the food riot as a regular part of the repertoire of popular protest going forward.[10] As an immediate consequence, however, the uprisings cut short the Alfonsín government's project to rebuild the republic in the terms of a democratic state that could put an end to the traditional separation of social justice and political freedoms.

The food riots took many by surprise. Yet zooming in on the dramatic end of the Alfonsín years forces a more critical assessment of the relationship between political crisis and structural adjustment and the onset of Argentina's neoliberal age. The potent combination of state terror in the 1970s, followed by inflation and ongoing recession in the decade that followed, contributed to a growing consensus for austerity over the course of the 1980s. These transformations were anything but abrupt. But it took the outbreak of hyperinflation and the weeklong food riots to elevate these ideas to a new common sense. The state response to the chaos of the final year of the Alfonsín presidency became proof that one social and economic order had ended and a new one begun.

Ultimately, the Alfonsín administration's broad program to reform every aspect of Argentine society fell far short of its original goals, with the exception of the consolidation of democracy itself. The tumult of 1989 did not lead to military takeover, but rather to a more constrained redefinition of the democratic future, which upheld neoliberal reforms as the only way to guarantee constitutional order and individual freedoms. In the fragile years following the end of the military regime, the grievances that ultimately compelled people to sack supermarkets exposed the unfulfilled promises of 1983 for a democratic society built on a foundation of social justice and rights—one that could ensure well-being and "could feed."

MAKING HYPERINFLATION

Thick sheets of humidity hang over Buenos Aires in the summer, when January temperatures can surge above 100 degrees Fahrenheit. The summer of 1989 broke records, though. An energy crisis that had begun the previous year prompted rotating power outages that lasted five to six hours at a time.[11] Throughout the capital and the surrounding suburbs, government offices and banks reduced their operations. Streetlights and traffic signals flickered off intermittently. Some joked that it was best to avoid riding in elevators in the early morning or evening, for fear of getting stuck until the power came back on.[12] The energy crisis tested the patience of the most unflappable urban residents and brought in a new year that began with an inauspicious start. But it foretold more dramatic events to come.

In the early morning hours of January 23, 1989, members of the leftist organization Movimiento Todos por la Patria (All for the Motherland Movement, MTP) attempted to occupy the Tablada military barracks, located just outside the capital limits.[13] A core group of MTP members had grown alarmed by the Alfonsín government's concessions to the armed forces and by the bravado of military officers affiliated with the far-right and ultranationalist *carapintada* movement. The most recent *carapintada* uprising, in December 1988 at the Villa Martelli barracks—the third and final during the Alfonsín presidency—had barely receded from public conversation.[14] The MTP believed a military coup was imminent. Their takeover of La Tablada was meant to thwart a coup and in doing so spark a popular rebellion. The hastily planned operation quickly spiraled out of control. The forty-six MTP members who stormed the barracks were no match for military tanks, gas, and firepower. Surrounded and with no way to retreat, by the next morning dozens were dead (many summarily executed), and the survivors were tortured on-site. Images of the dead circulated widely and recalled the guerrilla movements of the previous decade and the disproportionate repression of the state and the armed forces.[15] Going forward, La Tablada shaped how the unrest of the coming months would be interpreted by government officials in the service of inaugurating a new era of social and economic discipline.

For some, the violence with which 1989 began evoked memories of 1975, the year before the onset of the dictatorship, with the fate of constitutional government hanging in the balance. Its popular mandate eroded and its domestic support weakened, the Alfonsín administration had been losing support since its loss of provincial governorships and congressional seats in the 1987 legislative elections. For government officials, their main goal was to make it to the May 1989 presidential election, ensure a Radical Party victory if at all possible, and guarantee the peaceful transfer of constitutional power in December. These scenarios depended more than anything on managing an impending financial collapse. In the final week of January 1989, as La Tablada captivated national attention, Argentina's creditors called in $486.3 million dollars in payments.[16] That demand marked the first of a series of events that would deplete the dollar reserves of the Central Bank and end in hyperinflation. The Alfonsín administration oriented its priorities toward mitigating the worst effects of the economic crisis while attempting to maintain its tenuous alliances with domestic industrial and agricultural groups and Argentina's external creditors. Both efforts proved untenable.

During the final year of the Alfonsín presidency, authorities determined that they could no longer service the nation's foreign debts.[17] In 1983, Argentina's external debt hovered around $43 billion. By 1989, that figure had risen to approximately $65 billion.[18] Despite concessions to foreign lenders and pledges to advance the privatization of state enterprises and reduce the fiscal deficit, lending conditions proved unfeasible and politically unpopular. Argentina all but ceased payments to its creditors in April 1988. "Argentina won't pay and banks won't lend," concluded a representative from a US bank in Argentina. The only way out, he surmised, was for Argentina to follow the example of Brazil, where the government of José Sarney had recently enacted a series of austerity measures, and to "accept the menu" of structural adjustment.[19] In June 1988, the IMF declared Argentina "noncompliant," which barred the country from obtaining additional loans from the fund for the remainder of Alfonsín's term. Negotiations between Buenos Aires and Washington to secure additional funding stalled.[20] The IMF would not grant Argentina more credit until after Carlos Menem took office.

Isolated from foreign lending markets, Argentina's remaining hope for bailout funds was the World Bank, which continued to provide credit following the IMF announcement. The first installment of a promised $1.25 billion loan was set for February 1989.[21] But those funds never materialized. In the transition from the administration of Ronald Reagan to George H. W. Bush in the United States, Argentina lost one of its remaining allies, former treasury secretary James Baker.[22] Shortly after the Bush administration took office, the World Bank announced that it would be suspending the first $350 million loan installment. The news set off a swift chain of events. Commercial banks holding Argentina's debts demanded immediate payment and suspended short-term loans. Creditors began to dump their Argentine australes and to buy dollars, sparking a frantic run on the dollar, which rose 59 percent by the end of February 1989. The World Bank's announcement also had other consequences, not the least of which was the collapse of the "Plan Primavera," the Alfonsín administration's final stabilization plan, and the fragile alliances that held it together.

Launched in August 1988, the Plan Primavera was designed for the pragmatic purpose of avoiding hyperinflation before the presidential elections of May 1989. Among other measures, the stabilization plan devalued the currency, set renewable price and tariff accords, reduced import taxes, and fixed variable exchange rates on the dollar for commercial and banking transactions.[23] The economic team led by Juan Sourrouille also agreed to reduce state expenditures in accordance with the demands of international lenders and to take further steps to privatize state enterprises, including Aerolineas Argentinas and ENTeL (Empresa Nacional de Telecomunicaciones), the public phone company.[24] The success of the Plan Primavera also depended on a series of accords with national business, financial, and agricultural interest groups. As possibilities for external funding narrowed by mid-1988, the Alfonsín government was compelled to seek closer collaboration and support from the representatives of Argentine capital. The most significant of these alliances came through the Group of 8, a loose coalition of Argentina's largest banking, industrial, construction, and agro-export associations.[25] In broad strokes, the government called on business leaders to keep consumer prices in check and to halt capital flight by reinvesting their profits and dollars back into the country. In return, the state would commit to more stringent anti-inflationary measures, lower tariffs, and deeper structural reforms. While these measures sought to appease foreign creditors and domestic critics calling for liberalization, they reflected a steady move toward more orthodoxy since the 1985 announcement of the "wartime economy."

The Alfonsín government's relationship with economic interest groups, which had seen their influence in political life increase in the aftermath of the dictatorship, had been a fraught and an ongoing source of frustration throughout the decade. By 1988, one of the consequences of the last-ditch attempts at stabilization ended up bringing interest groups closer to state power and gave them greater sway over public decision making.[26] Though business leaders initially offered support for the Plan Primavera, in early 1989, when the World Bank cut off promised credits to Argentina, any remaining pacts collapsed. This left the Alfonsín government at the mercy of a powerful economic lobby that it had helped to strengthen. Within a few months, most members of the Group of 8 and other "captains of industry" openly threw their support behind the candidacy of Carlos Menem.

The making of hyperinflation in 1989 had its roots in a confluence of medium and long-term causes and internal and external factors. A decade of recession dating to the onset of military rule in the 1970s, which was exacerbated by crushing debt, the demands of external lending institutions, and balance of payment crises, eventually left Argentina with no outside sources of support. Likewise, state alliances with domestic interest groups that had the ability to set prices and to control internal markets increasingly hemmed in the Alfonsín government and emboldened the very conglomerates and business leaders most poised to profit from the outbreak of inflation. Beyond the purely economic realm, the government response to ongoing threats to institutional stability caused by military rebellions and La Tablada further eroded popular support for the Alfonsín administration. Combined with the uncertainties of the upcoming presidential election, these events touched off a brewing climate of hyperinflation.

DOLLAR FEVER

Government efforts proved incapable of halting hyperinflation during the first half of 1989. Month by month, prices continued to rise. Inflation—already at 17 percent in March—rose to 33 percent in April, 79 percent in May, and 116 percent by June, tipping into technical hyperinflation less than one month before the May 14 presidential election.[27] The economic news produced alarming effects, with a turnover of three economic ministers in six months, sharp devaluations of the local currency, and exchange rates that eventually shifted hour by hour.[28] Stopgap measures to stem the collapse only inflamed public ire and opened the door to widespread financial speculation, felt in the form of punishing austerity in the lives of ordinary individuals.

The dwindling dollar reserves of the Central Bank caused government officials the most concern as the steady bleeding out of US currency sped up during the first month of 1989.[29] Creditors and other firms bought up dollars, while exporters refused to liquidate their receipts in anticipation of a currency devaluation.[30] The "financial bicycle"—in which investors took advantage of Argentina's high interest rates to convert their dollars to australes and then back again for large profit margins—further emptied the coffers of the Central Bank. Juan Sourrouille and José Machinea, the president of the Central Bank, announced that Argentina did not have enough dollars to keep up with demand. In early February, Sourrouille withdrew the austral from exchange markets and created a free-floating dollar.[31] The measure, an attempt to stem the flow of cash from Argentina's reserves, sent the value of the austral plummeting. In one day, the dollar rose 33 percent.[32] The narrow streets of "la City," Buenos Aires's financial district, overflowed in a feverish scramble for dollars.[33]

In the weeks and months to come, a familiar scene repeated itself. Customers inundated banks and exchange houses beginning in the early morning hours each day, waiting in lines that stretched several blocks. They came, calculators and bankbooks in hand, to buy dollars, cash in on fixed-term deposits, and protect their savings in any way possible.[34] Short tempers and angry confrontations overwhelmed financial employees. "More than one bank teller might have lunched on valium," remarked one observer.[35] The run on the dollar triggered calls for the resignation of the entire government economic team from across the political spectrum. Yet no amount of head scratching or protest in front of exchange boards could allay the anxieties surrounding an ever-rising dollar. While individuals and small businesses saw their savings and paychecks shrink, many of Argentina's biggest firms were poised to profit through a combination of speculation and capital flight. By the end of February, close to US$1 billion had been transferred from Argentina to Uruguay, as firms such as the multinational food giant Cargill, which had played a leading role in discrediting state regulatory capacities during the Caso Mazzorín, and the grain processor Bunge & Born, sold their dollars in Montevidean markets.[36] Government officials denounced these actions as a "market coup," part of a deliberate attempt to debilitate the Alfonsín government through speculation and a massive transfer of wealth. Between January and July 1989, Argentina's Central Bank reserves dropped from US$2,463,500,000 to $112,000,000. Over that same six-month period, the price of the dollar jumped more than 3,600 percent.[37]

The run on the dollar was felt immediately in rising consumer prices. Following the announcement of the withdrawal of the austral from exchange markets in

February, basic goods such as milk and certain medicines jumped 30 percent in less than a week.[38] Though government functionaries insisted that the value of the dollar should not affect internal prices, the reality of a crashing austral led to a spike in the cost of staple goods that did not let up for the next six months. Officials called on consumers to denounce speculation on the front lines in the war against inflation. "Your attitude as an alert consumer is decisive. Collaborate. It is in self-defense," ran one communiqué from the Ministry of Economy.[39] But these combative pronouncements, including threats of sanctions against companies and vendors that raised prices, lacked teeth. At the end of February 1989, the Argentine Industrial Union (UIA) and the Argentine Chamber of Commerce (CAC)—two main partners in the Plan Primavera—announced their decision to withdraw from previous price accord agreements, which left the government with few remaining domestic allies and sent prices soaring. In February, the consumer price index rose by almost 10 percent over the previous month. Within this climate of economic uncertainty, troubling news from Venezuela reached Buenos Aires. The announcement by the recently inaugurated government of Carlos Andrés Pérez of an IMF-funded financing package set off a week of rioting and urban protests that left hundreds dead at the hands of state forces.[40] Reports of the Caracazo increased concerns that a social explosion along the lines of Venezuela might not be far off if inflation continued to rise.

"RED PEN" VERSUS "PRODUCTIVE REVOLUTION": THE 1989 PRESIDENTIAL ELECTION

As voters prepared to return to the polls to elect a president for the first successive transfer of constitutional power following the end of the dictatorship, the economic crisis emerged as the touchstone issue of the 1989 election. Despite the Alfonsín administration's desire to move the economy out of the center of politics, the emergency shaped the campaigns of the Radical and Peronist candidates. Eduardo Angeloz, the Radical Party nominee and governor of Córdoba, attempted to distance himself from a government that had been debilitated by recession and a steady loss of support. A proponent of free-market orthodoxy affiliated with the conservative wing of the Radical Party, Angeloz ran on a ticket calling for a *lápiz rojo* (red pen) to slash government spending and reduce inefficiency by privatizing state enterprises.[41] Angeloz's platform put him most closely in line with Álvaro Alsogaray, the presidential candidate and leader of the conservative Unión del Centro Democrático (UCeDé), who would eventually win 6.5 percent of the vote. As an outspoken critic of the Alfonsín government's fiscal policies—going so far as to call for the dismissal of Juan Sourrouille and his economic team—Angeloz initially enjoyed the support of international creditors and US officials fearful of a Peronist victory. But that support diminished with each of the Alfonsín administration's failed attempts at stabilization. Angeloz's appeals to middle-class voters, a traditional Radical Party base, also waned as the economic crisis battered middle-income sectors. Despite attempts to differentiate himself from Alfonsín, Angeloz's chances for victory were eclipsed by the growing popularity of his Peronist rival, Carlos Menem.

Carlos Menem's rise surprised many within and outside of the Peronist movement.[42] In July 1988, the two-time governor of La Rioja province bested Antonio Cafiero, the party president and governor of Buenos Aires, in the Justicialist Party's (PJ's) first direct primaries.[43] Like Cafiero, Menem was also affiliated with the Peronist Renovation. Since Peronism's defeat in 1983, the Renovators had taken steps to jettison industrial trade unions from the party's leadership and to democratize it through internal elections. In 1987, those efforts swept Renovation candidates into governorships throughout the country and seemed to all but secure Cafiero's 1989 run for the presidency. With his own presidential ambitions, Menem began to cultivate the support of an "old guard" of orthodox union bosses—the precise figures Renovators sought to displace. He also built alliances within the remade territorial bases of Peronism among the urban poor, which helped to extend his influence locally and nationally.[44]

Menem's carefully crafted image reclaimed the symbols and gestures of Peronist tradition.[45] One of his first campaign events took place in Berisso, "the cradle of Peronism" on the outskirts of La Plata, where workers had marched en masse on October 17, 1945, to demand Juan Perón's release from prison, bringing forth Peronism and establishing the working class as a main protagonist in national life.[46] Riding the country aboard his "Menem-mobile," Menem combined charisma and oratory skill with a promise to finish Perón's "inconclusive revolution." As a candidate, Menem drew sharp distinctions between his political project and that of other Peronist reformers, whom he accused of harboring liberal sympathies and an uncomfortable affinity with an *alfonsinista* vision of democratic life. "The people cannot live on democracy alone," he declared at a campaign rally in early 1989. "We don't want formal democracy just so that people can suffer and die from hunger."[47] Menem drove a wedge through the equation of liberal democracy and social rights, which shaped the progressive wing of the Radical Party and the Peronist Renovation. In doing so, he attempted to demonstrate that the Alfonsín government had failed to displace Peronism's dominion of social justice, while depicting Peronist Renovators as barely indistinguishable from their Radical counterparts. In the midst of the 1989 economic emergency, the culmination of a decade's worth of growing social inequalities, these ideas attracted voters among the new urban poor and a not insignificant portion of the middle classes.

But while Menem was promising a "productive revolution" and wage increases for labor, he was also taking the steps to transform Peronism into a market-oriented party. Shortly after he secured his nomination, he cultivated the support of Argentina's economic establishment with pledges to comply with the requirements of international lenders and to double down on free-market reforms.[48] Funding for his campaign came from the Argentine conglomerates Bunge & Born and Grupo Fortabat, whose directors went on to obtain positions in Menem's government.[49] While many of these negotiations took place beyond public view, Menem was often explicit in his vow to guide Argentina into the twenty-first century through an embrace of free-market reforms, an influx of foreign capital, and stronger ties with the United States. During a campaign speech in early 1989, he made some of those intentions clear. "Peronism has evolved," he began. "We cannot continue to live with the same systems as 40 years ago. . . . If not, we can see what is happening in the Soviet Union and in China, where Marxist principles have been completely buried. If it is like that in those countries, than it is even more necessary for nations that constantly evolve to not continue with the same systems that the times have completely passed by."[50] In the twilight of the Cold War and global socialism, Menem used the examples of China and the Soviet Union—nations on the cusp of their own eras of market reform—to issue a warning that Argentina risked being passed by in the worldwide transformation of capitalism if it did not embrace structural adjustment. At first glance, Menem's invocation of Peronist doctrine might seem at odds with his alliances among the *vendepatrias* of Argentina's economic elites. But according to Menem's formulation, there was no contradiction at all: it was Peronism alone that could usher in an era of necessary reforms for Argentina. Casting himself in the footsteps of Perón's inconclusive revolution, Menem's recourse to the memory of a Peronist past would ease the radical transformations to come and in the process put an end to forty years of a benefactor state first consolidated by Peronism itself.

A cursory look at the 1989 elections reveals how a neoliberal worldview had moved closer to the political center over the previous six years. This did not mean that free-market policies enjoyed broad social support or legitimacy, as the individual letter writers quoted in chapter 5 made clear. But the ongoing economic crisis lent itself to a belief in the inevitability of coming reforms. By 1989, despite the military's periodic threats, most voters believed Argentina's political democracy had been secured, though a key piece of the promise of 1983 was missing. The main candidates paid scant attention to human rights or the ethical foundations of a democratic republic, key pillars of Alfonsín's 1983 victory. Angeloz and Menem, in fact, openly discussed the possibility of amnesty for military leaders convicted in the 1985 trials. Indeed, the dominant message of the 1989 election upheld the free market as the primary path to achieving domestic peace.

"ANARCHY OF PRICES": LIVING IN HYPERINFLATION

The weeks leading up to the food riots were marked by growing waves of rumor, unease, and fruitless government initiatives to prevent the eruption of hyperinflation. Juan Sourrouille was forced to step down from his post as economic minister in late March. His replacement, Juan Carlos Pugliese, a former economic minister during the government of Arturo Illia and current head of the Chamber of Deputies, did not fair any better. During his first full week in office, the family basket rose 30 percent, along with an increase in layoffs that left families and individuals in dire straits. Pugliese's efforts to halt inflation with another currency devaluation led to a 65 percent spike in the value of the dollar in a matter of days.[51] His public lament about his fruitless attempts to negotiate with business leaders, most of whom had declared their support for Carlos Menem—"I speak to them from the heart and they answer me with their pockets"—revealed the impotence of the Alfonsín government during its final months in office. The newspaper *Clarín* began to refer to the economic panorama in April 1989 as the "Rodrigazo Radical," a reference to the fiscal spiral of 1975 that had given Argentines their first prolonged taste of hyperinflation. Reports of an imminent economic collapse set off rumors of food shortages and tense scenes in supermarkets, where some store owners had begun to post guards at the doors.[52]

Police throughout Buenos Aires province stepped up their monitoring of supermarkets. Officials at Police Intelligence headquarters in La Plata drafted detailed reports that charted the rising cost of the family basket from March to April. According to their calculations, the overall cost of feeding a family of four rose by 129 percent over this two-month period.[53] The price of staple goods such as eggs and pasta jumped 280 and 205 percent, respectively. Rough, hand-drawn tables plainly showed how salaries could not keep pace with inflation.[54] These reports read more like the economic indicators published by national statistical agencies than police missives. It is not clear where the figures came from or how they were calculated, but the close attention security forces paid to the prohibitive costs of staple goods spoke to the fact that food prices were at the heart of brewing social unrest. Officers speculated that a social explosion along the lines of the Venezuelan Caracazo might be around the corner.[55] Their reports described the overall scenario in April 1989 as an "anarchy of prices," battering the middle and lower classes with a steady "deterioration in quality of life." "This crisis," one memo concluded, "will derive serious social consequences difficult to repair over the long term."[56]

Argentines had lived with inflationary crises since the mid-1970s. But the everyday strategies of economizing used by poor people and the middle classes stopped working in the context of the 1989 hyperinflation.[57] Those with means and access to dollars were sheltered from austral devaluations, while salaried professionals and informal workers saw their monthly earnings diminish along with their purchasing power. Middle-income sectors had long protected their currency from fluctuations by investing in durable goods such as cars and appliances, and properties for the most well off. For growing numbers of urban residents, these defensive purchases were no longer an option. Commercial districts emptied of shoppers. Tailors, and repair shops for shoes, umbrellas, and electronics, however, reported an uptake in business as individuals attempted to salvage items for another year of use.[58]

As in other inflationary moments, the most acute effects were felt in the supermarket. Bulk shopping, stockpiling, and communal purchases direct from wholesale suppliers—common strategies to counteract rising prices—continued apace when possible. But most individuals were forced to alter their economic patterns. Shoppers quickly grew accustomed to purchasing only what was needed for that day's food preparation. Due to costumer demand, some grocers in Buenos Aires's most comfortable middle-class neighborhoods began to sell cooking oil portioned for individual meals. These adaptations demonstrated the resilience of consumers grown accustomed to currency fluctuations. But they also laid bare the impossibility of individual efforts to get ahead of increased costs and to counter the worst effects of inflation. Rapid price fluctuations eroded the energy, will, and patience of buyers and sellers alike. And they produced effects seen in other cases of twentieth-century hyperinflation, characterized as the "absence of parameters of reference" in daily economic life.[59] With currency devaluating on an hourly basis, calculating costs took on an air of fiction and a sense of the unreal. Time also took on different meaning in the rush to get rid of the local currency or to beat the price machine before new increases could take effect.[60] The outbreak of hyperinflation plunged people into poverty over the following months. According to data from the Instituto Nacional de Estadística y Censos (INDEC), the national statistics bureau, the percentage of people living below the poverty line in Buenos Aires and the metropolitan region increased from 19.7 percent in May 1989 to 38.3 percent in October of that same year. Day to day and hour by hour, the economic crisis challenged individuals' understanding of their place in the social world.[61]

Few were surprised when Carlos Menem beat Eduardo Angeloz in the May 14 presidential elections.[62] Yet Menem's victory did little to settle the economic turmoil. Layoffs, the suspension of social services, and the collapse of any predictability in terms of prices accelerated in the second half of May. Raúl Alfonsín spoke to the nation in one of his final televised addresses, on May 23. Since Menem's electoral victory, the Radical government and the incoming Peronist administration had begun to negotiate the possibility of an early transfer of power. When that first round of talks broke down, Alfonsín's entire cabinet resigned, and preparations began for an emergency plan to govern for the next six months. In his brief address, Alfonsín recognized the majority that had cast its vote in favor of Menem, and he reiterated that the "true test" of the transition would see him carry out his term with a peaceful transfer of constitutional power. The purpose of the address, however, was to prepare Argentines for the trying times ahead using a by then familiar refrain: "We are not only going to have a *wartime economy*. This will be a crisis government. We will carry out policies attuned to social issues, but it will be hard as all can imagine." The next day, news broke that looters had begun sacking supermarkets in the outskirts of Córdoba and Rosario.

ANATOMY OF A FOOD RIOT

The hundreds of food riots that spread throughout Argentina's major urban centers during the final week of May 1989 shocked the nation. Though the economic emergency that preceded the uprisings had been a long time coming, the scale and scope of popular fury unleashed by hyperinflation nonetheless took many by surprise, as it simultaneously exposed the plight of the urban poor in Argentina's declining industrial cities.

In the Greater Buenos Aires township of Quilmes, the first riots began on May 26 and reached their peak on May 30, with several simultaneous lootings of national supermarket chains. Quilmes had already played an outsized role in the food politics of post-dictatorship Argentina—first as the site of the soup kitchens organized by the local Catholic Church toward the end of the dictatorship, then as the launching site of the PAN food program, and now as one of the epicenters of the 1989 food riots. In the late afternoon of May 26, a group of about thirty people, mostly women and children, calmly entered a local supermarket and emptied shelves of basic goods such as sugar, milk, and dishtowels. As they left the store, police detained six people between the ages of nine and twenty-four, all residents of the nearby El Monte shantytown. When later questioned, those detained said that they had gone to the supermarket in response to a rumor that the owners were giving away free food and other merchandise to women.[63] The next day, similar incidents were reported throughout the township. A group of about twenty people demanded food at the entrance to the Llanesa supermarket.[64] At Supermercado Lorena, twenty-five women took goods, breaking windows as they retreated.[65] The crowds had also grown by the end of the second day. Around five hundred people gathered at the entrance of Cooperativa Unión and chanted at the police, "Can you live on your salary?" The crowd dispersed after about an hour, and no further incidents were reported.[66]

Over the next three days, dozens of food riots erupted in the area, drawing between thirty and several hundred individuals each. Police reports noted the strong presence of women and children, and a large number of those detained were minors.[67] May 30 was the most agitated day of uprisings in Greater Buenos Aires. In Quilmes and the surrounding towns, one looting per hour was reported by early afternoon.[68] Parents kept their children home from school amid fears that the uprisings would spread to lunchrooms and public buildings used as distribution centers for the PAN food program.[69] Nationwide, clashes between protesters and police left up to ten dead by the end of the day.

In the town of Wilde, one midday uprising on May 30 reflected the course of many of the riots in the area. Residents of the Villa Azul shantytown gathered at the entrance to El Más Gauchito, a local branch of a national supermarket chain with a strong presence in Greater Buenos Aires and La Plata. The crowd quickly swelled to one thousand people, demanding the immediate distribution of food. Women and children congregated at the front, shopping bags in hand. Police reports later noted that the majority of those present were mothers with their children, followed by a smaller group "of members of the masculine sex acting as rear guard."[70] Tensions were already high when a priest from Quilmes began negotiating with the store owners for the disbursement of basic goods such as bread, pasta, milk, and sugar from a delivery truck. These types of negotiations occurred frequently, with store owners agreeing to distribute food in exchange for crowds' leaving the stores untouched. Events took a bad turn once food distribution began. Conflicting accounts recall sporadic gunshots coming from nearby or from security forces, which sent people into a panic and caused a run on the food truck. The scene devolved from there into a chaotic scramble for goods as police began to fire on the crowd with rubber bullets. Most people fled for shelter. But a smaller group of young men faced off against the police, forming a barricade behind the railroad tracks that separated Villa Azul from the middle-class chalets on the other side. They set fire to tires, forming a roadblock until early evening.

No one died in Wilde that afternoon, although similar incidents the day before in San Miguel and Rosario had resulted in several deaths. The Wilde riot, however, was emblematic of many of the uprisings during the final week of May 1989. Large groups of women and children seeking food were the most visible faces of the riots, with men and adolescents armed with rocks and other projectiles confronting police. To outside observers, the lootings proceeded through violence and confusion. But behind the scenes investigators found that much of the food taken from stores was also used to supply soup kitchens, which sprang up to address critical need throughout Greater Buenos Aires during the first half of 1989.[71] Media coverage, however, overwhelmingly depicted looters as delinquents who pilfered electronics, alcohol, and other items. For example, the newspaper Clarín's coverage of the Wilde uprising described the outbreak of violence as a battle of "slum versus slum" and the distribution of food as if it were "[being done in] the middle of a zoo." Accompanying photos showed two women pulling each other's hair. This and other mainstream media coverage emphasized thinly veiled disdain for hungry poor people.[72]

Yet even in the midst of their alarming chaos, the riots contained an internal order. Their first aim was visibility. Almost all lootings took place in daylight, from the early afternoon to dusk. Patterns also emerged in the types of stores targeted, with large national supermarket firms being the most frequent focus. A police list of the uprisings in Quilmes and the surrounding towns showed that chains such as El Más Gauchito, Llaneza, and Supercoop were the most looted stores.[73] Supermarket chains located close to shantytowns and in poor urban neighborhoods often dominated shopping options in those areas. They represented the most conspicuous face of inflationary food prices and drew the ire of local residents. One woman who openly discussed her participation in several sackings in Quilmes explained that she and her neighbors only took from supermarket chains, in part because they "were insured." "We do not go to small retail stores [*comercios minoristas*]," she emphatically declared.[74] Small store owners in Quilmes shuttered their shops during the riots, though few reported serious damage.[75]

Basic food goods and items of *primera necesidad* (first necessity) were most frequently emptied from store shelves. While looters did steal cash registers, electronics, clothing, and appliances, police and media reporting tended to confirm that food was the prime aim of the sackings. Even during the most frightening uprisings in parts of Rosario, witnesses noted that *saqueadores* (looters) "carried off a considerable amount of food and left without violence. . . . [T]here were no insults or shouting, rather a certain conviction to exercise the taking of food."[76] Of course, violence was also a hallmark of the *saqueos*. But it tended to erupt after negotiations broke down between looters and store owners, or in response to threats of police force. In these contexts, any subsequent sacking "made sense" as a justified collective response to the threat of physical harm and individuals' inability to fulfill their basic needs.[77]

On the front lines were women. Coverage of the riots often pictured poor and working-class women accompanied by their children, the most vulnerable individuals affected by the crisis. This was perhaps not surprising. Women carried the burdens of balancing food budgets and stretching paychecks and other earnings. As the primary shoppers in many households, they endured rising food prices up close as they toiled to feed their families. "No one is sending us [to loot]," declared one mother who spoke freely about her participation in the riots in Quilmes. "We are doing this out of necessity because what we and our husbands make is not enough."[78] For many women, staving off hunger justified looting as an action of last resort. Another woman stated that she "robbed" because "we don't have anything to feed our children."[79] In her and other women's estimation, the act of taking food was a just due and a right, with hunger the motivating force.

The gendered dimensions of the crisis ran through the food riots and a series of simultaneous food-related protests during May 1989. From the May 14 presidential elections on, housewives' associations, *sociedades de fomento*, and neighborhood groups convened marches and protests to denounce the economic emergency. By and large, these were led by women. A march of the "empty bags" (*bolsas vacías*) organized by the Amas de Casa del País drew over a thousand women to the Plaza de Mayo with calls to "imprison the economic criminals!"[80] The gathering recalled the *cacerolazos* made famous by conservative women opposed to Salvador Allende's Popular Unity government in Chile.[81] But the group's main demands called on government officials to restore "price controls for the family basket" and a more equitable regulation of the economy. In Greater Buenos Aires, the Unión de Mujeres Argentina (UMA), an antifascist organization founded in 1947 that brought together various parties of the Left, organized several days of protests during the last week of May 1989. "Our goal is not to destabilize, as many accuse us," one UMA representative declared. "We only ask that the hope the people deposited in the ballot box is fulfilled, because when there is hunger there is no democracy."[82]

Read against the backdrop of the first years of democratic return, the food riots and mobilizations of May 1989 put into relief the limits of a social agenda initially outlined by the Alfonsín government that had failed to materialize. Seen from this vantage point, the goal to end hunger, which had so animated expectations at the onset of the democratic return, fell far short of those original aims. Indeed, in the midst of the prolonged hyperinflation of 1989, the need for food relief seemed more pressing than it had in 1983. At their most ethical center, the riots exposed extreme need and pushed to its outermost limit the demand for the basic human right to food and material well-being. The 1989 uprisings gave voice and visibility to the urban poor as a new political actor following years of political violence, industrial decline, and early experiments with austerity first put in motion by the military dictatorship. Over the coming decade, as the neoliberal era deepened and undid remaining protections, many of the groups and individuals that mobilized in 1989 would go on to define new social movements that sought to fulfill the unfinished promises of 1983.

THE ROAD TO AUSTERITY

At the start of the weeklong food riots, Buenos Aires police forces initially detailed looters' straightforward motivations: "Obviously, these events cannot be separated from the critical economic situation across the country, which has led the most unprotected sectors to obtain elemental necessities using tactics beyond the law." "Notwithstanding this," one report concluded, "we cannot rule out political motives behind this distressing situation."[83] As the protests accelerated and grew in number, police stepped up their use of force and began blaming the riots on leftist conspirators. Police claimed the May 30 riot in Wilde was the work of MAS (Movimiento al socialismo) activists based in Villa Azul.[84] In the Greater Buenos Aires township of Lanus, officers investigated a backpack containing a revolver and leftist publications belonging to a law student and the alleged ringleader of a series of riots in the area.[85] In Quilmes, security forces attempted to follow up on sightings of a young middle-class couple going door to door, calling on shantytown residents to join the riots.[86] They also recorded several anonymous phone calls to police stations with messages such as, "*Viva el ERP!* If you hadn't triumphed at La Tablada this wouldn't be happening right now."[87]

Reports like these prove difficult to confirm, though chances are many were embellished or fabricated.[88] Leftist organizations and parties did mobilize in the poorer urban neighborhoods of Greater Buenos Aires in May and June 1989. But as with the example of the Unión de Mujeres Argentina, their protests tended to revolve around demands for concrete basic needs, not armed revolution. Security forces had long planted evidence of left-wing conspiracies, and the level of detail recorded in police memos about leftist militants during the weeklong riots contrasts starkly with the sparse and rushed descriptions of the lootings themselves. The recent attack on La Tablada led officials to see elaborate conspiracies between "marginalized sectors" "directed by the Communist Party (PC) and other leftist activists" who would try to "occupy police stations, ministries, and other public offices . . . to sack supermarkets, [and] distribute arms throughout villas."[89] To be sure, the events at La Tablada heightened police awareness of any armed mobilization. Yet police reactions during the riots reveal how close security forces remained to the tactics of the previous decade as they attempted to connect a revolutionary vanguard of middle-class activists to inciting slum residents to riot. In May 1989, Cold War logics still justified the use of force and the surveillance of popular sectors.

For their part, government officials also repeated the claim that the riots were the work of the Left. Interior Minister Juan Carlos Pugliese, who in the most recent cabinet shake-up had left his post as minister of economy, described the food riots as a "sophisticated," "Trotskyist-styled" takeover intended to give rise to a new Caracazo fueled by popular indignation.[90] From Córdoba, the defeated UCR candidate Eduardo Angeloz claimed organized commandos were using women and children as shields to pilfer stores throughout the province, while recently elected Carlos Menem declared that rioters were "holding on to ideologies that [belonged in a] museum."[91] UCeDé leader Álvaro Alsogaray echoed that sentiment and admonished Argentines not to be swayed by "organized subversion."[92] Leaders of the nation's most influential political parties may have had their differences, but on the riots they found common ground. Their assessments left little room to view the uprisings as a popular collective response to hardship and grievances over the state's inability to repair the prolonged economic crisis. As the uprisings entered their sixth full day, Alfonsín declared a thirty-day state of siege, which both congressional chambers approved swiftly. While the state of exception facilitated expanded security measures, other social protections simultaneously broke down. The PAN food program, whose initial design was meant to put an end to extreme hunger, was suspended in parts of the country. Congress voted to increase the PAN budget, yet many suppliers refused to release goods because of the government's failure to pay for them.[93]

Ultimately, the political response to the riots, which connected the protests of popular sectors to expressions of the revolutionary Left, cemented a belief in austerity as the only viable resolution to Argentina's social and economic malaise. The wheels of this transition were already firmly in motion by May 1989. But widespread interpretations of the food riots as an outgrowth of "museum ideologies," to paraphrase Menem, only reinforced conclusions that a break with past forms of social and economic planning was not only necessary but inevitable. Accordingly, the food riots represented proof that the forty-year-old benefactor state—with its inability to feed its citizens and to avoid the inflationary crisis and social uprisings that followed—had reached its explosive end.

The food riots thus marked the negotiation of dual transitions: from one constitutionally elected government to another for the first time in six decades, and from a twentieth-century welfare state to neoliberalism. On May 30, the day of the most deadly rioting, Menem announced Miguel Ángel Roig, a former vice president of the agriculture conglomerate Bunge & Born, as his finance minister.[94] Bunge & Born had drawn the invective of two generations of Peronists as the quintessential *vendepatria* firm among Argentina's export-oriented elites. Plan BB, Menem's first economic program, named for the Bunge & Born managers who helped design it, called for a deepening of the market-oriented reforms already taking place. These included sharp currency devaluations, an acceleration of privatizations, and renewed debt talks with Argentina's creditors. Menem also fortified his alliances with the free-market boosters of the UCeDé, naming party leader Álvaro Alsogaray his chief adviser on debt negotiations with Washington, D.C., and his daughter, Senator María Julia, to lead the privatization of the state-run ENTeL phone utility. These high-level political nominations generated the most discussion in the aftermath of the food riots, but another appointment also made the news. To the post of domestic trade secretary, Menem named Alberto Albamonte, the UCeDé congressman who had catapulted the Caso Mazzorín into the public eye. In the year since the height of the scandal, Albamonte had managed to keep the infamous chickens—and himself—in the headlines.[95] Shortly after receiving Menem's offer, he announced that one of his first tasks would be to disband the Supply Law, the cornerstone regulatory measure of the state office he was set to lead. Though he never assumed the post of domestic trade secretary, Albamonte's nomination and his comments about his charge foretold economic transformations to come; the diagnosis of the state as the problem also included its solution. By the beginning of June 1989, negotiations had resumed for the early transfer of presidential power, and the management of the economic crisis was in the hands of the incoming Menem administration.

Alfonsín announced his resignation in a national address on June 12. Delivered in a hoarse voice punctuated by frequent coughing, his speech lacked the verve with which he had rallied enthusiastic crowds during his campaign and through the first years of his presidency.[96] There would be other opportunities for a reckoning with the achievements of his government. For now, he began, the economic crisis warranted the nation's full attention and made virtually impossible any measures that his government could take to avoid further suffering.[97] "These times demand energetic and unavoidable solutions," he stated as he vowed, in one of the final acts of his presidency, to support the passage of the economic laws proposed by the incoming Menem administration and to work toward a new round of debt negotiations. Midway through the somber address, when he declared that he would be stepping down on June 30, Alfonsín framed the decision as the fulfillment of a commitment he had made upon taking office in 1983. The peaceful transition of constitutional power, he concluded, depended on these "necessary economic decisions" to ensure democracy going forward.

Carlos Menem was inaugurated on July 8, 1989. The start of his presidency, however, did not put an end to hyperinflation. The cover of *Clarín* on the day he took office showed a portrait of a smiling Menem with Henry Kissinger, accompanied by the startling headline that prices had risen by 100 percent just the day before.[98] During Menem's first month in office, the price of consumer goods almost doubled again, while utilities such as gas, electricity, and telephone service soared by an average of 700 percent.[99] Sporadic rioting also continued throughout parts of Rosario and Tucumán. In August, Menem used presidential decree powers to push through an Economic Emergency and State Reform Law, which among other measures authorized deep cuts to state offices, the privatization of almost all public utilities, the end of special state subsidies, an overhaul of the Central Bank, and looser regulations on foreign investment.[100] Though these plans did not take effect right away, the emergency laws laid the path for neoliberal structural readjustment measures going forward and granted Menem greater presidential control over the entire process.

The economic laws and other high-profile events during the first months of Menem's government attempted to prepare Argentines for these coming changes. In October 1989, one week before he announced the first wave of pardons that would eventually free over two hundred military officials by the end of 1990, Menem orchestrated an elaborate repatriation of the remains of Juan Manuel Rosas.[101] The celebration of the polarizing nineteenth-century caudillo, revered by ultranationalists and conservative Peronists, was meant to promote national unity in the service of a new age of peace and prosperity.[102] Two days of ceremonies ended in Buenos Aires with a caravan carrying Rosas's remains and an escort of five thousand gauchos on horseback.[103] "In welcoming back Brigadier General don Juan Manuel de Rosas," Menem declared, "we say farewell to an old, wasteful, anachronistic and absurd nation. We say goodbye to a nation of disasters, myths, and false illusions."[104] The lavish reburial of Rosas, orchestrated against the backdrop of the ongoing crisis, sought to impose a forced reconciliation and a break with the past, to roll back human rights prosecutions, and to push forward radical market-oriented reforms.

It took almost two years for these transformations to get fully under way. Despite a brief respite from inflation at the start of the Menem presidency, another bout of hyperinflation and food rioting began in December 1989, followed a year later by a final *carapintada* uprising and a second round of pardons for those convicted during the 1985 trial of the juntas.[105] After a few additional false starts, in April 1991, Menem's third minister of economy, Domingo Cavallo, a former president of the Central Bank during the dictatorship and Menem's first foreign minister, set in motion "the miracle of the 1990s." His economic plan, known as "convertibility," pegged the peso to the dollar.[106] For a time, the plan resulted in average growth rates of 8 percent a year and a boom in consumer spending power. Market freedom, however, came at a considerable cost, undoing what remained of social programs and the benefactor state. The government financed this bonanza on a foundation of graft and corruption and by selling off its main assets to foreign investors, privatizing, among many other services, gas, telephone, airline, postal, water, subway, railroad, and electric utilities. As the public sector was purged, labor rights were dismantled, sparking the growth of an informal economy, massive inequalities, and a type of democracy entirely divested from its social roots.

Epilogue

Carrying Forward the Promise of 1983

Argentina's neoliberal democracy imploded at the beginning of the twenty-first century. In late December 2001, the country defaulted on $93 billion of its sovereign debt—the largest such default in history—amid nationwide protests against the local political class. The rallying cry of the uprisings, "que se vayan todos!" (throw them all out!), was a demand for the ouster of leaders and a rejection of a political system that had not been able to provide sustenance for its citizens. Protesters represented a broad cross section of victims of the "Argentine miracle." The flashpoints of national unrest drew thousands to the streets, from poor and working-class Argentines, to *cacerolazos* of middle-class residents, to highly organized movements of unemployed workers that had grown over the previous decade of austerity and rising inequality. Thirty-four people were killed during the weeklong revolt, many of them between December 19 and 20, the deadliest days of the uprisings.[1] The violence subsided with the resignation of then president Fernando de la Rúa, who fled the presidential palace in a helicopter.

To many observers, the events of December 2001 represented a stunning culmination of events. For much of the 1990s, Argentina had been the poster child for IMF-led structural readjustment. Raw memories of hyperinflation helped to ease the passage of radical, market-oriented reforms during the government of Carlos Menem (1989–1999), who touted the virtues of free enterprise and economic stability whatever the cost. The end of the Cold War led to diplomatic realignments and an era of "carnal relations" with the United States, as Menem termed his administration's cozy dealings with US leaders and the US-based financial institutions that increasingly dictated Argentina's fortunes. Buoyed for a time by public support for this project (and by a constitutional reform orchestrated by Menem, which allowed him to run for a second presidential term), Menem easily won ree-lection in 1995 on a promise to guide Argentina deeper into a prosperous age of global integration. The first half of the decade was a time of growth. Inflation that had battered the nation since the 1970s seemed, like the Cold War itself, a relic of history. In 1995, annual inflation hovered at 3.5 percent.[2]

But holding up the scaffolding of economic expansion and security was the steady erosion of social protections and the public sector. The privatization of state enter-prises and the liberalization of commodities and monetary policy went hand in hand with steep reductions in public employment and a rollback of historic protections in the labor code. While champions of this model signaled confidence in greater labor flexibility for Argentina's insertion into the world economy, rising rates of unem-ployment and cuts in health, education, and social spending led to shocking levels of income inequality and the end of dreams of a more egalitarian society built on a foundation of social rights. The mid-1990s saw an upsurge in social movements led by the sectors most impacted by the restructuring of the Argentine economy. In 1996, unemployed workers known as *piqueteros*—from the word *piquete*, for picket—made their debut protesting the privatization of state enterprises. In the southern province of Neuquén, former workers from the state oil company YPF blocked national highways, inaugurating a form of protest that replaced traditional labor mobilization as a site of contention and collective action. Workplace occupations and factory takeovers accelerated over the coming years nationwide.

The onset of recession in 1998 led to growing calls for a change of course, includ-ing for an end to convertibility, the monetary system of a pegged peso and dollar upon which the reforms of the 1990s had hinged. In 1999, after ten years in office, Menem was succeeded by the Alianza, a coalition government made up of the Rad-ical Party and the center-left FREPASO party. The Alianza presented itself as an alternative to Menem's neoliberal consensus, coming to power on a promise to put an end to unemployment and to reverse impoverishment.[3] Its full name—the Alli-ance for Work, Justice, and Education—proclaimed the democratic demands of the time. As president, however, Fernando de la Rúa, a conservative member of the Radical Party, soon reversed course and doubled down on austerity. A series of cor-ruption scandals and the resignation of the vice president, Carlos "Chacho" Álva-rez, in protest further tarnished the Alianza's legitimacy. By the start of the new millennium, more than 50 percent of the population lived below the poverty line.

The popular rebellion that swept Argentina at the start of this century led some observers to emphasize the newness of 2001. In fact, the crisis was decades in the making and had some striking parallels to the 1989 food riots. As Mónica Gordillo and Javier Auyero have shown, hunger was at the heart of many protesters' demands.[4] Middle-class urbanites banged noisily on their empty kitchen pots to denounce the effects of washed-up savings and austerity in their everyday lives. Approximately three hundred supermarkets were sacked nationwide over the course of a week.[5] Rioters declared lack of food and underfed children as compelling and righteous motives for their participation in looting. In the township of Quilmes, the inaugural site of the PAN food program and an epicenter of the 1989 *saqueos*, bishop Jorge Novak delivered his final sermon in 2001 with a sobering message. "We are painfully surprised by the widespread lack of bread in many Argentine households." Continuing, he asked, "How is it possible that in this day and age, there are still people who die from hunger, condemned to illiteracy, and without a roof over their heads? . . . How is it possible that at a time when grain harvests have reached exceptional levels there are still tables without bread? The true cause is a lack of work and the unjust administration of the community economy."[6] The bishop's lament on behalf of his parishioners sounded eerily similar to his condemnation of the social crisis at the end of the dictatorship and to the organization of the 1981 Hunger March, which marked a turning pointing in the popular struggle against the military regime. Novak's last sermon seemed to compress time, connecting the 2001 crisis to the unfulfilled promises of Argentina's post-dictatorship democracy inaugurated in 1983.

In 2001, citizens fought for the vision of democracy that had inspired constitutional return two decades before. Argentina's post-dictatorship future was built on triple pillars of social, human, and political rights. The Alfonsín government's pledge to restore the rule of law and to prosecute the armed forces was inextricably wedded to an expansive view of universal well-being. At its most ambitious, Argentina's first democratically elected government following the dictatorship attempted to reconcile a historic tradition of Latin American social republicanism with the coming post–Cold War and neoliberal age. Yet the roots of popular democratic expectations lay far beyond the imagination of one administration, the machinations of party committees, or the corridors of political power.

Despite the military regime's violent attempts to dismantle the welfare apparatus that had emerged at midcentury during Peronism, the imprint of this period of social rights remained intact. Throughout the 1980s, citizens pursued its legacies via demands for a democratic state that would ensure the basic human right to eat, among other rights and protections. Hunger emerged in the public sphere for the first time at the end of the dictatorship. And it was often through struggles over food that the promise of Argentina's new democracy played out, and through which it eventually came undone. The shock of there being thousands of malnourished victims of authoritarian rule prompted the first massive food distribution program in the nation's history. Officials designed the PAN food program as an exceptional, emergency measure that would be suspended as soon as economic recovery took place. When that failed to occur, critics cited the palliative nature of the aid program and its limited reach to fuel arguments against a wasteful state that needed to be streamlined due to its inability to fulfill basic needs. The Caso Mazzorín, with its government-purchased chickens, captivated national attention at a moment of economic duress. The scandal that ensued highlighted the structural changes to the Argentine economy initiated by the dictatorship and the Alfonsín government's limited ability to reverse course. In many ways, the hope for material well-being that had animated Argentina's democratic return was short lived, replaced by a belief in economic stability and growth. The food riots of 1989, the dramatic climax of months of hyperinflation, gave way to an imperfect consensus in favor of auster- ity. The consolidation of neoliberal democracy by a Peronist government in the 1990s marked the end of the postwar ideal of universal social rights.

Admittedly, this history ends on a somber note. Focusing on the less commonly examined episodes that impacted the everyday lives of Argentines in the 1980s, how- ever, restores a measure of contingency and complexity to the period between the inspiring moment of democratic return and the ideological and material ruptures of the subsequent decade. For many compelling reasons, scholars tend to emphasize the place of human rights prosecutions and institutional change at the center of Argen- tina's democratic transition. The social foundations that grounded the democratic return have not been the focus of histories of post-dictatorship Argentina—or Latin America—for good reason, in part: the ferocious inequalities that swept the region in the last decade of the twentieth century far outpaced rates of poverty and hardship in the 1980s. But the erasure of struggles to forge a more socially attuned democracy at the end of the dictatorship is itself a result of the gradual unraveling of the ambitious, rights-based project upon which Argentina's transition was conceived.

Returning anew to the 1980s beyond a traditional focus on military trials or electoral politics provides a clearer picture of the origins and articulation of new rights and needs in the years that followed. A decade of neoliberalism upended labor unions, social programs, and public institutions, but it did not erase the promise of 1983 or the idea of everyday rights that animated it. Expectations for the democratic return in the 1980s were radicalized in the 1990s by new social movements that challenged neoliberal reforms. This included many human rights organizations, which expanded their repertoires into the fields of social and eco- nomic justice. In point of fact, the promise of 1983 has been at the center of popular democratic struggles ever since.

The 2003 election of Néstor Kirchner, a Peronist governor from the southern province of Santa Cruz, brought the neoliberal experiment of the 1990s to an end. His government (2003–2007) and that of his wife and successor, Cristina Fernán- dez de Kirchner (2007–2015), came to power as part of the "pink tide" of left-wing and progressive governments that swept Latin America at the beginning of the twenty-first century. Taking over during the depths of Argentina's economic crisis, in many ways the Kirchners were the political heirs to Argentina's unfinished tran- sition to democracy. Their governments renegotiated Argentina's debt with inter- national creditors, restored pensions and unemployment benefits, and oversaw the historic reopening of trials to prosecute military officers responsible for human rights abuses during the dictatorship. Among other measures, these policies attempted to realize the incomplete projects of the "lost decade," perhaps none more important than the notion that the democratic state could be a vehicle for systematically improving the everyday lives of citizens.

When Raúl Alfonsín died in March 2009, at the age of eighty-two, mourners paraded through densely packed streets for a chance to pay their last respects to the former president. Against the backdrop of formal state honors, the processions, with their song and signage, recalled the grand mobilizations that had accompanied the onset of the Alfonsín presidency a quarter century before. Remembrances of Alfonsín seemed to cement his place in living memory as the bearer of civic virtues and political decency. The most overheard phrases described Alfonsín as "the great Argentine statesman," "a man of ethics," and "the father of democracy." These tributes revealed as much about the preoccupations of the present (primary among them being the divisive public arena of the Kirchner governments) as about the lived realities of his time in office. In death, Alfonsín assumed an exalted place in the pantheon of national leaders. To some degree, his status had already been secured by the inequities of the years following his presidency, which culminated in the inaugural crisis of this century. Memories of Alfonsín highlighted his administration's principal goal to forge a democratic republic beholden to the constitution and the rule of law. Recollections of the hard-won certainty of democratic longevity, however, overlooked the more ambitious aims of his years in office.

Paradoxically, Alfonsín was one of the first to fix this narrative with his own public memory making. In 1992, following a final wave of hyperinflation and on the eve of the inequalities of the coming decade, he offered a subtle but notable amendment to his iconic definition of democracy: "I believe that with democracy one eats, one is cured, one is educated," he said, "but it does not do miracles." With this revision, Alfonsín underscored the uncomfortable distance between the euphoria of constitutional return and the impact of years of economic tailspin. But the demands that Alfonsín's time in office generated never disappeared. The promises and pitfalls of his presidency have loomed over any project that attempts to unify social, human, and civic rights into a single agenda, from the Alianza to the Kirchner governments. Its legacy also resonates in ways that complicate Peronist narratives claiming exclusive ownership of the social realm, as it simultaneously exposes the narrowness of a liberal political vision. The recent resurgence of conservative and right-wing governments in Argentina and throughout the region has made this painfully clear. The current government of Mauricio Macri, a businessman and former mayor of Buenos Aires, has proven adept at wielding the language of rights and republicanism in the service of dismantling hard-won social protections. Three decades ago, Argentines believed that the end of military rule would restore a measure of material well-being and security to their lives. The pursuit of a democracy that can feed, educate, and heal remains as vital today as in 1983.

INTRODUCTION

1. Archivo General de la Nación/Departamento Archivo Intermedio (hereafter AGN/ DAI), Fondo Documental "Presidencia de la Nación. Secretaria Privada, Presidencia Alfonsín (1983–1989)," legajo 273–152.850.

2. The period of "democratic restoration" in South America most often refers to the return of democratic governments in Bolivia (1982), Argentina (1983), Brazil, (1985), Uruguay (1985), Paraguay (1989), and Chile (1990).

3. One of the most enduring works on democratic transitions in South America is *Transitions from Authoritarian Rule*, a five-volume Woodrow Wilson Center set edited by Guillermo O'Donnell, Philippe C. Schmitter, and Laurence Whitehead (Baltimore, MD: Johns Hopkins University Press, 1986). See also Juan Linz and Alfred Stepan, *Problems of Democratic Transitions and Consolidation: Southern Europe, South America, and Post-Communist Europe* (Baltimore, MD: The Johns Hopkins University Press, 1988); and Guillermo O'Donnell, *Counterpoints: Selected Essays on Authoritarianism and Democratization* (Notre Dame, IN: University of Notre Dame Press, 1999).

4. Argentina's return to democracy formed part of a regional and global moment of democratization during the final decades of the twentieth century. Democratic returns throughout Southern Europe and Latin America generated transnational scholarly networks and a vast body of comparative literature. In the late 1980s Eastern Europe was also incorporated into a growing number of comparative regional studies. See Linz and Stepan, *Problems of Democratic Transitions and Consolidation*; Adam Przeworski, *Democracy and the Market: Political and Economic Reforms in Eastern Europe and Latin America* (Cambridge, UK: Cambridge University Press, 1991); and Carlos H. Waisman and Raanan Rein, eds., *Spanish and Latin American Transitions to Democracy* (Brighton, UK: Sussex Academic Press, 2005).

5. Cecilia Lesgart, *Usos de la transición a la democracia: Ensayo, ciencia y política en la década del '80* (Rosario, Santa Fe: Homo Sapiens Ediciones, 2003).

6. O'Donnell, *Counterpoints*, xv.

7. Kathryn Sikkink, *The Justice Cascade: How Human Rights Prosecutions Are Changing the World*, The Norton Series in World Politics (New York: W.W. Norton & Company, 2011).

8. Elizabeth Jelin, *Los trabajos de la memoria* (Buenos Aires: Siglo XXI, 2002).

9. See Alison Brysk, *The Politics of Human Rights in Argentina: Protest, Change, and Democratization* (Stanford, CA: Stanford University Press, 1994); Margaret E. Keck and Kathryn Sikkink, *Activists Beyond Borders: Advocacy Networks in International Politics* (Stanford, CA: Stanford University Press, 1998); Winifred Tate, *Counting the Dead: The Culture and Politics of Human Rights Activism in Colombia* (Berkeley: University of California Press, 2007); and Patrick William Kelly, *Sovereign Emergencies: Latin America and the Making of Global Human Rights Politics* (New York: Cambridge University Press, 2018).

10. Recent and notable exceptions from outside Argentina include Bryan McCann, *Hard Times in the Marvelous City: From Dictatorship to Democracy in the Favelas of Rio de Janeiro* (Durham, NC: Duke University Press, 2014); Alejandro Velasco, *Barrio Rising: Urban Popular Politics and the Making of Modern Venezuela* (Oakland: University of California Press, 2015); Luis Van Isschott, *The Social Origins of Human Rights: Protesting Political Violence in Colombia's Oil Capital, 1919-2010* (Madison: University of Wisconsin Press, 2015); and Alison Bruey, *Bread, Justice, and Liberty: Grassroots Activism and Human Rights in Pinochet's Chile* (Madison: University of Wisconsin Press, 2018).

11. See Eduardo Elena, *Dignifying Argentina: Peronism, Citizenship, and Mass Consumption* (Pittsburgh: University of Pittsburgh Press, 2011); Natalia Milanesio, *Workers Go Shopping in Argentina: The Rise of Popular Consumer Culture* (Albuquerque: University of New Mexico Press, 2013); and Rebekah Pite, *Creating a Common Table in Twentieth-Century Argentina: Doña Petrona, Women, and Food* (Chapel Hill: University of North Carolina Press, 2013).

12. Influential studies include Jeffrey Pilcher, *The Sausage Rebellion: Public Health, Private Enterprise, and Meat in Mexico City, 1890-1917* (Albuquerque: University of New Mexico Press, 2006); Sandra Aguilar, "Nutrition and Modernity: Milk Consumption in 1940s and 1950s Mexico," in "Radical Foodways," special issue, *Radical History Review* 110 (Spring 2011): 36-58; and Heidi Tinsman, *Buying into the Regime: Grapes and Consumption in Cold War Chile and the United States* (Durham, NC: Duke University Press, 2014).

13. Pioneering theories of the "everyday" from the fields of history, sociology, and anthropology have helped inform this point. See E. P. Thompson, "The Moral Economy of the English Crowd in the Eighteenth Century," *Past and Present* 50 (February 1971): 76-136; Michel de Certeau, *The Practice of Everyday Life* (Berkeley: University of California Press, 1984); Arjun Appadurai, ed., *The Social Life of Things: Commodities in Cultural Perspective* (Cambridge, UK: Cambridge University Press, 1986); and Viviana Zelizer, *The Social Meaning of Money* (New York: Basic Books, 1994).

14. During the twentieth century constitutional governments were overthrown six times, in 1930, 1943, 1955, 1962, 1966, and 1976.

15. Aldo Marchesi, *Latin America's Radical Left: Rebellion and Cold War in the Global 1960s* (New York: Cambridge University Press, 2017).

16. For histories of the dictatorship, see Marguerite Feitlowitz, *A Lexicon of Terror: Argentina and the Legacies of Torture* (New York: Oxford University Press, 1999); and James

Brennan, *Argentina's Missing Bones: Revisiting the History of the Dirty War* (Oakland: University of California Press, 2018).

17. Paula Canelo, *La política secreta de la última dictadura Argentina: A 40 años del golpe de Estado (1976–1983)* (Buenos Aires: Edhasa, 2016).

18. The National Commission on the Disappearance of Persons (Comisión Nacional sobre la Desaparación de Personas, CONADEP), the investigative body charged with documenting the gross human rights violations of the regime that are recounted in *Nunca Más*, estimated that 8,690 individuals were still missing, though the authors conceded that the actual figure was most likely much higher. *Nunca Más: The Report on the Argentine National Commission on the Disappeared*, trans. Writers and Scholars International, Ltd. (New York: Farrar Straus Giroux, 1986), 447.

19. Recent works in this vein include Sebastián Carrasai, *The Argentina Silent Majority: Middle Classes, Politics, Violence, and Memory in the Seventies* (Durham, NC: Duke University Press, 2014); Federico Finchelstein, *The Ideological Origins of the Dirty War: Fascism, Populism, and Dictatorship in Twentieth Century Argentina* (New York: Oxford University Press, 2014); and David Sheinin, *The Consent of the Damned: Ordinary Argentinians in the Dirty War* (Gainesville: University Press of Florida, 2013).

20. These data can be found at http://nombres.historias.datos.gob.ar/nombre/Jorge%20Rafael/1978#seccion2.

21. Gerardo Aboy Carlés, *Las dos fronteras de la democracia argentina: La reformulación de las identidades políticas de Alfonsín a Menem* (Rosario, Santa Fe: Homo Sapiens Ediciones, 2001).

22. Matthew Karush, *Workers or Citizens: Democracy and Identity in Rosario, Argentina (1912–1930)* (Albuquerque: University of New Mexico Press, 2002).

23. Carlos Altamirano, "'La lucha por la idea': El proyecto de la renovación peronista," in Marcos Novaro and Vicente Palermo, eds., *La historia reciente: Argentina en democracia* (Buenos Aires: Edhasa, 2004), 59–74; and Steven Levitsky, *Transforming Labor-Based Parties in Latin America: Argentine Peronism in Comparative Perspective* (New York: Cambridge University Press, 2003).

CHAPTER ONE. THE BREAKDOWN OF AUTHORITARIAN RULE

1. Jorge Schvarzer, *La política económica de Martínez de Hoz* (Buenos Aires: Hyspamérica, 1986).

2. "Más de doscientos cincuenta niños se alimentan en comedores creados por el Padre Gardenal en Varela," *El Sol* (Quilmes), November 7, 1981.

3. Pierre Ostiguy and Warwick Armstrong, *La evolución del consumo alimenticio en la Argentina, 1974–1984* (Buenos Aires: Centro Editor de América Latina, 1987).

4. Hugo Vezzetti, *Pasado y presente: Guerra, dictadura y sociedad en la Argentina* (Buenos Aires: Siglo Veintiuno Editores, 2009).

5. Mario Rapoport, *Historia económica, política y social de la Argentina (1880–2003)* (Buenos Aires: Ariel, 2006); and Pablo Gerchunoff and Lucas Llach, *El ciclo de la ilusión y el desencanto: Un siglo de políticas económicas argentinas* (Buenos Aires: Ariel, 1998).

6. Paula Canelo, "La política contra la economía: Los elencos militares frente al plan económico de Martínez de Hoz durante el Proceso de Reorganización Nacional (1976–

1981)," in Alfredo Pucciarelli, ed., *Empresarios, tecnócratas y militares: La trama corporativa de la ultima dictadura* (Buenos Aires: Siglo XXI, 2004), 219–312.

7. Klaus Veigel, *Dictatorship, Democracy, and Globalization: Argentina and the Cost of Paralysis, 1973–2001* (University Park: Pennsylvania State University Press, 2009), 57.

8. The maintenance of public spending had less to do with the social conscience of military leaders at the head of industries and local office than with the economic protectionism of one sector of the armed forces, which feared the political impossibility of the full-scale eradication of pensions and social security. See Canelo, "La política contra la economía."

9. *Propaganda de la época de la dictadura militar argentina 1*, YouTube, published February 8, 2019, www.youtube.com/watch?v=zJS3CbmOWf4&NR=1. For a discussion of consumer campaigns and the junta's plan to create a new economic mentality during the dictatorship, see Daniel Fridman, "A New Mentality for a New Economy: Performing the Homo economicus in Argentina (1976–83)," *Economy and Society* 39, no. 2 (2010): 271–302.

10. Louise Walker, *Waking from the Dream: Mexico's Middle Classes after 1968* (Stanford, CA: Stanford University Press, 2013).

11. The social impact of this period of boom and bust was best captured in the film *Plata dulce*, which depicts the travails of two business partners and their struggling furniture factory in the midst of the economic bonanza. The most enduring scene shows one partner's incredulity as he returns to the factory late one night and realizes that he and his partner have been swindled. As he opens box after empty box in the warehouse, the comic incomprehension of a factory that no longer produces anything yet remains fully operational serves as a biting metaphor for the Argentine economy over the course of the dictatorship. Though the film takes place in a middle-class neighborhood of Buenos Aires, the story of one family's rise and fall in the new service-oriented economy captures the effects of the regime's economic philosophy that cut across region and social standing. Fernando Ayala and Juan José Jusid, dirs., *Plata dulce* (Aries Cinematográfica Argentina, 1982).

12. Marcos Novaro and Vicente Palermo, *La dictadura Militar, 1976–1983: Del golpe de estado a la restauración democrática* (Buenos Aires: Paidós, 2003), 357–388.

13. Created in July 1981, the Multipartidaria was a political coalition that brought together five of the leading political parties in Argentina: the Radical Party, the Justicialist Party (Peronist), the Intransigent Party (PI), the Christian Democratic Party, and the Movement for Integration and Development (MID).

14. "Primer documento de la Multipartidaria, Buenos Aires," July 14, 1981, http://servicios2.abc.gov.ar/docentes/efemerides/10dediciembre/descargas/democracia/multipartidaria.pdf. See also "Documento de la Multipartidaria, 28 de Julio de 1981," in Carlos Alberto Giacobone and Edit Gallo, eds., *Radicalismo: Un siglo al servicio de la Patria* (Buenos Aires: Archivo Histórico y Centro de Documentación, Unión Cívica Radical, 2004), 261–262.

15. Memoria Abierta, Archivo Oral, "Testimonio de Aída Bogo de Sartí," Buenos Aires, 2001; and Ulises Gorini, *La rebelión de las Madres: Historia de las Madres de la Plaza de Mayo* (Buenos Aires: Grupo Editorial Norma, 2010).

16. Pablo Pozzi, *La oposición obrera a la dictadura, 1976–1982* (Buenos Aires: Editorial Contrapunto, 1988).

17. Matthew Karush, *Musicians in Transit: Argentina and the Globalization of Popular Music* (Durham, NC: Duke University Press, 2017), especially ch. 5.

18. Federico Lorenz, *Los zapatos de Carlitos: Una historia de los trabajadores navales de Tigre en la década del setenta* (Buenos Aires: Grupo Editorial Norma, 2007).

19. Steven Levitsky, *Transforming Labor-Based Parties in Latin America: Argentine Peronism in Comparative Perspective* (New York: Cambridge University Press, 2003), 95.

20. Levitsky, *Transforming Labor-Based Parties*, 96.

21. "Trágica situación atraviesan los trabajadores de la zona," *El Sol* (Quilmes), July 24, 1985.

22. Obispado de Quilmes, Vicaria Episcopal para la Pastoral de Acción Social, Diócesis de Quilmes, "Una jornada de protesa: Un llamado apremiante del pueblo argentino al gobierno," Quilmes, Argentina, July 21, 1981.

23. El Archivo de la DIPPBA (Dirección de Inteligencia de la Policía de la Provincia de Buenos Aires) (hereafter Archivo DIPPBA), Mesa DE, Religioso, legajo no. 643, Aug. 1981, folio 849.

24. Archivo DIPPBA, Mesa DE, Religioso, legajo no. 643, Aug. 1981, folio 845.

25. Jennifer Adair, "Popular Politics, the Catholic Church, and the Making of Argentina's Transition to Democracy, 1978–1983," in Benjamin Bryce and David Sheinin, eds., *Making Citizens in Argentina* (Pittsburgh, PA: University of Pittsburgh Press, 2017), 161–179.

26. Archivo DIPPBA, Mesa DE, Religioso, legajo no. 643, Aug. 1981, folio 850.

27. Archivo DIPPBA, Mesa DE, Religioso, legajo no. 643, Aug. 1981, folio 850.

28. Archivo DIPPBA, Mesa DE, Religioso, legajo no. 643, Aug. 1981, folio 855–856.

29. Archivo DIPPBA, Mesa DE, Religioso, legajo no. 643, Aug. 1981, folio 857.

30. Archivo DIPPBA, Mesa DE, Religioso, Legajo no. 643, Aug. 1981, folio 894; and Archivo DIPPBA, Mesa DE, Religioso, legajo no. 643, Aug. 1981, folio 898.

31. Archivo DIPPBA, Mesa DE, Religioso, legajo no. 643, Aug. 1981, folio 878–881.

32. Archivo DIPPBA, Mesa DE, Religioso, legajo no. 643, Aug. 1981, folio 894.

33. Archivo DIPPBA, Mesa DE, Religioso, legajo no. 643, Aug. 1981, folio 895.

34. Susana Hintze, *Estrategias alimentarias de sobrevivencia: (Un estudio de caso en el Gran Buenos Aires)*, vols. 1–2 (Buenos Aires: Centro Editor de America Latina, 1989).

35. Archivo DIPPBA, Mesa DE, Religioso, legajo no. 643, Aug. 1981, folio 861.

36. Warwick Armstrong, "Hunger and Monetarism in Buenos Aires, 1976–1983: A Food Systems Approach," *Boletín de Estudios Latinoamericanos y del Caribe* 45 (December 1988): 29.

37. Ostiguy and Armstrong, *La evolución del consumo alimenticio*, 59.

38. Ostiguy and Armstrong, *La evolución del consumo alimenticio*, 48–52.

39. Ostiguy and Armstrong, *La evolución del consumo alimenticio*, 50.

40. Archivo DIPPBA, Mesa DE, Religioso, legajo no. 643, Aug. 1981, folio 902.

41. "La CGT Avellaneda-Lanus adhirió a la peregrinación a San Cayetano," *Diario El Sol* (Quilmes), 7 November 1981.

42. For the history of the land takeovers in Greater Buenos Aires in 1981, see Inés Izaguirre and Zulema Aristizábal, *Las tomas de tierra en la zona sur del Gran Buenos Aires* (Buenos Aires: Centro Editor de América Latina, 1988); Beatriz Cuenya et al., *Condiciones de habitat y de salud de los sectores populares: Un estudio piloto en el asentamiento San Martín de Quilmes* (Buenos Aires: Centro de Estudios Urbanos y Regionales, 1984); Pablo

Vommaro, "Las organizaciones sociales de base territorial y comunitaria en Quilmes: el caso de las tomas de tierra y asentamientos de 1981" (paper delivered at the IV Jornadas de Jóvenes Investigadores, Instituto Gino Germani, September 19–21, 2007); and Jorge Ossona, *Punteros, malandras y porongas: Ocupación de tierras y usos políticos de la pobreza* (Buenos Aires: Siglo Veintiuno Editores, 2014).

43. "Toma de tierras," *Revista Al Sur*, March 1982, 17.

44. Inés González Bombal, *Los vecinazos: Las protestas barriales en el Gran Buenos Aires (1982–1983)* (Buenos Aires: IDES, 1988). The majority of uprisings took place in the townships in the south and southwest parts of Greater Buenos Aires: Morón, Esteban Echeverría, Merlo, Tres de Febrero, Avellaneda, Lomas de Zamora, and Lanus. González Bombal's study centers on the acceleration of protests between October and December 1982. Nonetheless, she demonstrates a rich network of civil associations and contestation before the outbreak of the Malvinas War.

45. Archivo DIPPBA, Mesa DE, Quilmes, legajo No. 178, folio 348.

46. The Paz, Pan y Trabajo march took place on March 30, 1982. It was the second general strike led by Saúl Ubaldini. More than fifty thousand people protested in the center of Buenos Aires, denouncing the economic program of the dictatorship and calling for an end to the regime. Protests were coordinated throughout the country, and the regime exercised fierce repression, making over three thousand arrests.

47. The sovereignty of the Malvinas/Falkland Islands had been disputed between Great Britain and Argentina since the nineteenth century. The Malvinas War, as it became known, lasted from April 2 to June 14, 1984, and produced a surge of nationalism and a brief renewal of support for the regime. For histories of the war, see Federico Lorenz, *Las guerras por las Malvinas* (Buenos Aires: Edhasa, 2006); and Vicente Palermo, *Sal en las heridas: Malvinas en la cultura argentina contemporánea* (Buenos Aires: Sudamericana, 2007).

48. Lorenz, *Las Guerras por las Malvinas*. See also Juan Suriano and Eliseo Alvarez, *505 días que la Argentina olvidó: De la rendición de Malvinas al triunfo de Alfonsín* (Buenos Aires: Editorial Sudamericana, 2013).

49. *Clarín*, March 25, 1982. Inés González Bombal, "El diálogo político: La transición que no fue," Documento CEDES 61 (Buenos Aires: CEDES, 1991).

50. Paula Canelo, *La política secreta de la última dictadura Argentina: A 40 años del golpe de Estado (1976–1983).* (Buenos Aires: Edhasa, 2016).

51. For an overview of the role of military authorities, political parties, and human rights organizations during the months leading up to the elections in October 1983, see Suriano and Alvarez, *505 días que la Argentina olvidó,* 145–181.

52. Obispado de Quilmes, "Circular: 100 días de campaña de solidaridad," Quilmes, Argentina, April 11, 1982.

53. "Creo que es el egoísimo," *Clarín*, July 16, 1982.

54. *Gente*, July 1, 1982, quoted in Federico Lorenz, "Ungidos por el infortunio: Los soldados de Malvinas en la posdictadura; entre el relato heroico y la victimización," in Patricia Funes, ed., *Revolución, dictadura, y democracia: Logicas militantes y militares en la historia argentina en el contexto latinoamericano* (Buenos Aires: Imago Mundi, 2013), 230.

55. Marina Franco and Claudia Feld, eds. *Democracia hora cero: Actores, políticas y debates en los inicios de la posdictadura* (Buenos Aires: Fondo de Cultura Económica, 2015).

CHAPTER TWO. THE CAMPAIGN FOR A DEMOCRATIC ARGENTINA

1. Ana Pérez de Vera is most likely referring to Juan Perón's statement, "Mejor que decir es hacer, mejor que prometer es realizar." For the full version of Pérez de Vera's letter, in addition to an interview in which she explains her decision to vote for Raúl Alfonsín, see "Votó con una carta," *Gente* 18, no. 957 (November 24, 1983): 40–44.

2. See Roberto Gargarella, María Victoria Murrillo, and Mario Pecheny, eds., *Discutir Alfonsín* (Buenos Aires: Siglo Veintiuno Editories, 2010); and Juan Suriano and Eliseo Alvarez, *505 días que la Argentina olvidó: De la rendición de Malvinas al triunfo de Alfonsín* (Buenos Aires: Sudamericana, 2013).

3. Notable exceptions include Gabriel Kessler and Victor Armory "Imágenes de una socieded en crisis: Cuestión social, pobreza y desempleo," in Marcos Novaro and Vicente Palermo, eds., *La Historia reciente. Argentina en democracia* (Buenos Aires, Edhasa, 2004), 91–113; and Gabriel Vommaro, "La pobreza en transición: El redescubrimiento de la pobreza y el tratamiento estatal de los sectores populares en Argentina en los años 80," *Apuntes de Investigación del CECYP* 14, no. 19 (2011): 45–73.

4. "Raúl Alfonsín: El más joven de los viejos politicos," *Diario Popular* (Buenos Aires) January 14, 1979.

5. For the history of the UCR, see Ezequiel Gallo and Silvia Sigal's essay, "La Formación de los Partidos Políticos Contemporáneos—la UCR (1891–1916)," in Torcuato S. Di Tella et al., eds., *Argentina, Sociedad de Masas* (Buenos Aires: Eudeba, 1965), 24–76; David Rock, *Politics in Argentina: The Rise and Fall of Radicalism, 1890–1930* (New York: Cambridge University Press, 1975); and Paula Alonso, *Entre la Revolución y las urnas: Los orígenes de la UCR y la política argentina en los años '90* (Buenos Aires: Sudamericana-Universidad de San Andrés, 1994). For newer histories of radicalism, see Ana Virginia Persello, *Historia del Radicalismo* (Buenos Aires: Edhasa, 2007); Ezequiel Adamovsky, "Acerca de la relación entre el Radicalismo argentino y la 'clase media' (una vez más)," *Hispanic American Historical Review* 89, no. 2 (May 2009): 209–251; and Matthew Karush's examination of radicalism and working-class politics in Rosario during Argentina's first "transition to democracy" (1912–1930), *Workers or Citizens: Democracy and Identity in Rosario, Argentina (1912–1930)* (Albuquerque: University of New Mexico Press, 2002).

6. Julia Constenla, *Raúl Alfonsín: Biografía no desautorizada* (Buenos Aires: Vergara, 2009), 39.

7. Constenla, *Raúl Alfonsín*.

8. In 1957, the party divided over the issue of Peronism. One sector, the Radical Civic Union of the People (UCRP), led by Arturo Frondizi, was more inclined to work with Perón and to grant the movement some concessions, a factor that many believe contributed to Frondizi's election in 1958. The other faction, the Intransigent Radical Civic Union (Unión Cívica Radical Intransigente, UCRI), led by party boss Ricardo Balbín, supported efforts to "de-Peronize" the nation.

9. Balbín's comment was directed at Arturo Frondizi, leader of the UCRI. Most observers attribute Frondizi's 1958 presidential win to overtures he made to Perón in exile and his concessions to the Peronist opposition. For a discussion of the UCRI and UCRP rivalry, see Raúl Alfonsín, *Qué es el radicalismo* (Buenos Aires: Sudamérica, 1983), 186. Despite Balbín's early stance, however, by the early 1970s he had begun to make several overtures to

Peronism and to Perón himself. This was one of the reasons that Alfonsín eventually discontinued his support for Balbín.

10. "Manifiesto del Movimiento Renovador Nacional, 24 de Septiembre de 1972," Documento no. 57, in Carlos Alberto Giacabone and Edit Rosalía Gallo, eds., *Radicalismo: Un siglo al servicio de la Patria* (Buenos Aires: Archivo Histórico y Centro de Documentación, Unión Cívica Radical, Editorial Dunken, 2004), 221–226.

11. "Un candidato para el cambio," folleto, carpeta no. 2, *Raúl Alfonsín*, Biblioteca y Archivo Histórico de la UCR (hereafter Biblioteca UCR), no date.

12. José Antonio Díaz and Alfredo Leuco, *Los Herederos de Alfonsín* (Buenos Aires: Sudamericana/Planeta, 1987), 66.

13. Leopoldo Moreau, interview by author, Buenos Aires, Argentina, September 6, 2010.

14. Moreau, interview.

15. Oscar Muiño, *Alfonsín: Mitos y verdades del padre de la democracia* (Buenos Aires: Aguilar, 2013).

16. Persello, *Historia del Radicalismo*, 234.

17. Marcos Novaro and Vicente Palermo, *La dictadura Militar, 1976–1983*, Historia Argentina, vol. 9 (Buenos Aires: Paídos, 2003), 471.

18. Gerardo Aboy Carlés, *Las dos fronteras de la democracia argentina: La reformulación de las identidades políticas de Alfonsín a Menem* (Rosario: Homo Sapiens Ediciones, 2001), 168.

19. "No habrá solución sin fuerzas armadas democráticas, afirmó Raúl Alfonsín," *Clarín* (Buenos Aires), July 17, 1982.

20. Jesús Rodríguez, interview by author, Buenos Aires, Argentina, August 19, 2010.

21. "No habrá solución sin fuerzas armadas democráticas."

22. "No habrá solución sin fuerzas armadas democráticas."

23. "No habrá solución sin fuerzas armadas democráticas."

24. Suriano and Alvarez, *505 días que la Argentina olvidó*.

25. "El costo de la vida encareció un 13% en febrero; estudios sobre la canasta familiar," in Centro de Investigaciones Sociales sobre el Estado y la Administración (CISEA), *Argentina 1983* (Buenos Aires: Centro Editor de América Latina, 1984), 32.

26. Volantes campaña presidencial, "Alfonsín o lo de siempre," in Edit Rosalía Gallo, ed., *Propaganda Política de la UCR, Catálogo de imagines, 1890–1991* (Buenos Aires: Unión Cívica Radical, Biblioteca, Archivo Histórico y Centro de Documentación, 2010), CD-ROM.

27. New York Public Library, "Argentine Political Campaign Literature Collection, 1983," folder 21, "Unión Cívica Radical," folio 8.

28. Raúl Alfonsín, Oficina de Prensa, "Mensaje del 1 de Mayo," Biblioteca UCR, carpeta Alfonsín 1.

29. CISEA, *Argentina 1983*, 123.

30. "Discursos Históricos del Dr. Alfonsín: Ferro, Plaza de la República, Rosario," Biblioteca UCR, carpeta Alfonsín 1.

31. "Alfonsín constituye el hombre-intérprete de este momento histórico," *Voz del Interior*, January 23, 1983. Biblioteca UCR, carpeta Alfonsín 2.

32. Francisco Delich, "Desmovilizacion social, reestructuración obrera y cambio sindical," in Peter Waldmann and Ernesto Garzón Valdés, eds., *El Poder militar en la Argentina*,

1976–1981 (Buenos Aires: Editorial Galerna, 1983); and Pablo Pozzi, *Oposición obrera a la dictadura, 1976–1982* (Buenos Aires: Editorial Contrapunto, 1988).

33. "Contra los pactos a espaldas del pueblo, para afianzar la democracia: síntesis de la conferencia de prensa del Doctor Raúl Alfonsín, 2 de mayo de 1983," Biblioteca UCR, carpeta Alfonsín 2.

34. *La Prensa*, 30 April 1983, in CISEA, *Argentina 1983*, 156.

35. Alison Brysk, *The Politics of Human Rights in Argentina: Protest, Change, and Democratization* (Stanford, CA: Stanford University, 1994).

36. Claudia Feld, "La prensa de la transición ante el problema de los desaparecidos: El discurso del 'show del horror,'" in Claudia Feld and Marina Franco, eds., *Democracia Hora Cero: Actores, políticas y debates en los inicios de la posdictadura* (Buenos Aires: Fondo de Cultura Económica, 2015), 269–316.

37. Carlos Santiago Nino, *Radical Evil on Trial* (New Haven, CT: Yale University Press, 1998).

38. Raúl Alfonsín, *Memoria política: Transición a la democracia y derechos humanos* (Buenos Aires: Fondo de Cultura Económica de Argentina, 2004), 35.

39. Alfonsín, *Memoria Política*, 45.

40. Aboy Carles, *Las dos fronteras de la democracia argentina*.

41. For a brief summary of the landscape of Peronism during the campaign, see Novaro and Palermo, *La dictadura Militar*, 534–538.

42. Lúder served as interim president from September 13 to October 17, 1975, during which time he issued the decrees 2270/75 and 2272/75, authorizing the "annihilation" of subversion in the national territory.

43. Gabriel Vommaro, "Cuando el pasado es superado por el presente: Las elecciones presidencials de 1983 y la construcción de un nuevo tiempo político en la Argentina," in Alfredo Pucciarelli, ed., *Los años de Alfonsín: ¿El poder de la democracia o la democracia del poder?* (Buenos Aires: Siglo Veintinuno Ediores, 2006), 245–288.

44. New York Public Library, "Argentine Political Campaign Literature Collection, 1983," folder 21, "Unión Cívica Radical," folio 6.

45. New York Public Library, "Argentine Political Campaign Literature Collection, 1983," folder 21.

46. *1983: Spot campaña presidencial Raúl Alfonsín*, YouTube, published August 17, 2013, www.youtube.com/watch?v=AZRihtFjrcA.

47. Edgardo Catterberg, *Los argentinos frente a la politica: Cultura política y opinion pública en la transición argentina a la democracia* (Buenos Aires: Grupo Editorial Planeta, 1989).

48. New York Public Library, "Argentine Political Campaign Literature Collection, 1983," folder 12.

49. New York Public Library, "Argentine Political Campaign Literature Collection, 1983," folder 15.

50. "Publicidad política argentina," http://publicidadpolitica.com.ar/1983f/1983.htm (no longer an active link).

51. Jorge Cobos, interview by author, Quilmes, Argentina, April 24, 2009.

52. Cobos, interview.

53. *Humor*, June 21, 1983.

54. Moreau, interview.

55. "Discursos Históricos del Dr. Alfonsín: Ferro, Plaza de la República, Rosario," Biblioteca UCR, carpeta Alfonsín 1.

56. Alfonsín won the election with 51.75 percent of the vote. Ítalo Lúder gained 40.16 percent of the total votes. For a full breakdown of the results of the 1983 presidential and legislative elections, see https://recorriendo.elecciones.gob.ar/presidente1983.html#/4/1.

CHAPTER THREE. "WITH DEMOCRACY ONE EATS"

1. "En la argentina nadie pasa hambre," *Clarín*, April 14, 1983.

2. Patricia Aguirre, "El P.A.N.—Programa Alimentario Nacional—Informe sobre su implementación entre los años 1984 y 1989" (unpublished report, Buenos Aires, May 1990), 56.

3. Historical reconstructions of the PAN present several challenges. First, government records of the PAN were discarded in the early 1990s during the transfer of the Ministry of Health and Social Action from the administration of Raúl Alfonsín to Carlos Menem. Second, no official program evaluations were conducted throughout the duration of the PAN, making it difficult to gauge its reach or how well it worked to reverse the nutritional deficiencies of aid recipients. There is, however, a small bibliography on the PAN that relies on existing data and fieldwork from the 1980s. See Analía del Franco, "Consideraciones organizacionales acerca del PAN," in Bernardo Kliksberg, ed., *Como enfrentar la pobreza, estrategias y experiencias organizacionales inovadoras* (Buenos Aires: Grupo Editor Latinoamericano, 1989), 199–251; George Midre, "Bread or Solidarity? Argentine Social Policies, 1983–1990," *Journal of Latin American Studies* 24, no. 2 (May 1992): 343–373; and Víctor Sigal, *Aspectos de la implementación de una política pública: El caso PAN* (Buenos Aires: INAP, 1986). After the program had been suspended in 1990, Patricia Aguirre, an anthropologist who worked on its technical aspects, wrote an unpublished evaluation of the program, "El P.A.N.." The anthropologist Susana Hintze also wrote an ethnography on food strategies in Greater Buenos Aires that includes some of the only real-time interviews of PAN recipients: *Estrategias alimentarias de sobrevivencia: (Un estudio de caso en el Gran Buenos Aires)*, vols. 1–2 (Buenos Aires: Centro Editor de America Latina, 1989). Pierre Ostiguy and Warwick Armstrong published an extensive study on food and consumption during the dictatorship, which also briefly addresses the PAN: *La evolución del consumo alimenticio en la Argentina, 1974–1984: Un estudio empírico* (Buenos Aires: Centro Editor de America Latina, 1987).

4. See: Ana Virigina Persello, *Historia del Radicalismo* (Buenos Aires: Edhasa, 2007); and Matthew Karush, *Workers or Citizens: Democracy and Identity in Rosario, Argentina (1912–1930)* (Albuquerque: University of New Mexico Press, 2002).

5. María Victoria Murillo, "¿Las corporaciones o los votos?" in Roberto Gargarella, María Victoria Murillo, and Mario Pecheny, eds., *Discutir Alfonsín* (Buenos Aires: Siglo Veintiuno Editores, 2010), 139–159.

6. See Emilio Crenzel, *La historia politica del Nunca Más: La memoria de las desapariciones en la Argentina* (Buenos Aires: Siglo Veintiuno Editores Argentina, 2008).

7. For more on the relationship between the Alfonsín administration and the labor movement, see Ricardo Gaudio and Andrés Thompson, *Sindicalism peronista/gobierno radical: Los años del Alfonsín* (Buenos Aires: Fundación Friedrich Ebert & Folios Ediciones, 1990); Rosendo Fraga, *La cuestión sindical* (Buenos Aires: Centro de Estudios para la Nueva Minoria, 1990); Santiago Senén González and Fabián Bosoer, *La trama gremial 1983–1989: Crónica y testimonios* (Buenos Aires: Corregidor, 1993). For a discussion of the Mucci Law deliberations, see Juan Carlos Portantiero, "La concertación que no fue: De la Ley Mucci al Plan Austral," in José Nun and Juan Carlos Portantiero, eds., *Ensayos sobre la transición democrática argentina* (Buenos Aires: Puntosur Editores, 1987), 117–138.

8. Jessica Stites Mor, *Transition Cinema: Political Filmmaking and the Argentine Left since 1968* (Pittsburgh: University of Pittsburgh Press, 2012).

9. For a thorough listing of the most prominent laws and legislation passed by the Alfonsín administration during the first few months of the government, see Roberto Gargarella, "Democracia y derechos en los años de Raúl Alfonsín," in Roberto Gargarella, María Victoria Murillo, and Mario Pecheny, eds., *Discutir Alfonsín*, 25–28.

10. Aguirre, "El P.A.N.," 42.

11. Del Franco, "Consideraciones organizacionales acerca del PAN," 252.

12. *Publicidad del Programa Alimentario Nacional*, YouTube, published May 21, 2011, www.youtube.com/watch?v=gNcpUuLzrVs.

13. For an examination of immigrant social welfare networks, see Benjamin Bryce, "Paternal Communities: Social Welfare and Immigration in Argentina, 1880–1930," *Journal of Social History* 49, no. 1 (2015): 213–236.

14. David Rock, "Machine Politics in Buenos Aires and the Argentine Radical Party," *Journal of Latin American Studies* 4, no. 2 (November 1972): 251–252. See also Joel Horowitz, *Argentina's Radical Party and Popular Mobilization, 1916–1938* (University Park: Pennsylvania State University Press, 2008).

15. See Eduardo Elena, *Dignifying Argentina: Peronism, Citizenship, and Mass Consumption* (Pittsburgh: Pittsburgh University Press, 2011), esp. ch. 5; and Natalia Milanesio, "Food Politics and Consumption in Peronist Argentina," *Hispanic American Historical Review* 90, no. 1 (February 2010): 75–108.

16. Susana Novick, *IAPI: Auge y decadencia* (Buenos Aires: Centro Editor de America Latina, 1986).

17. Milanesio, "Food Politics," 85.

18. Juan Carlos Torre and Elisa Pastoriza, "La democratización del bienestar," in *Nueva historia argentina*, vol. 8, Juan Carlos Torre, ed., *Los años peronistas, 1943–1955* (Buenos Aires: Argentina: Editorial Sudamericana, 2002), 257–312.

19. Congreso de la Nación, República Argentina, *Diario de sesiones de la Cámara de Diputados de la Nación, 1983, Sesiones extraordianarias, Tomo I* (Buenos Aires, 1983), 1057.

20. Congreso de la Nación, *Diario de sesiones*, 1065.

21. Congreso de la Nación, *Diario de sesiones*, 1069.

22. Congreso de la Nación, *Diario de sesiones*, 1069.

23. Congreso de la Nación, *Diario de sesiones*, 1069.

24. Congreso de la Nación, *Diario de sesiones*, 1058.

25. Though Argentines had general knowledge of the food program, the details of the PAN remained on scraps of paper, having been vaguely sketched out over the course of sporadic meetings. The idea for the PAN dates to Alfonsín's visit to Europe in July 1983, in the middle of presidential campaigning. During a stop in Rome, he met with Arturo Goetz, an Argentine official at the Food and Agricultural Organization of the United Nations (FAO). According to Goetz and other specialists involved in the early design of the PAN, Alfonsín and Goetz hammered out the general design for the PAN hastily over the course of one evening. Alfonsín returned to Argentina with the outline of the program; however, the logistics of the PAN were not formalized until after the elections in October 1983. Arturo Goetz, interview by author, Buenos Aires, Argentina, April 14, 2009.

26. Congressional debates over passage of the PAN took place February 2–3, 1984. The program was approved initially for two years. It was extended twice—in January 1986 and December 1987—and officially suspended in January 1990. See Congreso de la Nación, *Diario de sesiones*, 1054–1074.

27. The PAN fell under the auspices of the Ministry of Health and Social Action. Aldo Neri, the minister in charge of coordinating the PAN, formed part of Alfonsín's old guard of associates. A physician by training and a respected public health specialist, Neri accompanied Alfonsín from the early days of the Renovation and Change movement. He brought together nutrition specialists, public health experts, and technical advisers to work on the PAN. Neri's recruits were either sympathetic to the goals of the new government or themselves Radical Party members. Though Neri formed part of Alfonsín's cabinet, the political face of the PAN was the Junta Coordinadora Nacional, a group of young Radical Party activists whose members also held high-ranking posts within the PAN infrastructure and ministry. While Neri's recruits and members of the Coordinadora may have shared Radical Party affinities, the two groups coexisted in an uneasy peace within the ministry. At the center of tensions was a rift between Neri's appointees, who had the technical knowledge required to run and evaluate the welfare program, and members of the Coordinadora, who hoped the PAN would help strengthen support for the Radical Party, especially in places like Greater Buenos Aires. Aldo Neri, interview by author, Buenos Aires, Argentina, November 25, 2008.

28. During the dictatorship, the production of socioeconomic indicators that were national in scope was limited. The most abundant data available came from the 1980 census. On their own, however, the census figures did not reveal many clues about the nutritional state of Argentines. Detailed evidence of hunger was scattered. Much of it came from the historically poorer northern provinces, where public health officials had long concentrated their efforts on the eradication of malnutrition. In 1983, the Center for the Study of Childhood Nutrition (CESNI) published a report on the health of Argentina's most marginalized youth. The report, which drew on hospital records and local field studies, offered a sobering glimpse into childhood malnutrition in specific locales, united by recurrent cycles of sickness, chronic disease, and in many cases premature death. The report's overall conclusions confirmed the lack of comprehensive data on a national level. Its authors put forward an urgent recommendation for a nationwide survey to tackle the problem of malnutrition and hunger. See CESNI, Centro de Estudios Sobre Nutrición Infantil, "Seminario sobre situación nutricional de los niños en Argentina," Publicación CESNI no. 2 (Buenos Aires: CESNI, August 1983).

29. Gabriel Vommaro, "La pobreza en transición: El redescubrimiento de la pobreza y el tratamiento estatal de los sectores populares en Argentina en los años 80," *Apuntes de Investigación del CECYP* 14, no. 19 (2011): 45–73.

30. INDEC (Instituto Nacional de Estadistica y Censos), *La pobreza en la Argentina: Indicadores de necesidades basicas insatisfechas a partir de los datos del Censo Nacional de Población y Vivienda 1980* (Buenos Aires: INDEC, 1984).

31. Maria del Carmen Banzas de Moreau, interview by author, Buenos Aires, Argentina, May 27, 2010.

32. Congreso de la Nación, *Diario de sesiones*, 244–245.

33. Congreso de la Nación, *Diario de sesiones*, 244.

34. Congreso de la Nación, *Diario de sesiones*, 245.

35. Fondo Comisión Nacional sobre la Desaparición de Personas, Archivo Nacional de la Memoria, Argentina, caja no. 28, "Programa Alimentario Nacional."

36. Fondo Comisión Nacional sobre la Desaparición de Personas, Caja no. 28.

37. Fondo Comisión Nacional sobre la Desaparición de Personas, Caja no. 28. In accordance with the regulations of the Archivo Nacional de la Memoria, I have omitted the full names of individuals mentioned in the archive's records.

38. Fondo Comisión Nacional sobre la Desaparición de Personas, Caja no. 28.

39. "15.000 familias carenciadas de Quilmes recibieron el PAN," *El Sol* (Quilmes), May 22, 1984.

40. "No queremos que el hambre golpee nuestras puertas," *El Sol* (Quilmes), April 4, 1984.

41. Eduardo Vides, interview by author, Quilmes, Argentina, April 3, 2009.

42. Aguirre, "El P.A.N.," 34.

43. Aguirre, "El P.A.N.," 34. In rural areas, PAN agents were each responsible for ensuring food aid for approximately two hundred families per month.

44. Catalina Vera, interview by author, Quilmes, Argentina, May 5, 2009.

45. Jorge Cobos, interview by author, Quilmes, Argentina, April 24, 2009.

46. Vera, interview.

47. Anonymous email message to author, April 14, 2009.

48. "Programa Alimentario Nacional: Evaluación de aspectos operativos y componentes de imagen: Encuesta nacional a beneficiarios del P.A.N." (Buenos Aires, August 1986).

49. Patricia Aguirre, interview by author, Buenos Aires, May 2, 2009.

50. Vera, interview.

51. *Primer manual para agentes del Programa Alimentario Nacional* (Buenos Aires: Ministerio de Salud y Acción Social, Gobierno de la República de Argentina, 1984), 4.

52. Carolina Barry, *Evita capitana: El Partido Peronista Femenino, 1949–1955* (Buenos Aires: Editorial Eduntref, 2009). For more on the role of women and social welfare legislation during the first period of Peronism, see Isabella Cosse, *Estigmas de nacimiento: Peronismo y orden familiar, 1945–1955* (Buenos Aires: Fondo de Cultura Económica—Universidad San Andrés, 2006); and Donna Guy, *Women Build the Welfare State: Performing Charity and Creating Rights in Argentina, 1880–1955* (Durham, NC: Duke University Press, 2008).

53. *Primer manual para agentes del Programa Alimentario Nacional*, 4.

54. New York Public Library, "Argentine Political Campaign Literature Collection, 1983," folder 21, "Unión Cívica Radical."

55. New York Public Library, folder 21.

56. Transcription of field notes by Brazilian anthropologist Carlos Cohelo Campino, a professor from the Instituto de Pesquisas Económicas de la Universidad de San Pablo. In 1986, he conducted fieldwork in Avellaneda and attended PAN meetings in a church located in the Villa Maciel neighborhood. The notes are quoted from Aguirre, "El P.A.N.," 25–27.

57. Sonia Alvarez, *Engendering Democracy in Brazil: Women's Movements in Transition Politics* (Princeton, NJ: Princeton University Press, 1990).

58. Vera, interview.

59. The following report is indicative of the type of memos that provincial police agents filed regarding the PAN in Quilmes. In addition to demonstrating the anxiety caused by the PAN, which warranted such detailed reporting, the police memos are also rich evidence of how the PAN functioned locally with the support of the church. "The P.A.N. . . . will be helping needy families in the Emergency Neighborhood of 'VILLA LUJAN' of the Partido de Quilmes, at the 'MADRE DE LA FE' Chapel, which will distribute the merchandise, located at the intersection of Primera Junta and Mozart, and part of the NUESTRA SENORA DE LUJAN church, located at the intersection of Primera Junta and Lavalle, with the Priest Xxx (M.S.T.M.). It will be known that said chapel has been outfitted with a reception office, authorized by Pbro. Xxxx (M.S.T.M.), for the entire month of April, which is being attended by Mrs. XXX of the 'VILLA LUJAN' neighborhood. It has been brought to our attention that the boxes will be delivered next week, with no exact date set as of yet." Archivo DIPPBA, Mesa Referencia, Factor Social, carpeta 6, legajo 18620, folio 29.

60. Steven Levitsky, *Transforming Labor-Based Parties in Latin America: Argentine Peronism in Comparative Perspective* (New York: Cambridge University Press, 2003).

61. In the Senate, Osvaldo Britos, a Peronist senator from the province of San Luis, was able to limit debates to the Comisión de Trabajo, over which he presided. For its part, the UCR believed it had enough votes in the Senate to secure the law, counting on the support of provincial parties. UCR officials from the Ministry of Labor resisted making concessions to Peronism during the debates because they believed that they would be able to secure the support of independents. Meanwhile, Britos was able to obtain the decisive vote of Elías Sapag of the Movimiento Popular de Neuquen. Sapag's vote against the measure sealed the fate of the Mucci Law. In April, Antonio Mucci was replaced as labor minister by Juan Manuel Casella. From the start, the Mucci Law encountered fierce opposition from the CGT, which reunited against the measure. On February 10, 1984, the CGT organized a march to coincide with the opening of the congressional debates. The CGT combined vociferous public outcries against the measure with a new strategy: union leaders began to lobby congress through the Comisión de Trabajo. As scholars have argued, the labor movement adopted a strategy of "organizational resource accumulation" beginning in the 1980s that helped unions negotiate and retain institutional benefits during the full-scale attack on labor during the 1990s under the Peronist government of Carlos Menem. See Murillo, "¿Las corporaciones o los votos?"

62. The first general strike took place in September 1984.

63. Steven Levitsky charts how this transformation occurred through the use of patronage resources: "Although the PJ lost the presidency in 1983, it won twelve governorships,

hundreds of mayoralties and provincial legislative seats, and thousands of city council seats. Holders of these offices gained immediate access to patronage resources. Local *punteros* who had previously gone to the unions for resources now turned to PJ government officials. PJ office holders built alliances with these *punteros*, creating *agrupaciones* whose principal bases were patronage, rather than unions. The *agrupaciones* became alternative party organizations, created at the margins of both the unions and the party bureaucracy. In stitching together the *agrupaciones* into larger, territorially based factions, party leaders essentially built 'parties on the side,' or informal organizations with which they would compete for power within Peronism. Upon gaining control of local parties, these informal organizations became the party organization, replacing the unions entirely." Levitsky, *Transforming Labor-Based Parties in Latin America*, 109–110.

64. The Renovación Peronista refers to the movement that emerged between 1983 and 1989 within the Justicialist Party (PJ) in the aftermath of the 1983 elections. The Renovators were a heterogeneous mix of Peronist leaders from across the nation that included progressive union leaders from the "25" faction, urban reformers, and provincial politicians. The most prominent members of the Renovation were Antonio Cafiero, Carlos Menem, Carlos Grosso, and José Manuel de la Sota. Intellectually, the ideas surrounding the Peronist Renovation found a home within the influential journal *Unidos*, directed, among others, by Carlos "Chacho" Alvarez and Mario Wainfeld. See Carlos Altamirano, "'La lucha por la idea': El proyecto de la renovación peronista," in Marcos Novaro and Vicente Palermo, eds., *La historia reciente: Argentina en democracia* (Buenos Aires: Edhasa, 2004), 59–74; Ana María Mustapic, "Del Partido Peronista al Partido Justicialista: Las transformaciones de un partido carismático," in Marcelo Cavarozzi, and Juan Manuel Abal Medina, eds., *El Asedio a la Política*, 137–162 (Rosario: Homo Sapiens, 2002); and Levitsky, *Transforming Labor-Based Parties in Latin America*.

65. Excerpt from speech given by Antonio Cafiero during the Plenario de la Renovación Justicialista, November 13, 1987, in Antonio Cafiero, *Testimonios: Del '45 y del 2000 también*. (Buenos Aires: Nuevo Hacer, Grupo Editor Latinoamericano, 1995), 66.

66. "Cajas del PAN en mal estado," *La Nación* (Buenos Aires), May 20, 1988.

67. *La Gaceta de Hoy* (Buenos Aires), 20 May 1985, quoted in Midre, "Bread or Solidarity?," 351.

68. Between 1984 and 1985, the cost of the program was approximately US$120 million. In 1986, the budget rose to US$206 million, with the World Bank estimating that 92 percent of those costs went to food purchases and 8 percent to program administration, which included food storage, transportation, and personnel. See World Bank, "Report No. 6555-AR: Argentina Population, Health and Nutrition Sector Review" (Washington, DC: The World Bank, 1987), 21.

69. This figure is based on the data calculated by the II Reunión Interministerial de Programas Alimentarias, published in Aguirre, "El P.A.N.," 74.

70. Aguirre, "El P.A.N.," 74.

71. Archivo DIPPBA, Mesa Referencia, Factor Social, carpeta 6, legajo 18620, folio 6.

72. Aguirre, "El P.A.N.," 42.

73. Archivo DIPPBA, Mesa Referencia, Factor Social, carpeta 6, legajo 18620, folio 14.

74. Archivo DIPPBA, Mesa Referencia, folio 3.

75. Archivo DIPPBA, Mesa Referencia, folio 8–9.

76. Cosse, *Estigmas de naciemiento*; and Brodwyn Fischer, *A Poverty of Rights: Citizenship and Inequality in Twentieth Century Río de Janeiro* (Stanford, CA: Stanford University Press, 2008).

77. Aguirre, "El P.A.N.," 42.

78. Aguirre, "El P.A.N.," 49–50. See also "Programa Alimentario Nacional: Evaluación."

79. INDEC (Instituto Nacional de Estadística y Censos), *La Pobreza en el conurbano bonarense* (Buenos Aires: INDEC, 1989), 49.

80. INDEC, *La Pobreza en el conurbano bonarense*, 50.

81. INDEC, *La Pobreza en el conurbano bonarense*, 24.

82. For the exact data of the household survey on the PAN, see INDEC, *La Pobreza en el conurbano bonarense*, 49–50; and Midre, "Bread or Solidarity?," 354.

83. Cobos, interview.

84. Archivo DIPPBA, Mesa Referencia, folio 12.

85. "El problema de los niños desnutridos se soluciona con el triunfo del Peronismo," *El Sol* (Quilmes), May 19, 1988.

86. "Para qué sirve el PAN?," *Clarín*, June 28, 1986.

CHAPTER FOUR. "CHERNOBYL CHICKENS"

1. See Daniel Azpiazu, Eduardo Basualdo, and Miguel Khavisse, *El nuevo poder económico en la Argentina de los años 80* (Buenos Aires: Editorial Legasa, 1986); Alfredo Pucciarelli, ed. *Empresarios, tecnócratas y militares: La trama corporativa de la última dictadura* (Buenos Aires: Siglo Veintiuno, 2004); Alejandro Grimson and Gabriel Kessler, *On Argentina and the Southern Cone: Neoliberalism and National Imaginations* (New York: Routledge, 2005); and Alexandre Roig, *La moneda imposible: La convertibilidad argentina de 1991* (Buenos Aires: Fondo de Cultura Económica, 2016).

2. Lauren Derby has also investigated the cultural symbolism of chicken and scandals involving its consumption in the context of the Dominican Republic. See Lauren Derby, "Gringo Chickens with Worms: Food and Nationalism in the Dominican Republic," in Gilbert Joseph, Catherine LeGrand, and Ricardo D. Salvatore, eds., *Close Encounters of Empire: Writing the Cultural History of US-Latin American Relations* (Durham, NC: Duke University Press, 1998), 451–493.

3. "No esperar milagros." *Clarín* (Buenos Aires), December 28, 1983.

4. Edgar Dosman, *The Life and Times of Raúl Prebisch* (Montreal: McGill-Queens Press, 2008).

5. "Peligrosa bomba de tiempo," *Clarín* (Buenos Aires), December 24, 1983.

6. See Mariana Heredia, *Cuando los economistas alcanzaron el poder (o cómo se gestó confiana en los expertos)* (Buenos Aires: Siglo Veintiuno Editores, 2015).

7. For more on the imprint of the Illia administration on the early fiscal policies of the Alfonsín government, see Julieta Pesce, "Política y economía durante el primer año del gobierno de Raúl Alfonsín: La gestión del ministro Grinspun," in Alfredo Pucciarelli, ed., *Los años de Alfonsín: ¿El poder de la democracia o la democracia del poder?* (Buenos Aires: Siglo Veintiuno, 2006), 367–412. See also Néstor Restivo and Horacio Rovelli, *El Accidente*

Grinspun: Un Ministro Desobediente, Claves Para Todos, series ed. José Nun (Buenos Aires: Capital Intelectual, 2011).

8. Pesce, "Política y economía durante el primer año del gobierno de Raúl Alfonsín," 379–381.

9. Raúl Alfonsín, "Hay cuentas que no cierran," December 29, 1982, Biblioteca UCR, carpeta Alfonsín No. 1.

10. Jorge Navarrete, "Foreign Policy and International Financial Negotiations: The External Debt and the Cartegena Consensus," *CEPAL Review*, no. 27 (December 1985): 7–25.

11. José Luis Machinea, interview, April 4, 2007 (video on CD), Archivo de Historia Oral de la Argentina Contemporánea, Programa de Historia Política del Instituto de Investigaciones Gino Germani (UBA), Centro de Documentación e Información (IIGG), Buenos Aires.

12. "Bankers Worried about Losses on Argentine Loans," *Washington Post*, March 6, 1984, A1.

13. In late September 1984, Argentina reached a preliminary agreement with the IMF and private lending banks, which issued another US$4 billion in loans. At the same time, private lending banks agreed to roll over more than $13 billion in outstanding loans that were due in 1985. For more background on the 1984 debt negotiations, see Klaus Veigel, *Dictatorship, Democracy, and Globalization: Argentina and the Cost of paralysis, 1973–2001* (University Park: Pennsylvania State University Press, 2009), 144.

14. Pesce, "Política y economía durante el primer año del gobierno de Raúl Alfonsín," 392.

15. "Todos los mitos politicos sobrevivirán?" *Clarín* (Buenos Aires), 18 March 1984.

16. Eduardo Elena has examined the relationship between wages and prices and daily life dating back to the first Peronist period. See "Peronist Consumer Politics and the Problem of Domesticating Markets in Argentina, 1943–1955," *Hispanic American Historical Review* (February 2007): 111–149.

17. "Coincidencia en la críticas," *Clarín* (Bueno Aires), March 10, 1984.

18. Pablo Martínez, "La veda de carne: Al final todos enojados," *Revista Somos*, March 23, 1984.

19. Mario Rapoport, *Historia económica, política y social de la Argentina (1880–2003)* (Buenos Aires: Ariel, 2006), 707.

20. Veigel, *Dictatorship, Democracy, and Globalization*, 144.

21. Quoted from Gerardo Aboy Carlés, *Las dos fronteras de la democracia argentina: La reformulación de las identidades políticas de Alfonsín a Menem* (Buenos Aires: Homo Sapiens Ediciones, 2001), 173.

22. William Robinson, *Promoting Polyarchy: Globalization, US Intervention, and Hegemony* (New York: Cambridge University Press, 1996). For a more recent attempt to historicize the multiple histories of neoliberalism, see "Genealogies of Neoliberalism," special issue, *Radical History Review*, no. 112 (Winter 2012).

23. David Harvey, *A Brief History of Neoliberalism* (Oxford: Oxford University Press, 2005), 1.

24. Archivo Histórico de Radio y Televisión Argentina (hereafter Archivo Histórico RTA), *Alfonsín en Estados Unidos: Respuesta a Reagan y discurso*, March 20, 1985, www .archivorta.com.ar/asset/alfonsin-en-estados-unidos-respuesta-a-reagan-y-discurso-1985/.

25. "A Heartfelt Cry from Alfonsín on Debt Crisis," *New York Times*, March 24, 1985.

26. Azpiazu et al., *El nuevo poder económico en la Argentina*.

27. José Nun and Mario Lattuada, *El gobierno de Alfonsín y las corporaciones agrarias* (Buenos Aires: Manatial, 1991); and Ricardo Ortiz and Martín Schorr, "La economía política del gobierno de Alfonsín: Creciente subordinación al poder económico durante la 'década perdida'" in Pucciarelli, ed., *Los años de Alfonsín*, 291–333.

28. Ricardo Mazzorín, interview by author, Buenos Aires, Argentina, April 9, 2009.

29. Heredia, *Cuando los economistas alcanzaron el poder*; and Juan Sourrouille, interview, September 14, 2005 (video on CD), Archivo de Historia Oral de la Argentina Contemporánea, Programa de Historia Política del Instituto de Investigaciones Gino Germani (UBA), Centro de Documentación e Información (IIGG), Buenos Aires.

30. The Rodrigazo refers to the set of draconian economic measures instituted in June 1975 by Celestino Rodrigo, the minister of economy during the government of Isabel Perón. The policies, which included a wage freeze and a massive increase in the cost of public services, prompted an inflationary spike and spelled the beginning of the end of Perón's government. See Néstor Restivo and Raúl Dellatorre, *El Rodrigazo: El lado oscuro del ajuste que cambió la Argentina* (Buenos Aires: Capital Intelectual, 2016).

31. "Discurso del Señor Presidente de la Nación, Dr. Raúl R. Alfonsín, desde el balcón de la casa del gobierno, el día 26 de abril de 1985," in *Discursos presidenciales: Recopilación de discursos, mensajes y conferencias de prensa efectuadas por el señor presidente de la nación, doctor Raúl Ricardo Alfonsín* (Buenos Aires: Secretaria de Información Pública, Dirección General de Difusión, 1985), 2:107, www.lanic.utexas.edu/larrp/pm/sample2/argentin /alfonsin/851253d.html. For the film version of the speech, see Archivo Histórico RTA, *Discurso de Alfonsín: Defense de la democracia y economía de guerra*, www.archivorta.com.ar /asset/cadena-nacional-discurso-de-alfonsin-defensa-de-la-democracia-y-economia-de -guerra-26-04-1985/.

32. "Discurso del Señor Presidente de la Nación," 2:109 (emphasis added).

33. "Discurso del Señor Presidente de la Nación," 2:109.

34. "Discurso del Señor Presidente de la Nación," 2:113.

35. Greg Grandin, *Empire's Workshop: Latin America, the United States, and the Rise of the New Imperialism* (New York: Metropolitan Books, 2006).

36. Veigel, *Dictatorship, Democracy, and Globalization: Argentina and the cost of paralysis*, 152.

37. Fundación de Investigaciones Económicas Latinoamericanas (FIEL), *Control de precios e inflación: La experiencia argentina reciente* (Buenos Aires: Ediciones Manatial, 1990), 36.

38. Mario Brodherson, interview, December 8, 2005 (video on CD), Archivo de Historia Oral de la Argentina Contemporánea, Programa de Historia Política del Instituto de Investigaciones Gino Germani (UBA), Centro de Documentación e Información (IIGG), Buenos Aires.

39. Rapoport, *Historia económica, política y social de la Argentina*, 707.

40. Veigel, *Dictatorship, Democracy, and Globalization*, 153.

41. "Mensaje de la Secretaria de Información Pública," *El Sol* (Quilmes), July 4, 1985.

42. "Impactos en el costo de vida," *Clarín*, July 2, 1986, 20.

43. "Sobreprecios del 30% en las carnecerias," *Clarín*, June 12, 1986, 22.

44. Resolutions authorizing the first poultry purchases and imports can be found in *Boletín Oficial de la República Argentina*, April 30–June 9, 1986.

45. Roy Hora, *The Landowners of the Argentine Pampas: A Social and Political History, 1860–1945* (New York: Oxford University Press, 2001).

46. Osvaldo Barsky and Jorge Gelman, *Historia del agro argentino: Desde la conquista hasta finales del siglo XX* (Buenos Aires: Mondadori, 2001), 438–440.

47. See Nun and Lattuada, *El gobierno de Alfonsín y las corporaciones agrarias*.

48. "A3: 'Nota del 27/05/85. Dirigida por C.E.P.A. (Centro de Empresas Procesadoras Avícolas. Entidad que nucléa [*sic*] el 92% de las empresas habilitadas por el S.E.N.A.S.A. al Sr. Secretario de Comercio Interior. Ing. Julio A. Mendez (Nota No. 42/85),'" Ministerio de Economía, Secretaría de Comercio Interior, "Expediente al Señor Juez Dr. Miguel Guillermo Pons" (Buenos Aires, July 7, 1988).

49. "A8: 'Nota del 17/05/85 del Sr. Gobernador de la Pcia. De Entre Rios. Sr. Sergio Montiel al Sr. Ministro de Economía. Dr. Juan Vital Sourrouille,'" Ministerio de Economía, Secretaría de Comercio Interior, "Expediente al Señor Juez Dr. Miguel Guillermo Pons" (Buenos Aires, July 7, 1988).

50. A9: 'Telegrama del 29/07/85, del Sr. Manuel Sarria. Presidente de la Asociación de Hoteles, Restorantes y Confiterías, dirigida al Sr. Secretario de Comercio Interior. Ing. Julio A. Méndez,'" Ministerio de Economía, Secretaría de Comercio Interior, "Expediente al Señor Juez Dr. Miguel Guillermo Pons" (Buenos Aires, July 7, 1988).

51. "Estimaciones de existencias ganaderas, producción, y consumo de carne vacuna," Ministerio de Economía, Secretaría de Comercio Interior, "Expediente al Señor Juez Dr. Miguel Guillermo Pons" (Buenos Aires, July 7, 1988).

52. "A6: 'Nota del 05/07/85 de CARGILL S.A.C.I., dirigida al Sr. Ministro de Economía. Dr. Juan Vital Sourrouille.'" Ministerio de Economía, Secretaría de Comercio Interior, "Expediente al Señor Juez Dr. Miguel Guillermo Pons" (Buenos Aires, July 7, 1988).

53. Ricardo Mazzorín, interview by author, Buenos Aires, Argentina, April 9, 2009; and Ricardo Mazzorín, interview, May 12, 2005 (video on CD), Archivo de Historia Oral de la Argentina Contemporánea, Programa de Historia Política del Instituto de Investigaciones Gino Germani (UBA), Centro de Documentación e Información (IIGG), Buenos Aires.

54. For seventy-two hours they halted deliveries of livestock to markets and suspended all bank transactions.

55. "El paro agropecuario dio comienzo," *Clarín*, June 9, 1986.

56. "Descartan una posible liberación de precios," *Clarín*, June 20, 1986.

57. The poultry imports were authorized by the power granted to the domestic trade secretary via the 1974 Supply Law (Law 20.680). Passed just days before the death of Juan Perón in the middle of his third presidential term, among other mechanisms, the law granted the executive authority to modify import tariffs and subsidies, limit exports, and guarantee supply in case of economic emergency by forcing producers to maintain the production and distribution of certain goods and services. The law also sanctioned penalties for firms that artificially inflated prices, provoked shortages of goods, or otherwise impinged on the "general welfare."

58. Héctor Ruiz Núñez, "Pollos Mazzorín: Lo que no se dijo," *Humor*, no. 223, July 1988, 28.

59. Marcos Novaro, *Argentina en el fin de siglo: Democracia, mercado y nación (1983–2001)*, Historia Argentina, vol. 10 (Buenos Aires: Paidós, 2009), 276.

60. "Comer es inflacionario," *Somos*, July 6, 1988, 20–21.

61. "Acusan al los empresarios por el alza de precios," *Clarín*, May 25, 1988.

62. "Comer es inflacionario," *Somos*, July 6, 1988, 20–21.

63. "Reportaje: Del Consumo," *Clarín*, May 29, 1988.

64. "Cuanto cuesta? Deme medio," *Clarín*, April 17, 1988.

65. "Estimaciones de existencias ganaderas, producción, y consumo de carne vacuna," Ministerio de Economía, Secretaría de Comercio Interior, "Expediente al Señor Juez Dr. Miguel Guillermo Pons" (Buenos Aires, July 7, 1988).

66. For an account of how the "pollos de Mazzorín" first came to light, see Romina Manguel and Javier Romero, *Vale todo: Biografia no autorizada de Daniel Hadad* (Buenos Aires: Ediciones B Argentina, Grupo Zeta, 2004), 58–69.

67. Comisión de Comercio Interior, H. Camara de Diputados Taquígrafos, Buenos Aires, June 9, 1988, 182.

68. Comisión de Comercio Interior, H. Camara de Diputados Taquígrafos, Buenos Aires, June 9, 1988, 14/20–21.

69. See chapter 3.

70. "Plataforma electoral: La solución al país, Unión del Centro Democrático."

71. Alberto Albamonte, "El inicio de la UCEDE" (Buenos Aires), 6 (unpublished manuscript, n.d.).

72. "El pollo Ricardo: Cuál sera el destino final de la aves importadas; cajas del PAN o relleno sanitario; Las explicaciones de Ricardo Mazzorín, Secretario de Comercio Interior," *Somos*, June 15, 1988, 40–41.

73. "Discuten la credibilidad del plan," *Clarín*, May 27, 1988, 22.

74. Cámara de Diputados, República Argentina, Comisión de Comercio Interior, H. Camara de Diputados Taquígrafos, Buenos Aires, June 2, 1988, 21.

75. Cámara de Diputados, H. Camara de Diputados Taquígrafos, 22.

76. Albamonte, "El inicio de la UCEDE," 12.

77. Cámara de Diputados, H. Camara de Diputados Taquígrafos, 92.

78. Cámara de Diputados, H. Camara de Diputados Taquígrafos, 12.

79. Cámara de Diputados, H. Camara de Diputados Taquígrafos, 271.

80. Cámara de Diputados, H. Camara de Diputados Taquígrafos, 32.

81. Cámara de Diputados, H. Camara de Diputados Taquígrafos, 211.

82. *Humor*, no. 222, June 1988.

83. Héctor Ruiz Núñez, "Pollos Mazzorín: lo que no se dijo," *Humor*, no. 223, July 1988, 28.

84. *Humor*, no. 222, June 1988.

85. Enrique Vásquez, "No ocurren casualidades en la Argentina," *Humor*, no. 222, June 1988.

86. Vásquez, "No ocurren casualidades en la Argentina."

87. *Clarín*, May 29, 1988.

88. Archivo Histórico RTA, *Cúpula empresaria apoya el plan antiinflacionario de Alfonsín, 1988*, www.archivorta.com.ar/asset/cupula-empresaria-apoya-el-plan-antiinflacionario -de-alfonsin-1988/.

89. Archivo Histórico RTA, *Cúpula empresaria apoya el plan antiinflacionario de Alfonsín.*

90. Archivo Histórico RTA, *Cúpula empresaria apoya el plan antiinflacionario de Alfonsín.*

91. Héctor Ruiz Núñez, "Pollos Mazzorín: Lo que no se dijo," *Humor*, no. 223, July 1988, 28.

92. Archivo Histórico RTA, *El palacio de la risa*, www.archivorta.com.ar/asset/el-palac io-de-la-risa-06-09-1993/.

CHAPTER FIVE. "DEAR MR. PRESIDENT"

A previous version of this chapter was published as "Democratic Utopias: The Argentine Transition to Democracy through Letters, 1983–1989," *The Americas* 72, no. 2 (April 2015): 221–247. Reprinted with permission, COPYRIGHT: © Academy of American Franciscan History 2015.

1. The letters on which this chapter is based are housed in the Archivo General de la Nación/Departamento Archivo Intermedio (hereafter AGN/DAI), Fondo Documental "Presidencia de la Nación. Secretaria Privada (1983–1989)." I have omitted the last names of letter writers to protect their identities. Though Raúl Alfonsín received letters from all over the country, the letters analyzed in this article were sent from Buenos Aires and the surrounding suburbs. Unless otherwise noted, all translations are mine. AGN/DAI, "Presidencia Alfonsín," legajo 306, 123.371.

2. These questions have guided investigations of the epistolary tradition in Latin America since the colonial period, which historians have mined for understandings of popular culture, national sentiment, and government administration, among others. Specific studies on the history and practice of letter writing have largely focused on the colonial period up through the nineteenth century. See, for example, John Lockhart and Enrique Otte, *Letters and People of the Spanish Indies, Sixteenth Century* (Cambridge: Cambridge University Press, 1976); and John Lockhart's essay, "Letters and People to Spain," in his *Of Things of the Indies: Essays Old and New in Early Latin American History* (Stanford, CA: Stanford University Press, 1999), 81–97. Kathryn Burns has looked at the politics of writing in *Into the Archive: Writing and Power in Colonial Peru* (Durham, NC: Duke University Press, 2010). For the nineteenth century, scholars have examined letter writing as an integral part of nation building. Key works in this regard include Angel Rama, *The Lettered City*, trans. and ed. John Chasteen (Durham, NC: Duke University Press, 1996); Sarah Chambers, "*Letters and Salons: Women Reading and Writing the Nation in the Nineteenth Century*," in Sarah Castro-Klarén and John Chasteen, eds., *Beyond Imagined Communities: Reading and Writing the Nation in Nineteenth-Century Latin America* (Baltimore, MD: Johns Hopkins University Press, 2003), 54–83; and William French, "'Cartas y cartas, compadre . . .': Love and Other Letters from Río Frío," in William H. Beezley and Linda Ann Curcio, eds., *Latin American Popular Culture Since Independence*, 2nd ed. (Lanham, MD: Rowman & Littlefield, 2012), 68–84.

3. For the twentieth century, an era characterized by growing literacy rates, letter writing has been frequently analyzed as evidence of popular political participation. See Sueann

Caulfield, *In Defense of Honor: Morality, Modernity, and Nation in Early Twentieth-Century Brazil* (Durham, NC: Duke University Press, 2000); Joel Wolfe, "Father of the Poor or Mother of the Rich? Getulio Vargas, Industrial Workers, and Constructions of Class, Gender, and Populism in São Paulo, 1930–1954," *Radical History Review* 58 (Winter 1994): 80–111; Brodwyn Fischer, *A Poverty of Rights: Citizenship and Inequality in Twentieth-Century Rio de Janeiro* (Stanford, CA: Stanford University Press, 2008); Lauren Derby, "In the Shadow of the State: The Politics of Denunciation and Panegyric During the Trujillo Regime in the Dominican Republic, 1940–1958," *Hispanic American Historical Review* 83, no. 2 (May 2003): 295–344; and Adolfo Gilly and Rhina Roux, eds., *Cartas a Cuauhtémoc Cárdenas* (Mexico City: Colección Problemas de México, Ediciones Era, 1989).

4. My discussion of the moral economy of democracy takes off from E. P. Thompson's groundbreaking analysis of food riots in eighteenth-century England. He presents moral economy as "a consistent traditional view of social norms and obligations, of the proper economic functions of several parties within the community, which, taken together, can be said to constitute the moral economy of the poor" (79); E. P. Thompson, "The Moral Economy of the English Crowd in the Eighteenth Century," *Past and Present* 50 (February 1971): 76–136.

5. The exact number of letters sent to Alfonsín over the course of his presidency is unknown, and because there has been no official attempt to systematize the correspondence, it is difficult to speak of a representative sample. While Alfonsín received thousands of letters over the course of his presidency, it is most likely that the number did not surpass the amount of correspondence sent to Evita and Juan Perón. Some estimate that the Eva Perón Foundation received, on average, twelve thousand letters per day. Evita was famous for personally responding to letters, often meeting individually with petitioners. In contrast, as Eduardo Elena notes in his study of letters sent to Perón during the "Perón Wants to Know Campaign," it was often unclear what happened to letters addressed to Perón once they arrived at government offices. The same was true of the popular correspondence sent to Alfonsín, which only rarely received a response from one of his secretaries.

6. Though Alfonsín received letters from across Argentina, this chapter examines those sent from Buenos Aires and the surrounding metropolitan suburbs. The findings are based on readings of approximately eight hundred letters from each year of the Alfonsín presidency (1983–1989).

7. AGN/DAI, "Presidencia Alfonsín," legajo 90, 20229/84.

8. AGN/DAI, "Presidencia Alfonsín," legajo 90, 20283/84.

9. AGN/DAI, "Presidencia Alfonsín," legajo 90, 20224/84.

10. AGN/DAI, "Presidencia Alfonsín," legajo 33, 7636-1-003 ("opposite of what the IMF tells you!"); and AGN/DAI, "Presidencia Alfonsín," legajo 90, 1735/84 (northern province of Tucumán).

11. AGN/DAI, "Presidencia Alfonsín," legajo 3, 28994/84.

12. AGN/DAI, "Presidencia Alfonsín," legajo 90, 20215/84.

13. This letter from Alfonsín's secretary, dated early 1984, was the only "official" response I encountered in the archives. It seems likely that this type of form letter was only sent during the first few months of the Alfonsín presidency, at the height of the greatest amount of support for the recently inaugurated democratic government. AGN/DAI, "Presidencia Alfonsín," legajo 90, 20115/84.

14. For an overview of the state of the Argentine economy at the end of the military regime, see Klaus Veigel, *Dictatorship, Democracy, and Globalization: Argentina and the Cost of Paralysis, 1973–2001* (University Park: Pennsylvania State University Press, 2009).

15. Gabriel Kessler and Silvia Sigal, "La hiperinflación en Argentina: Comportamientos y representaciones sociales," in Darío Canton and Jorge Raúl Jorat, eds., *La Investigación social en Argentina a 40 años de la refundación del Instituto de Sociología* (Buenos Aires: Instituto de Investigaciones Gino Germani y Oficina de Publicaciones del CBC, Universidad de Buenos Aires, 1997), 155–187.

16. AGN/DAI, "Presidencia Alfonsín," legajo 90, 17349/84. María de los Remedios de Escalada de San Martín was the wife of independence leader José de San Martín. She organized the support of women from Mendoza to donate their jewels to help finance the independence movement.

17. AGN/DAI, "Presidencia Alfonsín," legajo 8, 22028/84.

18. See chapter 3 for an overview of the law's provisions.

19. Kessler and Sigal, "La hiperinflación en Argentina."

20. Human rights groups paired disappointment about setbacks to justice with pointed criticism of the administration's handling of the military and human rights policy. The movement galvanized support to pressure the government to make good on its promises to prosecute the crimes of the regime. Meanwhile, the first rumblings of military discontent struck an ominous chord for the fate of newly restored institutions.

21. AGN/DAI, "Presidencia Alfonsín," legajo 90, 44199-9-0005.

22. AGN/DAI, "Presidencia Alfonsín," legajo 35, 457/8324.

23. Mariano Plotkin, *Mañana es San Perón: A Cultural History of Perón's Argentina* (Wilmington, DE: Scholarly Resources Inc., 1993), 158.

24. Eduardo Elena, "What the People Want: State Planning and Political Participation in Peronist Argentina," *Journal of Latin American Studies* 37, no. 1 (2005): 81–108. Omar Acha has also investigated the letters to Perón as evidence of the creation of a distinctly new political society. Omar Acha, "Sociedad civil y sociedad política durante el primer peronismo," *Desarrollo Económico* 44, no. 174 (July–September 2004): 199–230. See also Donna Guy, *Creating Charismatic Bonds in Argentina: Letters to Juan and Eva Perón* (Albuquerque: University of New Mexico Press, 2016).

25. Daniel James, *Resistance and Integration: Peronism and the Argentine Working Class, 1946–1976* (New York: Cambridge University Press, 1988); and Jeff Gould, *To Lead as Equals: Rural Protest and Political Consciousness in Chinandega, Nicaragua, 1912–1979* (Chapel Hill: University of North Carolina Press, 1990).

26. Natalia Milanesio, *Workers Go Shopping in Argentina: The Rise of Popular Consumer Culture* (Albuquerque: University of New Mexico Press, 2013); and Eduardo Elena, *Dignifying Argentina: Peronism, Citizenship, and Mass Consumption* (Pittsburgh: University of Pittsburgh Press, 2011).

27. My discussion of clientelism is informed by Javier Auyero's ethnographic study of patron-client networks in the shantytowns of Buenos Aires. In contrast to studies that emphasize the negative aspects of clientelism, Auyero examines the historical and sociological roots of clientelism as a series of "informal problem-solving networks" that helps residents mitigate extreme forms of poverty and exclusion. Javier Auyero, *Poor People's*

Politics: Peronist Survival Networks and the Legacy of Evita (Durham, NC: Duke University Press, 2000.

28. For more on the Argentine debates, see Mario Rapoport, *Historia económica, política y social de la Argentina (1880–2003)* (Buenos Aires: Ariel, 2006). For a regional view of these debates, see Paul Drake, ed., *Money Doctors, Foreign Debts, and Economic Reforms in Latin America from the 1890s to the Present*. (Wilmington, DE: Scholarly Resources, 1994).

29. AGN/DAI, "Presidencia Alfonsín," legajo 40, 58604/84.

30. AGN/DAI, "Presidencia Alfonsín," legajo 90, 44210/84.

31. AGN/DAI, "Presidencia Alfonsín," legajo 417, 116390/87.

32. Elizabeth Jelin, "Los derechos humanos: Entre el estado y la sociedad," in *Nueva Historia Argentina*, vol. 10, Juan Suriano, ed., *Dictadura y Democracia (1976–2001)* (Buenos Aires: Editorial Sudamericana, 2005), 507–557.

33. The law stipulated a sixty-day statute of limitations, after which no further charges could be brought against military officers suspected of crimes. Though the government hoped Full Stop would appease the military, the strategy backfired: more than four hundred new cases were filed by the deadline in February 1987.

34. The only crimes exempted from the Due Obedience and Full Stop Laws were the theft of babies stolen from mothers who were detained or disappeared.

35. The bibliography on human rights policy during the 1980s is as rich as it is vast. In general, authors have identified the Alfonsín government as unsuccessfully walking a "middle line" that attempted to balance the human rights movement and armed forces, ending up alienating both. See Carlos Acuña and Catalina Smulovitz, *¿Ni olvido ni perdón? Derechos humanos y tensiones cívico-militares en la transición argentina* (Buenos Aires: CEDES, 1991); Allison Brysk, *The Politics of Human Rights in Argentina: Protest, Change, and Democratization* (Stanford, CA: Stanford University Press, 1994); Elizabeth Jelin, "La política de la memoria: El movimiento de derechos humanos y la construcción democrática en la Argentina," in Carlos Acuña and Adama Przeworksi, eds., *Juicio, castigo y memorias: Derechos humanos y justicia en la política argentina* (Buenos Aires: Nueva Visión, 1995); and Carlos Nino, *Radical Evil on Trial* (New Haven, CT: Yale University Press, 1998). For a general review of the literature and its main arguments, see Marcos Novaro, "Formación, desarrollo y declive del consenso alfonsinista sobre derechos humanos," in Roberto Gargarella, María Victoria Murillo, and Mario Pecheny, eds., *Discutir Alfonsín* (Buenos Aires: Siglo Veintiuno Editories, 2010), 41–65.

36. AGN/DAI, "Presidencia Alfonsín," legajo 269, 109639.

37. AGN/DAI, "Presidencia Alfonsín," legajo 3/8/11, 10794/84.

38. AGN/DAI, "Presidencia Alfonsín," legajo 3/8/11, 10794/84.

39. AGN/DAI, "Presidencia Alfonsín," legajo 417, 116397.

40. AGN/DAI "Presidencia Alfonsín," legajo 46, 124.262.

41. AGN/DAI "Presidencia Alfonsín," legajo 46, 124.307.

42. AGN/DAI "Presidencia Alfonsín," legajo 34, 149.93.

43. AGN/DAI "Presidencia Alfonsín," legajo, 270, 273.370.

44. Claudia Hilb, "La Tablada: El último acto de la guerrilla setentista," *Lucha armada en la Argentina* 3, no. 9 (2007): 4–22.

45. Sergio Serulnikov, "When Looting Becomes a Right: Urban Poverty and Food Riots in Argentina," in "Social Movements and Political Change in Latin America: 2," special issue, *Latin American Perspectives* 21, no. 3 (Summer 1994): 72.

46. AGN/DAI, "Presidencia Alfonsín," legajo 20, 154.003.

47. Rapoport, *Historia económica, política y social de la Argentina*, 707.

48. "Mensaje Presidencial a la Asamblea Legislativa," May 1, 1989,http://lanic.utexas .edu/larrp/pm/sample2/argentin/alfonsin/893875t.html.

49. AGN/DAI, "Presidencia Alfonsín," legajo 20, 153.560.

50. AGN/DAI, "Presidencia Alfonsín," legajo 20, 153.560.

51. "'Robamos para darles comida a nuestros hijos,' dicen saqueadoras de Quilmes"; and "Saqueos: Acusan a la extrema izquierda," *Diario El Sol*, 30 May 1989.

52. AGN/DAI, "Presidencia Alfonsín," legajo 274, 152.774.

CHAPTER SIX. DEMOCRATIC PASTS, NEOLIBERAL FUTURES

1. "Se llevan comestibles de diversos comercios en Rosario y Córdoba," *Clarín*, May 25, 1989.

2. Nicolás Iñigo Carrera, María Celia Cotarelo, Elizabeth Gómez, and Federico M. Kindgard, "La revuelta argentina 1989–1990," Documento de Trabajo, no. 4 (Buenos Aires: PISMA, 1995), 45.

3. For a discussion of the role of *saqueos* in Argentine history, see Gabriel DiMeglio and Sergio Serulnikov, eds., *La larga historia de los saqueos en la argentina de la independencia hasta nuestros días* (Buenos Aires: Siglo XXI, 2017); see also Sergio Serulnikov's chapter in that same volume on the 1989 uprisings: "Como si estuvieran comprando: Los saqueos de 1989 y la irrupción de la nueva cuestión social," 137–176.

4. "Sigue el acoso a los supermercados," *Crónica*, May 26, 1989.

5. María Rosa Neufeld and María Cristina Cravino, "Los saqueos y las ollas populares de 1989 en el Gran Buenos Aires: Pasado y presente de una experiencia formativa," *Revista de antropología* 44, no. 2 (2001): 147–172.

6. Mario Rapoport, *Historia económica, política y social de la Argentina (1880–2003)* (Buenos Aires: Ariel, 2006), 752.

7. Oscar Martínez, "El escenario: Febrero-julio de 1989; Terrorismo económico y deses-tabilización política," in Atilio Borón, et al., eds., *El Menemato: Radiografía de dos años del gobierno de Carlos Menem* (Buenos Aires: Ediciones Letra Buena, 1991), 13–46.

8. Claudia Hilb, "La Tablada: El último acto de la guerrilla setentista," *Lucha armada en la Argentina* 3, no. 9 (2007): 4–22.

9. E. P. Thompson, "The Moral Economy of the English Crowd in the Eighteenth Century," *Past and Present*, no. 50 (February 1971): 76–136; and Raj Patel and Philip McMichael, "A Political Economy of the Food Riot," *Review: A Journal of the Fernand Braudel Center* 32, no. 1 (2009): 9–35.

10. Serulnikov, "Como si estuvieran comprando."

11. The energy crisis, which was most severe in Buenos Aires and Greater Buenos Aires, was sparked by a combination of drought and the breakdown of hydroelectric facilities, aging infrastructure, and problems with the Atucha and Embalse nuclear power plants.

12. "Power Supply Going Down in Argentina," *New York Times*, January 5, 1989.

13. Hilb, "La Tablada"; Vera Carnovale, "De Entre Todos a La Tablada: Redefiniciones y permanencias del ideario setentista," *Pol/His* 6, no. 12 (2013): 244–264.

14. For a brief account of the *carapintada* uprising at the Villa Martelli barracks, see Marcos Novaro, *Argentina en el fin del siglo: Democracia, mercado y nación (1983–2001)* (Buenos Aires: Paidós, 2009), 298–299.

15. David Sheinin, "La Tablada Attack and the Erosion of Civil Rights in Argentina," *Middle Atlantic Review of Latin American Studies* 1, no. 1 (2017): 77–96.

16. Martínez, "El escenario," 22.

17. See Eduardo Basualdo, *Estudios de historia económica argentina: Desde mediados del siglo XX a la actualidad* (Buenos Aires: Siglo Veintiuno Editores, 2010).

18. Matías Kulfas and Martín Schorr, *La deuda externa argentina: Diagnóstico y lineamientos propositivos para su reestructuración* (Buenos Aires: Fundación OSDE-CIEP, 2003), 130.

19. "Ni dólares ni drama," *Somos*, February 1, 1989, 47.

20. Juan Sourrouille, interview, September 14, 2005 (video on CD), Archivo de Historia Oral de la Argentina Contemporánea, Programa de Historia Política del Instituto de Investigaciones Gino Germani (UBA), Centro de Documentación e Información (IIGG), Buenos Aires. For more on these negotiations, see Klaus Veigel, *Dictatorship, Democracy, and Globalization: Argentina and the Cost of Paralysis, 1973–2001* (University Park: Pennsylvania State University Press, 2009), 164.

21. Martinez, "El escenario," 21.

22. Baker was the architect of the so-called Baker Plan, which prescribed orthodoxy and free-market reforms for the debtor nations of Latin America, helping to set off a decade of economic stagnation in the region. Baker's replacement, Nicholas Brady, quickly aligned with directors of the IMF and the World Bank, who objected to additional credits for Argentina.

23. For a concise overview of the Plan Primavera, see Fundación de Investigaciones Económicas Latinoamericanas (FIEL), *Control de precios e inflación: La experiencia argentina reciente* (Buenos Aires: Ediciones Manatial 1990), 45–47.

24. Rodolfo Terragno, Minister of Public Works, announced plans for the privatization of ENTel on March 18, 1988. The Alfonsín government proposed the partial privatization of the company, with 40 percent being transferred to the Spanish company Telefónica Nacional. The plan stalled in the face of Peronist congressional opposition and the protests of several unions. In November 1990, the government of Carlos Menem eventually privatized 60 percent of the company. It was among the largest and most prominent privatizations of the early 1990s.

25. The so-called Group of 8 was made up of the Unión Industrial Argentina (UIA), la Sociedad Rural (SRA), la Bolsa de Comercio de Buenos Aires, la Cámara Argentina de Comercio (CAC), la Asociación de Bancos de la República Argentina (ABRA), Asociación de Bancos de la Argentina (ADEBA), Unión Argentina de la Construcción (UAC), and la Cámara Argentina de la Construcción (CACon). See Ricardo Ortiz and Martín Schorr, "La economía política del gobierno de Alfonsín: Creciente subordinación al poder económico durante la 'década perdida,'" in Alfredo Pucciarelli, ed., *Los años de Alfonsín: ¿El*

poder de la democracia o la democracia del poder? (Buenos Aires: Siglo Veintiuno Editores, 2006), 462.

26. Ortiz and Schorr, "La economía política del gobierno de Alfonsín," 472.

27. Fundación de Investigaciones Económicas Latinoamericanas, *Control de precios e inflación*, 47.

28. From January to July 1989, there were three ministers of economy: Juan Vital Sourrouille, who served from February 1985 to March 31, 1989; Juan Carlos Pugliese, who served from March 31 to May 14, 1989; and Jesús Rodriguez, who served from May 14 to July 8, 1989.

29. Some estimates place the loss of dollar reserve at approximately US$900,000,000 between January and February 1989.

30. Veigel, *Dictatorship, Democracy, and Globalization*, 167.

31. On these changes, see "Imprevisto feriado bancario y cambiario dispusieron para hoy," *Clarín*, February 6, 1989; and "Medidas salientes," *Clarín*, February 7, 1989.

32. "Brusco incremento del dólar apuntala las tasas de interés," *Clarín*, February 8, 1989.

33. "El pulso de la City," *La Nación*, February 7, 1989.

34. "Confusión, expectativas, y largas filas, características de la City," *La Nación*, February 8, 1989.

35. "Una mañana agitada," *Clarín*, February 8, 1989.

36. Martínez, "El escenario," 26.

37. Martínez, "El escenario," 42.

38. "Inquietud por la evolución de precios," *Clarín*, February 13, 1989.

39. Ministerio de Economia, Secretaria de Comercio Interior, "Los precios no tienen que aumentar," February 1989.

40. Fernando Coronil and Julie Skurski, "Dismembering and Remembering the Nation: The Semantics of Political Violence in Venezuela," *Comparative Studies in Society and History* 33, no. 2 (April 1991): 288–337; and Alejandro Velasco, *Barrio Rising: Urban Popular Politics and the Making of Modern Venezuela* (Oakland: University of California Press, 2015), ch. 7.

41. Ana Virginia Persello, *Historia del radicalismo* (Buenos Aires: Edhasa, 2007), 306–308.

42. For more on the rise of Carlos Menem and transformations within the Peronist Party, see Gerardo Aboy Carlés, "De Malvinas al menemismo: Renovación y contrarrenovación en el peronismo," *Revista Sociedad*, no. 10 (November 1996): 5–31; James McGuire, *Peronism without Perón: Unions, Parties and Democracy in Argentina* (Stanford, CA: Stanford University Press, 1997); and Ana María Mustapic, "Del Partido Peronista al Partido Justicialista: Las transformaciones de un partido carismático," in Marcelo Cavarozzi and Juan Manuel Abal Medina, eds., *El asedio a la política: Los partidos latinoamericanos en la era neoliberal* (Rosario: Homo Sapiens Ediciones, 2002).

43. See Steven Levitsky, "Crisis and Renovation: Institutional Weakness and the Transformation of Argentina Peronism," in Steven Levitsky and María Victoria Murrillo, eds., *Argentine Democracy: The Politics of Institutional Weakness* (State College: Pennsylvania State University Press, 2006), 181–206.

44. Javier Auyero, *Poor People's Politics: Peronist Survival Networks and the Legacy of Evita* (Durham, NC: Duke University Press, 2000).

45. Menem's perception of himself as the heir to Perón has been the subject of much study. See Gabriela Cerutti and Sergio Ciancaglini, *El Octavo Círculo: Crónica y entretelones del poder menemista* (Buenos Aires: Editorial Planeta Argentina, 1991). Menem frequently peppered his language with passages from Perón's writings and speeches. In particular, he was fond of recalling and embellishing his brief meeting with Perón when he was a young politician. Cerutti and Ciancaglini trace how this meeting took on epic proportions during Menem's campaign.

46. "Como en el 45 pero distinto," *Página 12*, April 24, 1988.

47. "Menem dijo que no sólo de democracia viven los pueblos," *La Nación*, February 8, 1989.

48. Ana Castellani and Alejandro Gaggero, "Estado y grupos económicos en la Argentina de los noventa," in Alfredo Pucciarelli, ed., *Los años de Menem: La construcción del orden neoliberal* (Buenos Aires: Siglo Veintiuno Ediciones, 2011).

49. The first two economic ministers of Menem's administration were leading figures from Bunge & Born.

50. "Hay que cumplir con la deuda y cambiar métodos, dijo Menem," *Clarín*, January 2, 1989.

51. "Anuncian la reforma cambiariara con una importante devaluación," *Clarín*, April 4, 1989.

52. "Agitación en supermercados," *Clarín*, April 14, 1989; "Custodia en los supermercados," *Clarín*, April 21, 1989; and "Inquietantes rumores en todo el país," *Diario Popular*, April 20, 1989.

53. El Archivo de la DIPPBA (Dirección de Inteligencia de la Policía de la Provincia de Buenos Aires) (hereafter Archivo DIPPBA, Mesa De, Factor Social, legajo 567, April 1989, folio 20.

54. Archivo DIPPBA, Mesa De, Factor Social, legajo 567, April 1989, folio 21.

55. Archivo DIPPBA, Mesa De, Factor Social, legajo 567, April 1989, folio 1.

56. Archivo DIPPBA, Mesa De, Factor Social, legajo 567, April 1989, folio 8.

57. Gabriel Kessler and Silvia Sigal, "La hiperinflación en Argentina: comportamientos y representaciones sociales" in Darío Canton and Jorge Raúl Jorat, eds. *La Investigación social en Argentina a 40 años de la refundación del Instituto de Sociología* (Buenos Aires: Instituto de Investigaciones Gino Germani y Oficina de Publicaciones del CBC, Universidad de Buenos Aires, 1997), 155–187.

58. "Acá no se tira nada," *Clarín*, May 13, 1989.

59. For more on living during times of hyperinflation in contemporary Latin America, see Maureen O'Dougherty, *Consumption Intensified: The Politics of Middle Class Daily Life in Brazil* (Durham, NC: Duke University Press, 2002), 53.

60. Kessler and Sigal, "La hiperinflación en Argentina," 159.

61. O'Dougherty, *Consumption Intensified*.

62. Carlos Menem won the election with 47.49 percent of the vote. Eduardo Angeloz received 37.03 percent and Alvaro Alsogaray of the UCeDé, 6.53 percent. For the full election results, see Ministerio del Interior, Obras Públicas y Vivienda, Dirección Nacional Electoral, "Total pais," https://recorriendo.elecciones.gob.ar/presidente1989.html#/4/1.

63. Archivo DIPPBA, Mesa De, Factor Social, legajo 567, May 1989, folio 184.

64. Archivo DIPPBA, Mesa De, Factor Social, legajo 567, May 1989, folio 170.

65. Archivo DIPPBA, Mesa De, Factor Social, legajo 567, May 1989, folio 170.

66. Archivo DIPPBA, Mesa De, Factor Social, legajo 567, May 1989, folio 171.

67. Archivo DIPPBA, Mesa De, Factor Social, legajo 567, May 1989, folio 229.

68. Archivo DIPPBA, Mesa De, Factor Social, legajo 567, May 1989, folio 303–304.

69. Archivo DIPPBA, Mesa De, Factor Social, legajo 567, May 1989, folio 297.

70. Archivo DIPPBA, Mesa De, Factor Social, legajo 567, May 1989, folio 300.

71. Neufeld and Cravino, "Los saqueos y las ollas populares de 1989 en el Gran Buenos Aires."

72. "De como se entregó alimentos a cambio de evitar un saqueo: Un pacto, un estallido," *Clarín*, May 31, 1989.

73. Archivo DIPPBA, Mesa De, Factor Social, legajo 567, May 1989, folio 290.

74. "'Robamos para darle de comer a nuestros hijos,' dicen saqueadoras de Quilmes," *Diario El Sol* (Quilmes), May 30, 1989.

75. "Temor en comercios minoristas," *Diario El Sol* (Quilmes), May 29, 1989.

76. Archivo DIPPBA, Mesa De, Factor Social, legajo 567, May 1989, folio 128.

77. For a discussion of the question of collective violence in the context of food riots, see Javier Auyero, *Routine Politics and Violence in Argentina: The Gray Zone of State Power* (New York: Cambridge University Press, 2007), 135.

78. "'Robamos para darle de comer a nuestros hijos.'"

79. "'Robamos para darle de comer a nuestros hijos.'"

80. "'Cacerolazo de amas de casa en plaza de mayo," *Clarín*, May 27, 1989.

81. See Camilo Trumper's analysis of the "March of the Empty Pots" in chapter 2 of his *Ephemeral Histories: Public Art, Politics, and the Struggle for the Streets in Chile* (Oakland: University of California Press, 2016).

82. "Protestas a la cacerola," *Sur*, May 24, 1989.

83. Archivo DIPPBA, Mesa De, Factor Social, legajo 567, May 1989, folio 145.

84. Archivo DIPPBA, Mesa De, Factor Social, legajo 567, May 1989, folio 300.

85. Archivo DIPPBA, Mesa De, Factor Social, legajo 567, May 1989, folio 189.

86. Archivo DIPPBA, Mesa De, Factor Social, legajo 567, May 1989, folio 240.

87. Archivo DIPPBA, Mesa De, Factor Social, legajo 567, May 1989, folio 191.

88. For a discussion of working with declassified police and intelligence reports, see Louise Walker and Tanalís Padilla, eds., "Spy Reports: Content, Methodology and Historiography in Mexico's Recently-opened Secret Police Archives," special issue, *Journal of Iberian and Latin American Research* 19, no. 1 (July 2013).

89. Archivo DIPPBA, Mesa De, Factor Social, legajo 567, April 1989, folio 27–28.

90. "Pugliese responsibilizó de los desmanes a la ultraizquierda," *La Nación*, May 30, 1989.

91. "Saquearon en Rosario unos 20 supermercados," *La Prensa*, May 29, 1989 (pilfer stores throughout the province); and "Extienden su desborde el extremism y la protesta," *La Prensa*, May 31, 1989 ("holding on to ideologies that [belonged in a] museum").

92. "Condenan los saqueos a los supermercados," *La Nación*, May 31, 1989.

93. "Podrían suspender el abastecimiento al PAN," *Clarín*, May 26, 1989.

94. Roig died shortly after assuming his post in July 1989. He was replaced by Néstor Rapanelli, another Bunge & Born executive.

95. "Albamonte será el titular de Comercio Interior de Menem," *Ambito Financiero*, June 6, 1989.

96. The full text of Alfonsín's speech can be found in "Alfonsín anunció su renuncia para el 30 de junio y forzó un acuerdo," *Ambito Financiero*, June 13, 1989.

97. "Alfonsín anunció su renuncia para el 30 de junio y forzó un acuerdo."

98. *Clarín*, July 8, 1989.

99. Rapoport, *Historia económica, política y social de la Argentina*, 752.

100. Rapoport, *Historia económica, política y social de la Argentina*, 787.

101. Menem had already discussed plans for an amnesty before his election. On October 8, 1989, he pardoned 216 military officers and 64 civilians. The announcement of the pardons also included plans for a second round, which occurred in December 1990, following a final military uprising. The second round of pardons freed the main junta leaders, as well as prominent members of the left-wing Montoneros organization.

102. For a discussion of the repatriation of Rosas, see chapter 4 in Brenda Werth, *Theater, Performance, and Memory Politics in Argentina* (New York: Palgrave Macmillan, 2010).

103. "Homenaje desde el puerto a la Recoleta," *Clarín*, October 1, 1989.

104. "Homenaje desde el puerto a la Recoleta"; and "Meném llamó a eliminar el sectarismo al recibir los restos de Rosas," *Clarín*, October 1, 1989.

105. Novaro, *Argentina en el fin de siglo*, 341.

106. Alexandre Roig, *La moneda imposible: La convertibilidad argentina de 1991* (Buenos Aires: Fondo de Cultura Económica, 2016).

EPILOGUE

1. This number is based on figures cited in Javier Auyero, *Routine Politics and Violence in Argentina: The Gray Zone of State Power* (New York: Cambridge University Press, 2007). For a detailed analysis of the December 2001 uprisings, see Nicolás Iñigo Carrera and María Celia Cotarelo, "Génesis y desarrollo de la insurrección espontánea de diciembre de 2001 en Argentina," in Gerardo Caetano, ed., *Sujetos sociales y nuevas formas de protesta en la historia reciente de América Latina* (Buenos Aires: CLASCO, 2006), 49–92. And for a report on the 2001 uprisings presented to the Inter-American Commission on Human Rights, see Centro de Estudios Legales y Sociales (CELS), "La protesta social en la Argentina durante diciembre del 2001" (Buenos Aires: Centro de Estudios Legales y Sociales, 2002), www.cels .org.ar/common/documentos/protesta_social_en_argentina_mar2002.pdf.

2. Ronaldo Munck, "Introduction: A Thin Democracy," in "Argentina Under Menem," special issue, *Latin American Perspectives* 24, no. 6 (November 1997): 9.

3. For more on the Alianza government, see Alfredo Pucciarelli and Ana Castellani, eds., *Los años de la alianza: La crisis del orden neoliberal* (Buenos Aires: Siglo Veintiuno, 2015).

4. Mónica Gordillo, "La violencia anunciada: El ruido de las ollas vacías en 2001," in Gabriel DiMeglio and Sergio Serulnikov, eds., *La larga historia de los saqueos en la Argen-*

tina: *De la independencia a nuestros días* (Buenos Aires: Siglo Veintiuno Editores, 2017), 201–225; and Auyero, *Routine Politics and Violence in Argentina*, 135–137.

5. Auyero, *Routine Politics and Violence in Argentina*, 6.

6. Jorge Novak, "Homilía en la Solemnidad del Cuerpo y Sangre de Cristo, 2001: Ultima homilía pública," in Eduardo de la Serna, ed., *Padre Obispo Jorge Novak, svd.: Amigo de los pobres, profeta de la esperanza* (Buenos Aires: Editorial Guadalupe, 2002), 388–389.

BIBLIOGRAPHY

ARCHIVES CONSULTED

Archivo de Historia Oral de la Argentina Contemporánea, Programa de Historia Política del Instituto de Investigaciones Gino Germani, Universidad de Buenos Aires (UBA)

Archivo de la DIPPBA (Dirección de Inteligencia de la Policía de la Provincia de Buenos Aires)
Mesa A: comunal, estudiantil, prensa (1981–1991)
Mesa B: económico, gremial, laboral (1981–1991)
Mesa DE: religioso (1981–1991)
Mesa Referencia: factor social (1983–1990)

Archivo General de la Nación Argentina
Departamento Archivo Intermedio: "Presidencia de la Nación. Secretaria Privada, Presidencia Alfonsín (1983–1989)"

Archivo Histórico de Radio y Televisión Argentina (RTA)

Archivo Nacional de la Memoria, Argentina
Fondo Comisión Nacional sobre la Desaparición de Personas

Biblioteca y Archivo Histórico de la Unión Cívica Radical (UCR)
"Carpetas Alfonsín," 1–2 (1965–1999)

Memoria Abierta, Archivo Oral

Ministerio de Economía, Secretaria Comercio Interior, 1985–1988

New York Public Library
"Argentine Political Campaign Literature Collection, 1983"

Obispado de Quilmes
  "Homilias, Circulares, Mensajes" (1981–1989)
Personal archives of Patricia Aguirre
Personal archives of Elizabeth Jelin
Personal archives of Catalina Vera

PERIODICALS

Ámbito Financiero (1983–1989)

Boletín Oficial de la República Argentina (1984–1989)

Clarín (1978–1990)

Ciudad Futura (1988–1991)

Compartiendo (1980–1983)

Diario Popular (1979)

Gente (1982–1989)

Humor (1983–1989)

La Nación (1983–1988)

La Prensa (1989)

The New York Times (1983–1989)

Página 12 (1987–1989)

Revista Al Sur (1982)

El Sol (1978–1989)

Somos (1984–1989)

Tiempo Argentino (1983–1984)

The Washington Post (1987–1988)

INTERVIEWS

Patricia Aguirre

Alberto Albamonte

Maria del Carmen Banzas de Moreau

Jorge Cobos

Arturo Goetz

Ricardo Mazzorín

Leopoldo Moreau

Aldo Neri

Enrique Nosiglia

Jesús Rodríguez

Catalina Vera

Eduardo Vides

PUBLISHED PRIMARY AND SECONDARY MATERIALS

Aboy Carlés, Gerardo. "De Malvinas al menemismo: Renovación y contrarrenovación en el peronismo." *Revista Sociedad*, no. 10 (November 1996): 5–31.

———. *Las dos fronteras de la democracia argentina: La reformulación de las identidades políticas de Alfonsín a Menem*. Rosario: Homo Sapiens Ediciones, 2001.

Abrad, César Tcach, and Celso Rodríguez. *Illia: Un sueño breve*. Buenos Aires: Edhasa, 2006.

Acha, Omar. "Sociedad civil y sociedad política durante el primer peronismo." *Desarrollo Económico* 44, no. 174 (July–September 2004): 199–230.

Acuña, Carlos, and Adam Przeworski, eds. *Juicio, castigos y memorias: Derechos humanos y la justicia en la política argentina*. Buenos Aires: Ediciones Nueva Visión, 1995.

Acuña, Carlos, and Catalina Smulovitz. *¿Ni olvido ni perdón? Derechos humanos y tensiones cívico-militares en la transición argentina*. Buenos Aires: CEDES, 1991.

Acuña, Marcelo Luis. *Alfonsín y el poder económico: El fracaso de la concertación y los pactos corporativos entre 1983 y 1989*. Buenos Aires: Ediciones Corregidor, 1995.

Adair, Jennifer. "Democratic Utopias: The Argentine Transition to Democracy through Letters, 1983–1989." *The Americas* 72, no. 2 (April 2015): 221–247.

———. "Popular Politics, the Catholic Church, and the Making of Argentina's Transition to Democracy, 1978–1983." In Benjamin Bryce and David Sheinin, eds., *Making Citizens in Argentina*, 161–179. Pittsburgh: University of Pittsburgh Press, 2017.

Adamovsky, Ezequiel. "Acerca de la relación entre el Radicalismo argentino y la 'clase media' (una vez más)." *Hispanic Amercian Historial Review* 89, no. 2 (May 2009): 209–251.

———. *Historia de la clase media argentina: Apogeo y decadencia de una ilusión, 1919–2003*. Buenos Aires: Planeta, 2009.

Adelman, Jeremy, ed. *Colonial Legacies: The Problem of Persistence in Latin American History*. New York: Routledge, 1999.

Aguilar, Sandra. "Nutrition and Modernity: Milk Consumption in 1940s and 1950s Mexico." In "Radical Foodways," special issue, *Radical History Review* 110 (Spring 2011): 36–58.

Aguirre, Patricia. "El P.A.N.—Programa Alimentario Nacional—Informe sobre su implementación entre los años 1984 y 1989." Unpublished report. Buenos Aires, May 1990.

Albamonte, Alberto. "El inicio de la UCEDE" (Buenos Aires). Unpublished manuscript in author's possession, n.d.

Alfonsín, Raúl. *Ahora, mi propuesta política*. Buenos Aires: Sudamericana/Planeta, 1983.

———. *Democracia y consenso*. 1st ed. Buenos Aires: Corregidor, 1996.

———. *Inédito: Una batalla contra la dictadura (1966–1972)*. Buenos Aires: Editorial Legasa, 1986.

————. *Memoria política: Transición a la democracia y derechos humanos.* 1st ed. Buenos Aires: Fondo de Cultura Económica de Argentina, 2004.

————. *Qué es el radicalismo.* Buenos Aires: Sudamericana, 1983.

Alonso, Paula. *Entre la Revolución y las urnas: Los orígenes de la UCR y la política argentina en los años '90.* Buenos Aires: Sudamericana-Universidad de San Andrés, 1994.

Altamirano, Carlos. "'La lucha por la idea': El proyecto de la renovación peronista." In Marco Novaro and Vicente Palermo, eds., *La historia reciente: Argentina en democracia,* 59–74. Buenos Aires: Edhasa, 2004.

Alvarez, Sonia. *Engendering Democracy in Brazil: Women's Movements in Transition Politics.* Princeton, NJ: Princeton University Press, 1990.

Alvear, Idelber. *The Untimely Present: Postdictatorial Latin American Fiction and the Task of Mourning.* Durham, NC: Duke University Press, 1999.

Andrews, George Reid, and Herrick Chapman, eds. *The Social Construction of Democracy, 1870–1990.* New York: New York University Press, 1995.

Appadurai, Arjun, ed. *The Social Life of Things: Commodities in Cultural Perspective.* Cambridge, UK: Cambridge University Press, 1986.

Aricó, José. *La cola del diablo: Itinerario de Gramsci en América Latina.* Buenos Aires: Puntosur, 1988.

Armstrong, Warwick. "Hunger and Monetarism in Buenos Aires, 1976–1983: A Food Systems Approach." *Boletin de Estudios Latinoamericanos y del Caribe* 45 (December 1988): 29–45.

Aruguete, Eugenia. *De la recuperación de la democracia a la profundización de los legados dictatoriales: Concentración del poder económico y afianzamiento político de la gran burguesía en la Argentina de los ochenta.* Buenos Aires: Ediciones Cooperativas, 2010.

Auyero, Javier. *Contentious Lives: Two Argentine Women, Two Protests, and the Quest for Recognition.* Durham, NC: Duke University Press, 2003.

————. *Poor People's Politics: Peronist Survival Networks and the Legacy of Evita.* Durham, NC: Duke University Press, 2000.

————. *Routine Politics and Violence in Argentina: The Gray Zone of State Power.* New York: Cambridge University Press, 2007.

Ayala, Fernando, and Juan José Jusid. *Plata dulce.* Aries Cinematográfica Argentina, 1982.

Azpiazu, Daniel, Eduardo Basualdo, and Miguel Khavisse. *El nuevo poder económico en la Argentina de los años 80.* Buenos Aires: Editorial Legasa, 1986.

Barry, Carolina. *Evita capitana: El Partido Peronista Femenino, 1949–1955.* Buenos Aires: Editorial Eduntref, 2009.

Barsky, Osvaldo, and Jorge Gelman. *Historia del agro argentino: Desde la conquista hasta finales del siglo XX.* Buenos Aires: Mondadori, 2001.

Basualdo, Eduardo. *Estudios de historia económica argentina: Desde mediados del siglo XX a la actualidad.* Buenos Aires: Siglo Veintiuno Editories, 2010.

Bethell, Leslie, and Ian Roxborough. *Latin America Between the Second World War and the Cold War, 1944–1948.* Cambridge, UK: Cambridge University Press, 1992.

Blaustein, Eduardo, and Martín Zubieta, eds. *Decíamos ayer: La prensa argentina bajo el proceso.* Buenos Aires: Ediciones Colihue, 1998.

Botana, Natalio R. *El orden conservado: La política argentina entre 1880 y 1916.* Buenos Aires: Hyspamérica, 1985.

Brennan, James. *Argentina's Missing Bones: Revisiting the History of the Dirty War.* Oakland: University of California Press, 2018.

———, ed. *Peronism and Argentina.* Wilmington, DE: SR Books, 1998.

———. "Prolegomenon to Neoliberalism: The Political Economy of Populist Argentina, 1943–1976." *Latin American Perspectives* 34, no. 3 (May 2007): 49–66.

Brenta, Noemí. *Argentina atrapada: Historia de las relaciones con el FMI, 1956–2006.* Buenos Aires: Ediciones Cooperativas, 2008.

Bruey, Alison. *Bread, Justice, and Liberty: Grassroots Activism and Human Rights in Pinochet's Chile.* Madison: University of Wisconsin Press, 2018.

Bryce, Benjamin. "Paternal Communities: Social Welfare and Immigration in Argentina, 1880–1930," *Journal of Social History* 49, no. 1 (2015): 213–236.

Brysk, Allison. *The Politics of Human Rights in Argentina: Protest, Change, and Democratization.* Stanford, CA: Stanford University Press, 1994.

Buchanan, Paul G. "Exorcising Collective Ghosts: Recent Argentine Writings on Politics, Economics, Social Movements, and Popular Culture." *Latin American Research Review* 25, no. 7 (1990): 177–203.

Burgos, Raúl. *Los gramscianos argentinos: Cultura y política en la experiencia de Pasado y Presente.* Buenos Aires: Siglo XXI Editores de Argentina, 2004.

Burns, Kathryn. *Into the Archive: Writing and Power in Colonial Peru.* Durham, NC: Duke University Press, 2010.

Cafiero, Antonio. *Testimonios: Del '45 y del 2000 también.* Buenos Aires: Nuevo Hacer, Grupo Editor Latinoamericano, 1995.

Caimari, Lila. *Perón y la iglesia católica: religión, estado y sociedad en la Argentina, 1943–1955.* Buenos Aires: Grupo Editorial Planetas, Emecé, 2010.

Cámara de Diputados, República Argentina, Comisión de Comercio Interior, H. Camara de Diputados Taquígrafos, Buenos Aires, Argentina, 1988.

Canelo, Paula. "La política contra la economía: Los elencos militares frente al plan económico de Martínez de Hoz durante el Proceso de Reorganización Nacional (1976–1981)." In Alfredo Pucciarelli, ed., *Empresarios, tecnócratas y militares: La trama corporativa de la ultima dictadura,* 219–312. Buenos Aires: Siglo XXI, 2004.

———. *La política secreta de la última dictadura Argentina: A 40 años del golpe de Estado (1976–1983).* Buenos Aires: Edhasa, 2016.

Cardoso, Fernando Henrique, and Enzo Faletto. *Dependency and Development in Latin America.* Translated by Marjory Mattingly Urquidi. Berkeley: University of California Press, 1979.

Carnovale, Vera. "De Entre Todos a La Tablada: Redefiniciones y permanencias del ideario setentista," *Pol/His* 6, no. 12 (2013): 244–264.

Carrasai, Sebastián. *The Argentina Silent Majority: Middle Classes, Politics, Violence, and Memory in the Seventies.* Durham, NC: Duke University Press, 2014.

Cardoso, Fernando Henrique. *Autoritarismo e Democratização.* Rio de Janeiro: Paz e Terra, 1975.

Castellani, Ana. *Estado, empresas, y empresarios: La construcción de ámbitos privilegiados de acumulación entre 1966 y 1989.* Buenos Aires: Prometeo Libros, 2009.

Castellani, Ana, and Alejandro Gaggero. "Estado y grupos económicos en la Argentina de los noventa." In Alfredo Pucciarelli, ed., *Los años de Menem: La construcción del orden neoliberal,* 263–292. Buenos Aires: Siglo Veintiuno Ediciones, 2011.

Catterberg, Edgardo. *Los argentinos frente a la política: cultura política y opinion pública en la transición argentina a la democracia.* Buenos Aires: Grupo Editorial Planeta, 1989.

Caulfield, Sueann. *In Defense of Honor: Morality, Modernity, and Nation in Early Twentieth-Century Brazil.* Durham, NC: Duke University Press, 2000.

Cavarozzi, Marcelo. *Autoritarismo y democracia.* Buenos Aires: Centro Editor de América Latina, 1983.

———. "Peronism and Radicalism: Argentina's Transitions in Perspective." In Paul Drake and Eduardo Silva, eds., *Elections and Democratization in Latin America,* 143–174. San Diego: Center for Latin American and Iberian Studies, 1986.

Cavarozzi, Marcelo, and Juan Manuel Abal Medina, eds. *El asedio a la política: Los partidos latinoamericanos en la era neoliberal.* Rosario: Homo Sapiens Ediciones y Konrad Adenauer Stiftung, 2002.

Caviglia, Mariana. *Dictadura, vida cotidiana y clases medias.* Buenos Aires: Prometeo Libros, 2006.

Centro de Estudios Legales y Sociales (CELS). "La protesta social en la Argentina durante diciembre del 2001." Buenos Aires: Centro de Estudios Legales y Sociales, 2002.

Centro de Investigaciones Sociales sobre el Estado y la Administración (CISEA). *Argentina 1983.* Buenos Aires: Centro Editor de América Latina,1984.

Cerutti, Gabriela, and Sergio Ciancaglini. *El Octavo Círculo: Crónica y entretelones del poder menemista.* Buenos Aires: Editorial Planeta Argentina, 1991.

CESNI, Centro de Estudios Sobre Nutrición Infantil. "Seminario sobre situación nutricional de los niños en Argentina." Publicacíon CESNI no. 2. Buenos Aires: CESNI, August 1983.

Chambers, Sarah. "Letters and Salons: Women Reading and Writing the Nation in the Nineteenth Century." In Sarah Castro-Klarén and John Chasteen, eds., *Beyond Imagined Communities: Reading and Writing the Nation in Nineteenth-Century Latin America,* 54–83. Baltimore, MD: Johns Hopkins University Press, 2003.

Cheresky, Isidoro. *La inovación política: Política y derechos en la Argentina contemporánea.* Buenos Aires: EUDEBA, 1999.

Collier, David, ed. *The New Authoritarianism in Latin America.* Princeton, NJ: Princeton University Press, 1979.

Comisión Nacional sobre la Desaparación de Personas (CONADEP). *Nunca Más: The Report on the Argentine National Commission on the Disappeared.* Translated by Writers and Scholars International, Ltd. New York: Farrar Straus Giroux, 1986.

Congreso de la Nación, República Argentina. *Diario de sesiones de la Cámara de Diputados de la Nación, 1983: Sesiones extraordianarias, Tomo I.* Buenos Aires: n.p., 1983.

Constenla, Julia. *Raúl Alfonsín: Biografía no desautorizada.* Buenos Aires: Vergara, 2009.

Coronil, Fernando, and Julie Skurski. "Dismembering and Remembering the Nation: The Semantics of Political Violence in Venezuela." *Comparative Studies in Society and History* 33, no. 2 (April 1991): 288–337.

Cosse, Isabella. *Estigmas de nacimiento: Peronismo y orden familiar, 1946–1955.* Sección de obras de historia. Buenos Aires: Fondo de Cultura Económica—Universidad San Andrés, 2006.

Craviotto, José A. *Historia de Quilmes: Desde sus origenes hasta 1941.* La Plata, Argentina: Provincia de Buenos Aires, Ministerio de Educación, Publicaciones del Archivo Historico de la Provincia, "Doctor Ricardo Levene," 1967.

Crenzel, Emilio. *La historia política del Nunca Más: La memoria de las desapariciones en la Argentina*. Buenos Aires: Siglo Veintiuno Editores Argentina, 2008.

Cuenya, Beatriz, et al. *Condiciones de habitat y de salud de los sectores populares: Un estudio piloto en el asentamiento San Martín de Quilmes*. Buenos Aires: Centro de Estudios Urbanos y Regionales, 1984.

Dahl, Robert. *Polyarchy: Participation and Opposition*. New Haven, CT: Yale University Press, 1971.

de Certeau, Michel. *The Practice of Everyday Life*. Berkeley: University of California Press, 1984.

De la Serna, Eduardo, ed. *Padre Obispo Jorge Novak, svd: Amigo de los pobres, profeta de la esperanza*. Buenos Aires: Editorial Guadalupe, 2002.

Del Franco, Analia. "Consideraciones organizacionales acerca del PAN." In Bernardo Kliksberg, ed., *Como enfrentar la pobreza, estrategias y experiencias organizacionales inovadoras*, 199–251. Buenos Aires: Grupo Editor Latinoamericano, 1989.

Del Mazzo, Gabriel. *Radicalismo: Notas sobre su historia y su doctrina (1922–1952)*. Buenos Aires: Raigal, 1955.

Delich, Francisco. "Demovilización social, reestructuración obrera y cambio sindical." In Peter Waldmann and Ernesto Garzón Valdés, eds., *El Poder militar en la Argentina, 1976–1981*, 101–116. Buenos Aires: Editorial Galerna, 1983.

Derby, Lauren. "Gringo Chickens with Worms." In Gilbert Joseph, Catherine LeGrand, and Ricardo D. Salvatore, eds., *Close Encounters of Empire: Writing the Cultural History of US-Latin American Relations*, 451–493. Durham, NC: Duke University Press, 1998.

———. "In the Shadow of the State: The Politics of Denunciation and Panegyric During the Trujillo Regime in the Dominican Republic, 1940–1958." *Hispanic American Historical Review* 83, no. 2 (May 2003): 295–344.

Di Riz, Liliana. *Radicales y peronistas: El Congreso Nacional entre 1983 y 1989*. Buenos Aires: Centro Editor de América Latina, Instituto de Investigaciones de la Facultad de Ciencias Sociales de la Universidad de Buenos Aires, 1994.

Di Stefano, Roberto, and Loris Zanatta. *Historia de la iglesia argentina: Desde la conquista hasta finales del siglo XX*. Buenos Aires: Grupo Grijalbo Modadori, 2000.

Díaz, Elías. *Estado de derecho y sociedad democrática*. Madrid: *Cuadernos para el diálogo*, 1973.

Díaz, José Antonio, and Alfredo Leuco. *Los Herederos de Alfonsín*. Buenos Aires: Sudamericana/Planeta, 1987.

DiMeglio, Gabriel, and Sergio Serulnikov, eds. *La larga historia de los saqueos en la Argentina. De la Independencia hasta nuestros días*. Buenos Aires: Siglo Veintiunio Editores, 2017.

Diocesis de Quilmes, Subcomisión para el conocimiento de la realidad socieconómica política y cultural. *Realidad Humana y Social de la Diocesis de Quilmes*. Quilmes, September 1982.

"Discurso del Señor Presidente de la Nación, Dr. Raúl R. Alfonsín, desde el balcón de la casa del gobierno, el día 26 de abril de 1985." In *Discursos presidenciales: Recopilación de discursos, mensajes y conferencias de prensa efectuadas por el señor presidente de la nación, doctor Raúl Ricardo Alfonsín*, 2:107. Buenos Aires: Secretaria de Información Pública,

Dirección General de Difusión, 1985. www.lanic.utexas.edu/larrp/pm/sample2/argen tin/alfonsin/851253d.html.

Dos Santos, Theotonio. "The Structure of Dependence." *The American Economic Review* 60, no. 2 (May 1970): 231–236.

Dosman, Edgar. *The Life and Times of Raúl Prebisch*. Montreal: McGill-Queens Press, 2008.

Drake, Paul, ed. *Money Doctors, Foreign Debts, and Economic Reforms in Latin America from the 1890s to the Present*. Wilmington, DE: Scholarly Resources, 1994.

Elena, Eduardo. *Dignifying Argentina: Peronism, Citizenship, and Mass Consumption*. Pittsburgh: Pittsburgh University Press, 2011.

———. "Peronist Consumer Politics and the Problem of Domesticating Markets in Argentina, 1943–1955." *Hispanic American Historical Review* (February 2007): 111–149.

———. "What the People Want: State Planning and Political Participation in Peronist Argentina." *Journal of Latin American Studies* 37, no. 1 (2005): 81–108.

Escobar, Arturo. *Encountering Development: The Making and Unmaking of the Third World*. Princeton, NJ: Princeton University Press, 1995.

Escobar, Arturo, and Sonia E. Alvarez, eds. *The Making of Social Movements in Latin America: Identity, Strategy, and Democracy*. Boulder, CO: Westview Press, 1992.

Esquivel, Juan Cruz. *Detrás de los muros: La iglesia católica en tiempos de Alfonsín y Menem (1983–1999)*. Buenos Aires: Universidad Nacional de Quilmes, 2004.

Etchemendy, Sebastián, and Ruth B. Collier. "Down but Not Out: Union Resurgence and Segmented Neocorporatism in Argentina, 2003–2007." *Politics and Society* 35, no. 3 (September 2007): 363–401.

Feitlowitz, Marguerite. *A Lexicon of Terror: Argentina and the Legacies of Torture*. New York: Oxford University Press, 1999.

Feld, Claudia. "La prensa de la transición ante el problema de los desaparecidos: El discurso del 'show del horror.'" In Claudia Feld and Marina Franco, eds., *Democracia Hora Cero: Actores, políticas y debates en los inicios de la posdictadura*, 269–316. Buenos Aires: Fondo de Cultura Económica, 2015.

Finchelstein, Federico. *The Ideological Origins of the Dirty War: Fascism, Populism, and Dictatorship in Twentieth Century Argentina*. New York: Oxford University Press, 2014.

Fischer, Brodwyn. *A Poverty of Rights: Citizenship and Inequality in Twentieth Century Río de Janeiro*. Stanford, CA: Stanford University Press, 2008.

Fiszbein, Ariel, and Paula Inés Giovagnoli. "Hambre en la argentina." *Desarrollo Económico* 43, no. 172 (2004): 637–656.

Fraga, Rosendo. *La cuestión sindical*. Buenos Aires: Centro de Estudios para la Nueva Minoria, 1990.

Franco, Marina, and Claudia Feld, eds. *Democracia hora cero: Actores, políticas y debates en los inicios de la posdictadura*. Buenos Aires: Fondo de Cultura Económica, 2015.

French, William. "'Cartas y cartas, compadre . . .': Love and Other Letters from Río Frío." In William H. Beezley and Linda Ann Curcio, eds., *Latin American Popular Culture Since Independence*, 2nd ed., 68–84. Lanham, MD: Rowman & Littlefield, 2012.

Fridman, Daniel. "A New Mentality for a New Economy: Performing the Homo economicus in Argentina (1976–83)." *Economy and Society* 39 no. 2 (2010): 271–302.

Fundación de Investigaciones Económicas Latinoamericanas (FIEL). *Control de precios e inflación: La experiencia argentina reciente*. Buenos Aires: Ediciones Manatial, 1990.

Gallo, Edit Rosalía, ed. *Propaganda Política de la UCR, Catálogo de imágenes, 1890–1991.* Buenos Aires: Unión Cívica Radical, Biblioteca, Archivo Histórico y Centro de Documentación, 2010. CD-ROM.

Gallo, Ezequiel, and Silvia Sigal. "La Formación de los Partidos Políticos Contemporáneos—la UCR (1891–1916)." In Torcuato S. Di Tella et al., eds., *Argentina, Sociedad de Masas*, 24–76. Buenos Aires: Eudeba, 1965.

Gargarella, Roberto, María Victoria Murrillo, and Mario Pecheny, eds. *Discutir Alfonsín.* Buenos Aires: Siglo Veintiuno Editories, 2010.

Gaudio, Ricardo, and Andrés Thompson. *Sindicalismo peronista/gobierno radical: Los años del Alfonsín.* Buenos Aires: Fundación Friedrich Ebert & Folios Ediciones, 1990.

Gerchunoff, Pablo, and Lucas Llach. *El ciclo de la ilusión y el desencanto: Un siglo de políticas económicas argentinas.* Buenos Aires: Ariel, 1998.

Germani, Gino. *Política y sociedad en una época de transición: De la sociedad tradicional a la sociedad de masas.* Buenos Aires: Editorial Paídos, 1965.

Giacobone, Carlos Alberto, and Edit Gallo, eds. *Radicalismo: Un siglo al servicio de la Patria.* Buenos Aires: Archivo Histórico y Centro de Documentación, Unión Cívica Radical, 2004.

Gilly, Adolfo, and Rhina Roux, eds. *Cartas a Cuauhtémoc Cárdenas.* Mexico City: Colección Problemas de México, Ediciones Era, 1989.

Golbert, Laura. *De la sociedad de beneficencia a los derechos sociales.* Buenos Aires: Ministerio de Trabajo, Empleo y Seguridad Social, 2010.

González Bombal, Inés. "El diálogo politico: La transición que no fue." Documento CEDES 61. Buenos Aires: CEDES, 1991.

———. *Los vecinazos: Las protestas barriales en el Gran Buenos Aires (1982–1983).* Buenos Aires: IDES, 1988.

Gordillo, Mónica. "La violencia anunciada: El ruido de las ollas vacías en 2001." In Gabriel DiMeglio and Sergio Serulnikov, eds., *La larga historia de los saqueos en la Argentina: De la independencia a nuestros días*, 201–225. Buenos Aires: Siglo Veintiuno Editores, 2017.

Gorelik, Adrián. *La grilla y el parque: Espacio público y cultura urbana en Buenos Aires, 1887–1936.* Buenos Aires: Universidad Nacional de Quilmes, 1998.

Gorini, Ulises. *La rebelión de las madres: Historia de Las Madres de la Plaza de Mayo.* Buenos Aires: Grupo Editorial Norma, 2010.

Gould, Jeff. *To Lead as Equals: Rural Protest and Political Consciousness in Chinandega, Nicaragua, 1912–1979.* Chapel Hill: University of North Carolina Press, 1990.

Gramsci, Antonio. *Selections from the Prison Notebooks.* London: Electric Book Co., 2001.

Grandin, Greg. *Empire's Workshop: Latin America, the United States and the Rise of the New Imperialism.* New York: Metropolitan Books, 2006.

———. "The Instruction of Great Catastrophe: Truth Commissions, National History, and State Formation in Argentina, Chile, and Guatemala." *The American Historical Review* 110, no. 1 (February 2005): 46–67.

———. *The Last Colonial Massacre: Latin America in the Cold War.* Chicago: University of Chicago Press, 2004.

Grimson, Alejandro, and Gabriel Kessler. *On Argentina and the Southern Cone: Neoliberalism and National Imaginations.* New York: Routledge, 2005.

Guissani, Pablo. *Por qué Doctor Alfonsín?* Buenos Aires: Planeta/Sudamericana, 1987.

Guy, Donna. *Creating Charismatic Bonds in Argentina: Letters to Juan and Eva Perón.* Albuquerque: University of New Mexico Press, 2016.

―――. *Women Build the Welfare State: Performing Charity and Creating Rights in Argentina, 1880–1955.* Durham, NC: Duke University Press, 2008.

Halperín Donghi, Tulio. *La larga agonía de la Argentina peronista.* Buenos Aires: Ariel, 1994.

Haney, Lynne. *Inventing the Needy: Gender and the Politics of Welfare in Hungary.* Berkeley: University of California Press, 2002.

Harvey, David. *A Brief History of Neoliberalism.* New York: Oxford University Press, 2005.

Heredia, Mariana. *Cuando los economistas alcanzaron el poder (o cómo se gestó confianza en los expertos).* Buenos Aires: Siglo Veintiuno Editores, 2015.

Herra, Francisco. *Qué es la Coordinadora.* Buenos Aires: Editorial Galerna, 1985.

Hilb, Claudia. "La Tablada: El último acto de la guerrilla setentista." *Lucha armada en la Argentina* 3, no. 9 (2007): 4–22.

Hintze, Susana. *Estrategias alimentarias de sobrevivencia: (Un estudio de caso en el Gran Buenos Aires).* Vols. 1–2. Buenos Aires: Centro Editor de America Latina, 1989.

Hite, Katherine, and Paola Cesarini, eds. *Authoritarian Legacies and Democracy: Latin America and Southern Europe.* Notre Dame, IN: University of Notre Dame Press, 2004.

Hora, Roy. *The Landowners of the Argentine Pampas: A Social and Political History, 1860–1945.* New York: Oxford University Press, 2001.

Horowitz, Joel. *Argentina's Radical Party and Popular Mobilization, 1916–1938.* University Park: Pennsylvania State University Press, 2008.

INDEC (Instituto Nacional de Estadística y Censos). *La Pobreza en el conurbano bonarense.* Buenos Aires: INDEC, 1989.

―――. *La pobreza en la Argentina: Indicadores de necesidades basicas insatisfechas a partir de los datos del Censo Nacional de Población y Vivienda 1980.* Buenos Aires: INDEC, 1984.

―――. *Qué es el Gran Buenos Aires?* Buenos Aires: INDEC, 2003.

Iñigo Carrera, Nicolás, and María Celia Cotarelo. "Génesis y desarrollo de la insurrección espontánea de diciembre de 2001 en Argentina." In Gerardo Caetano, ed., *Sujetos sociales y nuevas formas de protesta en la historia reciente de América Latina,* 49–92. Buenos Aires: CLASCO, 2006.

Iñigo Carrera, Nicolás, María Celia Cotarelo, Elizabeth Gómez, and Federico M. Kindgard. "La revuelta argentina 1989–1990." Documento de Trabajo, no. 4. Buenos Aires: PISMA, 1995.

Isuani, Ernesto A., and Emilio Tenti, eds. *Estado democrático y política social.* Buenos Aires: Editorial Universitaria de Buenos Aires, 1989.

Izaguirre, Inés. "Imagen de clase en los partidos políticos argentinos: El caso del radicalismo." *Revista Latinoamericana de Sociología* 3, no. 2 (July 1967): 196–231.

Izaguirre, Inés, and Zulema Aristizábal. *Las tomas de tierra en la zona sur del Gran Buenos Aires.* Conflictos y procesos de la Historia Argentina Contemporánea. Buenos Aires: Centro Editor de América Latina, 1988.

James, Daniel. *Resistance and Integration: Peronism and the Argentine Working Class, 1946–1976.* New York: Cambridge University Press, 1988.

Jelin, Elizabeth. "La política de la memoria: El movimiento de derechos humanos y la construcción democrática en la Argentina." In Carlos Acuña and Adama Przeworski, eds., *Juicio, castigo y memorias: Derechos humanos y justicia en la política argentina*. Buenos Aires: Nueva Visión, 1995.

———. "Los derechos humanos: Entre el estado y la sociedad." In *Nueva Historia Argentina*, vol. 10, Juan Suriano, ed., *Dictadura y Democracia (1976–2001)*, 507–557. Buenos Aires: Editorial Sudamericana, 2005.

———, ed. *Los nuevos movimientos sociales: Derechos humanos, Obreros, Barrios*. Buenos Aires: Biblioteca Política Argentina, 1985.

———. *Los trabajos de la memoria*. Buenos Aires: Siglo XXI, 2002.

Jelin, Elizabeth, and Eric Hershberg, eds. *Constructing Democracy: Human Rights, Citizenship and Society in Latin America*. Boulder, CO: Westview Press, 1996.

Joseph, Gilbert M., ed. *Reclaiming the Political in Latin American History: Essays from the North*. Durham, NC: Duke University Press, 2001.

Joseph, Gilbert M., and Daniela Spenser, eds. *In From the Cold: Latin America's New Encounter with the Cold War*. Durham, NC: Duke University Press, 2008.

Karush, Matthew. *Musicians in Transit: Argentina and the Globalization of Popular Music*. Durham, NC: Duke University Press, 2017.

———. *Workers or Citizens: Democracy and Identity in Rosario, Argentina (1912–1930)*. Albuquerque: University of New Mexico Press, 2002.

Keck, Margaret E., and Kathryn Sikkink. *Activists Beyond Borders: Advocacy Networks in International Politics*. Stanford, CA: Stanford University Press, 1998.

Kedar, Claudia. *The International Monetary Fund in Latin America: The Argentine Puzzle in Context*. Philadelphia, PA: Temple University Press, 2013.

Kelly, Patrick William. *Sovereign Emergencies: Latin America and the Making of Global Human Rights Politics*. New York: Cambridge University Press, 2018.

Kessler, Gabriel, and Victor Armory. "Imágenes de una sociedad en crisis: Cuestión social, pobreza y desempleo." In Marcos Novaro and Vicente Palermo, eds., *La Historia reciente: Argentina en democracia*, 91–113. Buenos Aires, Edhasa, 2004.

Kessler, Gabriel, and Silvia Sigal. "La hiperinflación en Argentina: Comportamientos y representaciones sociales." In Dario Canton, and Jorge Raúl Jorrat, eds., *La Investigación social en Argentina a 40 años de la refundación del Instituto de Sociología*, 155–187. Buenos Aires: Instituto de Investigaciones Gino Germani y Oficina de Publicaciones del CBC, Universidad de Buenos Aires, 1997.

Kulfas, Matías, and Martín Schorr. *La deuda externa argentina: Diagnóstico y lineamientos propositivos para su reestructuración*. Buenos Aires: Fundación OSDE-CIEP, 2003.

Laclau, Ernesto. *Politics and Ideology in Marxist Theory: Capitalism, Fascism, and Populism*. London: Verso, 1977.

Laclau, Ernesto, and Chantal Mouffe. *Hegemony and Socialist Strategy: Towards a Radical Democratic Politics*. London: Verso, 1985.

Lesgart, Cecilia. *Usos de la transición a la democracia: Ensayo, ciencia y política en la década del '80*. Rosario, Santa Fe: Homo Sapiens Ediciones, 2005.

Levitsky, Steven. *Transforming Labor-Based Parties in Latin America: Argentine Peronism in Comparative Perspective*. New York: Cambridge University Press, 2003.

Levitsky, Steven, and María Victoria Murillo, eds. *Argentine Democracy: The Politics of Institutional Weakness.* State College: Pennsylvania State University Press, 2006.

Liberti, Luis O. SVD, ed. *Jorge Novak: Testigo y sembrador de esperanza.* Buenos Aires: Editorial Guadalupe, 2006.

Linz, Juan, and Alfred Stepan, eds. *The Breakdown of Democratic Regimes: Latin America.* Baltimore, MD: Johns Hopkins University Press, 1978.

———. *Problems of Democratic Transition and Consolidation: Southern Europe, South America, and Post-Communist Europe.* Baltimore, MD: Johns Hopkins University Press, 1996.

Lockhart, John. "Letters and People to Spain." In *Of Things of the Indies: Essays Old and New in Early Latin American History,* 81–97. Stanford, CA: Stanford University Press, 1999.

Lockhart, John, and Enrique Otte. *Letters and People of the Spanish Indies, Sixteenth Century.* Cambridge, UK: Cambridge University Press, 1976.

Lorenz, Federico. *Las guerras por las Malvinas.* Buenos Aires: Edhasa, 2006.

———. *Los zapatos de Carlitos: Una historia de los trabajadores navales de Tigre en la década del setenta.* Buenos Aires: Grupo Editorial Norma, 2007.

———. "Ungidos por el infortunio: Los soldados de Malvinas en la posdictadura; entre el relato heroico y la victimización." In Patricia Funes, ed., *Revolución, dictadura, y democracia: Logicas militantes y militares en la historia argentina en el contexto latinoamericano,* 225–246. Buenos Aires: Imago Mundi, 2013.

Loveman, Brian, and Thomas M. Davies, eds. *The Politics of Antipolitics: The Military in Latin America.* Lincoln: University of Nebraska Press, 1978.

Manguel, Romina, and Javier Romero. *Vale todo: Biografía no autorizada de Daniel Hadad.* Buenos Aires: Ediciones B Argentina, Grupo Zeta, 2004.

Marchesi, Aldo. *Latin America's Radical Left: Rebellion and Cold War in the Global 1960s.* New York: Cambridge University Press, 2017.

Markarian, Vania. *Left in Transformation: Uruguayan Exiles and the Latin American Human Rights Networks, 1967–1984.* New York: Routledge, 2005.

Martínez, Oscar. "El escenario: Febrero–julio de 1989; Terrorismo económico y desestabilización política." In Atilio Borón et al., eds., *El Menemato: Radiografía de dos años del gobierno de Carlos Menem,* 13–46. Buenos Aires: Ediciones Letra Buena, 1991.

McCann, Bryan. *Hard Times in the Marvelous City: From Dictatorship to Democracy in the Favelas of Rio de Janeiro.* Durham, NC: Duke University Press, 2014.

McGuire, James W. *Peronism without Perón: Unions, Parties, and Democracy in Argentina.* Stanford, CA: Stanford University Press, 1997.

Merklen, Denis. *Pobres ciudadanos: Las clases populares en la era democrática, Argentina, 1983–2003.* Buenos Aires: Gorla, 2005.

Midre, George. "Bread or Solidarity? Argentine Social Policies, 1983–1990." *Journal of Latin American Studies* 24, no. 2 (May 1992): 343–373.

Mignone, Emilio F. *Derechos humanos y sociedad: El caso argentino.* Buenos Aires: Centro de Estudios Legales y Sociales and Ediciones del Pensamiento Nacional, 1991.

———. *Witness to the Truth: The Complicity of Church and Dictatorship in Argentina.* Maryknoll, NY: Orbis Books, 1988.

Milanesio, Natalia. "Food Politics and Consumption in Peronist Argentina." *Hispanic American Historical Review* 90, no. 1 (February 2010): 75–108.

——. "Gender and Generation: The University Reform Movement in Argentina, 1918." In "Kith and Kin: Interpersonal Relationships and Cultural Practices," special issue, *Journal of Social History* 39, no. 2 (Winter 2005): 505–529.

——. *Workers Go Shopping in Argentina: The Rise of Popular Consumer Culture.* Albuquerque: University of New Mexico Press, 2013.

Mintz, Sidney, and Christine Dubois. "The Anthropology of Food and Eating." *Annual Review of Anthropology* 31 (2002): 99–119.

Moore, Barrington. *Social Origins of Dictatorship and Democracy: Lord and Peasant in the Making of the Modern World.* Boston: Beacon Press, 1966.

Mora y Araujo, Manuel. "La naturaleza de la coalición alfonsinista." In Natalio R. Botana, et al., eds., *La Argentina Electoral*, 89–107. Buenos Aires: Editorial Sudamericana, 1985.

Morales Solá, Joaquín. *Asalto a la ilusion.* Buenos Aires: Planeta, 1990.

Morero, Sergio, Ariel Eidelman, and Guido Lichtman, eds. *La noche de los bastones largos.* Buenos Aires: Nuevohacer, 2002.

Moyn, Samuel. *The Last Utopia: Human Rights in History.* Cambridge, MA: Belknap, 2010.

Muiño, Oscar. *Alfonsín: Mitos y verdades del padre de la democracia.* Buenos Aires: Aguilar, 2013.

——. *La otra juventud: Protagonistas y relato de la Junta Coordinadora Nacional de la Juventud Radical (1968–1983).* Buenos Aires: Corregidor, 2011.

——. *Los días de la Coordinadora: Políticas, ideas, medios y sociedad (1968–1983).* Buenos Aires: Corregidor, 2011.

Munck, Ronaldo. "Introduction: A Thin Democracy." In "Argentina Under Menem," special issue, *Latin American Perspectives* 24, no. 6 (November 1997): 5–21.

Murillo, María Victoria. "¿Las corporaciones o los votos?" In Roberto Gargarella, María Victoria Murillo, and Mario Pecheny, eds., *Discutir Alfonsín*, 139–159. Buenos Aires: Siglo Veintiuno Editories, 2010.

Murmis, Miguel, and Juan Carlos Portantiero. *Estudios sobre los origenes del Peronismo.* Buenos Aires: Siglo XXI Ediciones, 2004.

Mustapic, Ana María. "Del Partido Peronista al Partido Justicialista: Las transformaciones de un partido carismático." In Marcelo Cavarozzi, and Juan Manuel Abal Medina, eds., *El asedio a la política: Los partidos latinoamericanos en la era neoliberal*, 137–162. Rosario: Homo Sapiens Ediciones, 2002.

Navarrete, Jorge. "Foreign Policy and International Financial Negotiations: The External Debt and the Cartegena Consensus." *CEPAL Review*, no. 27 (December 1985): 7–25.

Neufeld, María Rosa, and María Cristina Cravino. "Los saqueos y las ollas populares de 1989 en el Gran Buenos Aires: Pasado y presente de una experiencia formativa." *Revista de antropología* 44, no. 2 (2001): 147–172.

Nino, Carlos Santiago. *Radical Evil on Trial.* New Haven, CT: Yale University Press, 1998.

Novak, Jorge. "Homilía en la Solemnidad del Cuerpo y Sangre de Cristo, 2001: Ultima homilía pública," in Eduardo de la Serna, ed., *Padre Obispo Jorge Novak, svd.: Amigo de los pobres, profeta de la esperanza*, 388–389. Buenos Aires: Editorial Guadalupe, 2002.

Novaro, Marcos. *Argentina en el fin del siglo: Democracia, mercado y nación (1983-2001).* Historia Argentina, vol. 10. Buenos Aires: Paídos, 2009.

———. "Formación, desarrollo y declive del consenso alfonsinista sobre derechos humanos." In Roberto Gargarella, María Victoria Murillo, and Mario Pecheny, eds., *Discutir Alfonsín*, 41–65. Buenos Aires: Siglo Veintiuno Editories, 2010.

Novaro, Marcos, and Vicente Palermo, eds. *Historia reciente: Argentina en democracia*. Buenos Aires: Edhasa, 2004.

———. *La dictadura Militar, 1976–1983: Del golpe de estado a la restauración democrática*. Historia Argentina, vol. 9. Buenos Aires: Paidós, 2003.

Novick, Susana. *IAPI: Auge y decadencia*. Buenos Aires: Centro Editor de América Latina, 1986.

Nun, José. *Crisis económica y despidos en masa: Dos estudios de casos*. Buenos Aires: Editorial Legasa, 1989.

Nun, José, and Mario Lattuada. *El gobierno de Alfonsín y las corporaciones agrarias*. Buenos Aires: Manatial, 1991.

Nun, José, and Juan Carlos Portantiero, eds. *Ensayos sobre la transición democrática en la Argentina*. Buenos Aires: Puntosur S.R.L., 1987.

O'Donnell, Guillermo. *Counterpoints: Selected Essays on Authoritarianism and Democratization*. Notre Dame, IN: University of Notre Dame Press, 1999.

———. "Illusions about Consolidation." *Journal of Democracy* 7, no. 2 (April 1996): 34–51.

———. *Modernization and Bureaucratic-Authoritarianism*. Berkeley: University of California Press, 1973.

O'Donnell, Guillermo, Philippe C. Schmitter, and Laurence Whitehead, eds. *Transitions from Authoritarian Rule: Prospects for Democracy*; *Transitions from Authoritarian Rule: Southern Europe*; *Transitions from Authoritarian Rule: Latin America*; *Transitions from Authoritarian Rule: Comparative Perspectives*; and *Transitions from Authoritarian Rule: Tentative Conclusions about Uncertain Democracies*. Woodrow Wilson Center series. 5 vols. Baltimore, MD: Johns Hopkins University Press, 1986.

O'Dougherty, Maureen. *Consumption Intensified: The Politics of Middle Class Daily Life in Brazil*. Durham, NC: Duke University Press, 2002.

Ortiz, Ricardo, and Martín Schorr. "La economía política del gobierno de Alfonsín: Creciente subordinación al poder económico durante la 'década perdida.'" In Alfredo Pucciarelli, ed., *Los años de Alfonsín: ¿El poder de la democracia o la democracia del poder?*, 291–333. Buenos Aires: Siglo Veintiuno Editores, 2006.

Ossona, Jorge. *Punteros, malandras y porongas: Ocupación de tierras y usos políticos de la pobreza*. Buenos Aires: Siglo Veintiuno Editores, 2014.

Ostiguy, Pierre, and Warwick Armstrong. *La evolución del consumo alimenticio en la argentina, 1974–1984*. Buenos Aires: Centro Editor de América Latina, 1987.

Palermo, Vicente. *Sal en las heridas: Malvinas en la cultura argentina contemporánea*. Buenos Aires: Sudamericana, 2007.

Patel, Raj, and Philip McMichael. "A Political Economy of the Food Riot." *Review: A Journal of the Fernand Braudel Center* 32, no. 1 (2009): 9–35.

Perelmiter, Luisina. *Burocracia plebeya: La trastienda de la asistencia social en la argentina*. Buenos Aires: UNSAM Edita de Universidad Nacional de General San Martín, 2016.

Persello, Ana Virginia. *Historia del Radicalismo*. Buenos Aires: Edhasa, 2007.

Pesce, Julieta. "Política y economía durante el primer año del gobierno de Raúl Alfonsín: La gestión del ministro Grinspun." In Alfredo Pucciarelli, ed., *Los años de Alfonsín: ¿El*

poder de la democracia o la democracia del poder?, 367–412. Buenos Aires: Siglo Veintiuno, 2006.

Pilcher, Jeffrey M. *Food in World History*. New York: Routledge, 2006.

———. *¡Que vivan los tamales! Food and the Making of Mexican Identity*. Albuquerque:
University of New Mexico Press, 1998.

———. *The Sausage Rebellion: Public Health, Private Enterprise, and Meat in Mexico City,
1890–1917*. Albuquerque: University of New Mexico Press, 2006.

Pite, Rebekah. *Creating a Common Table in Twentieth-Century Argentina: Doña Petrona,
Women, and Food*. Chapel Hill: University of North Carolina Press, 2013.

Pittaluga, Roberto. "Apuntes para pensar la historia del pasado reciente." *El Rodaballo:
Revista de política y cultura* 10, no. 15 (Winter 2004): 61–63.

Piven, Francis Fox, and Richard A. Cloward. *Regulating the Poor: The Functions of Public
Welfare*. New York: Pantheon Books, 1971.

Plotkin, Mariano. *Mañana es San Perón: A Cultural History of Perón's Argentina*. Wilmington, DE: Scholarly Resources Inc., 1993.

Portantiero, Juan Carlos. "Dominant Classes and Political Crisis in Argentina Today." *Latin
American Perspectives* 1, no. 3 (1974): 93–121.

———. "La concertación que no fue: De la Ley Mucci al Plan Austral." In José Nun and Juan
Carlos Portantiero, eds., *Ensayos sobre la transición democrática argentina*, 117–138. Buenos Aires: Puntosur Editores, 1987.

———. *La producción de un orden: ensayos sobre la democracia entre el estado y la sociedad*.
Buenos Aires: Ediciones Nueva Visión, 1988.

Pozzi, Pablo. *La oposición obrera a la dictadura, 1976–1982*. Buenos Aires: Editorial Contrapunto, 1988.

Primer manual para agentes del Programa Alimentario Nacional. Buenos Aires: Ministerio
de Salud y Acción Social, Gobierno de la República de Argentina, 1984.

"Programa Alimentario Nacional: Evaluación de aspectos operativos y componentes de
imagen; Encuesta nacional a beneficiarios del P.A.N." Buenos Aires, August 1986.

Przeworski, Adam. *Democracy and the Market: Political and Economic Reforms in Eastern
Europe and Latin America*. Cambridge, UK: Cambridge University Press, 1991.

Pucciarelli, Alfredo, ed. *Empresarios, tecnócratas y militares: La trama corporativa de la
última dictadura*. Buenos Aires: Siglo Veintiuno, 2004.

———, ed. *Los años de Alfonsín: ¿El poder de la democracia o la democracia del poder?* Buenos Aires: Siglo Veintiuno Editores, 2006.

———, ed. *Los años de Menem: La construcción del orden neoliberal*. Buenos Aires: Siglo
Veintiuno Ediciones, 2011.

Pucciarelli, Alfredo, and Ana Castellani, eds. *Los años de la alianza: La crisis del orden neoliberal*. Buenos Aires: Siglo Veintiuno, 2015.

Puiggrós, Adriana. *Neoliberalism and Education in the Americas*. Boulder, CO: Westview
Press, 1999.

Rama, Angel. *The Lettered City*. Translated and edited by John Chasteen. Durham, NC:
Duke University Press, 1996.

Rapoport, Mario. *Historia económica, política y social de la Argentina (1880–2003)*. Buenos
Aires: Ariel, 2006.

Restivo, Néstor, and Raúl Dellatorre. *El Rodrigazo: El lado oscuro del ajuste que cambió la Argentina*. Buenos Aires: Capital Intelectual, 2016.

Restivo, Néstor, and Horacio Rovelli. *El Accidente Grinspun: Un Ministro Desobediente*. Claves Para Todos. Series editor José Nun. Buenos Aires: Capital Intelectual, 2011.

Robinson, William. *Promoting Polyarchy: Globalization, US Intervention and Hegemony*. Cambridge, UK: Cambridge University Press, 1996.

Rock, David. "Machine Politics in Buenos Aires and the Argentine Radical Party." *Journal of Latin American Studies* 4, no. 2 (November 1972): 233–256.

———. *Politics in Argentina: The Rise and Fall of Radicalism, 1890–1930*. New York: Cambridge University Press, 1975.

Roig, Alexandre. *La moneda imposible: La convertibilidad argentina de 1991*. Buenos Aires: Fondo de Cultura Económica, 2016.

Romero, José Luis. *Buenos Aires: Historia de cuatro siglos*. Buenos Aires: Grupo Editor Altamira, 2000.

Roniger, Luis, and Mario Sznajder. *The Legacy of Human Rights Abuses in the Southern Cone: Argentina, Chile, and Uruguay*. Oxford: Oxford University Press, 1999.

Roxborough, Ian. "Unity and Diversity in Latin American History." *Journal of Latin American Studies* 16, no. 1 (May 1984): 1–26.

Rudé, George. *The Crowd in History*. New York: Wiley, 1964.

Schedler, Andreas. "What Is Democratic Consolidation?" *Journal of Democracy* 9, no. 2 (April 1998): 91–107.

Scheper-Hughes, Nancy. *Death Without Weeping: The Violence of Everyday Life in Brazil*. Berkeley: University of California Press, 1993.

Schvarzer, Jorge. *La política económica de Martínez de Hoz*. Buenos Aires: Hyspamérica, 1986.

Scott, James C. *The Moral Economy of the Peasant: Rebellion and Subsistence in Southeast Asia*. New Haven, CT, and London: Yale University Press, 1976.

———. *Weapons of the Weak: Everyday Forms of Peasant Resistance*. New Haven, CT, and London: Yale University Press, 1985.

Senén González, Santiago, and Fabián Bosoer. *La trama gremial 1983–1989: Crónica y testimonios*. Buenos Aires: Corregidor, 1993.

Serulnikov, Sergio. "Como si estuvieran comprando. Los saqueos de 1989 y la irrupción de la nueva cuestión social." Gabriel DiMeglio and Sergio Serulnikov, eds. *La larga historia de los saqueos en la argentina de la independencia hasta nuestros días*. Buenos Aires: Siglo XXI, 2017, 137–176.

———. "When Looting Becomes a Right: Urban Poverty and Food Riots in Argentina." In "Social Movements and Political Change in Latin America: 2," special issue, *Latin American Perspectives* 21, no. 3, (Summer 1994): 69–89.

Sheinin, David. *The Consent of the Damned: Ordinary Argentinians in the Dirty War*. Gainesville: University Press of Florida, 2013.

———. "La Tablada Attack and the Erosion of Civil Rights in Argentina." *Middle Atlantic Review of Latin American Studies* 1, no. 1 (2017): 77–96.

Sigal, Víctor. *Aspectos de la implementación de una política pública: El caso PAN*. Buenos Aires: INAP, 1986.

Sikkink, Kathryn. *The Justice Cascade: How Human Rights Prosecutions Are Changing the World*. The Norton Series in World Politics. New York: W.W. Norton & Company, 2011.

Southwell, Myriam. "Con la democracia se come, se cura, se educa: Disputas en torno a la transición y las posibilidades de una educación democrática." In Antonio Camou, Cristina Tortti, and Aníbal Viguera, eds., *La argentina democrática: los años y los libros*, 307–334. Buenos Aires: Prometeo Libros, Universidad Nacional de la Plata, 2007.

Stawski, Martín Esteban. *Asistencia social y buenos negocios: Política de la Fundación Eva Perón, 1948–1955*. Colección bitácora argentina. Buenos Aires: Argentina: Imago Mundi, 2009.

Stites Mor, Jessica. *Transition Cinema: Political Filmmaking and the Argentine Left since 1968*. Pittsburgh: University of Pittsburgh Press, 2012.

Suriano, Juan, and Eliseo Alvarez. *505 días que la Argentina olvidó: De la rendición de Malvinas al triunfo de Alfonsín*. Buenos Aires: Sudamericana, 2013.

Svampa, Maristella. *La sociedad excluyente: La Argentina bajo el signo del neoliberalismo*. Buenos Aires: Taurus, 2005.

Svampa, Maristella, and Sebastián Pereyra. *Entre la ruta y el barrio: La experiencia de las organizaciones piqueteras*. Buenos Aires: Editorial Biblos, 2009.

Tadesco, Laura. *Democracy in Argentina: Hope and Disillusion*. London: Frank Cass Publishers, 1998.

Tate, Winifred. *Counting the Dead: The Culture and Politics of Human Rights Activism in Colombia*. Berkeley: University of California Press, 2007.

Tedesco, Juan Carlos. *Educación y sociedad en la Argentina (1880–1900)*. Buenos Aires: Centro Editor de América Latina, 1982.

Terán, Oscar. *En busca de la ideología argentina*. Buenos Aires: Catálogos, 1986.

Thompson, E. P. *The Making of the English Working Class*. New York: Vintage Books, 1963.

———. "The Moral Economy of the English Crowd in the Eighteenth Century." *Past and Present*, no. 50 (February 1971): 76–136.

Tinsman, Heidi. *Buying into the Regime: Grapes and Consumption in Cold War Chile and the United States*. Durham, NC: Duke University Press, 2014.

Torre, Juan Carlos, and Elisa Pastoriza. "La democratización del bienestar." In *Nueva historia argentina*, vol. 8, Juan Carlos Torre, ed., *Los años peronistas, 1943–1955*, 257–312. Buenos Aires: Editorial Sudamericana, 2002.

Trumper, Camilo. *Ephemeral Histories: Public Art, Politics, and the Struggle for the Streets in Chile*. Oakland: University of California Press, 2016.

Van Isschott, Luis. *The Social Origins of Human Rights: Protesting Political Violence in Colombia's Oil Capital, 1919–2010*. Madison: University of Wisconsin Press, 2015.

Veigel, Klaus. *Dictatorship, Democracy, and Globalization: Argentina and the Cost of Paralysis, 1973–2001*. University Park: Pennsylvania State University Press, 2009.

Velasco, Alejandro. *Barrio Rising: Urban Popular Politics and the Making of Modern Venezuela*. Oakland: University of California Press, 2015.

Vezzetti, Hugo. *Pasado y presente: Guerra, dictadura y sociedad en la argentina*. Buenos Aires: Siglo Veintiuno Editores, 2009.

Vitelli, Guillermo. *Cuarenta años de inflación en la Argentina*. Buenos Aires: Editorial Edhasa, 1986.

Vommaro, Gabriel. "Cuando el pasado es superado por el presente: Las elecciones presiden-cials de 1983 y la construcción de un nuevo tiempo político en la Argentina." In Alfredo Pucciarelli, ed., *Los años de Alfonsín: ¿El poder de la democracia o la democracia del poder?*, 245–288. Buenos Aires: Siglo Veintinuno Ediores, 2006.

——. "La pobreza en transición: El redescubrimiento de la pobreza y el tratamiento estatal de los sectores populares en Argentina en los años 80." *Apuntes de Investigación del CECYP* 14, no. 19 (2011): 45–73.

Vommaro, Pablo. "Las organizaciones sociales de base territorial y comunitaria en Quilmes: El caso de las tomas de tierra y asentamientos de 1981." Paper delivered at the "IV Jorna-das de Jovenes Investigadores," Instituto Gino Germani, September 19–21, 2007.

Waisman, Carlos H., and Raanan Rein, eds. *Spanish and Latin American Transitions to Democracy*. Brighton, UK: Sussex Academic Press, 2005.

Waldman, Peter, and Natalio Botana. *El impacto de la inflación en la sociedad y la política*. Buenos Aires: Editorial Tesis, Instituto Torcuato di Tella, 1988.

Walker, Louise. *Waking from the Dream: Mexico's Middle Classes after 1968*. Stanford, CA: Stanford University Press, 2013.

Walker, Louise, and Tanalís Padilla, eds. "Spy Reports: Content, Methodology and Histori-ography in Mexico's Recently-Opened Secret Police Archives," special issue, *Journal of Iberian and Latin American Research* 19, no. 1 (July 2013).

Werth, Brenda. *Theater, Performance, and Memory Politics in Argentina*. New York: Pal-grave Macmillan, 2010.

Williams, Raymond. *Culture and Society: 1780–1950*. New York: Harper & Row, 1966.

Wolfe, Joel. "Father of the Poor or Mother of the Rich? Getulio Vargas, Industrial Workers, and Constructions of Class, Gender, and Populism in São Paulo, 1930– 1954." *Radical History Review* 58(Winter 1994): 80–111.

World Bank. "Report No. 6555-AR: Argentina Population, Health and Nutrition Sector Review." Washington, DC: The World Bank, 1987.

Zelizer, Viviana. *The Social Meaning of Money*. New York: Basic Books, 1994.

Zimmermann, Eduardo. *Los liberales reformistas: La cuestión social en la Argentina, 1890– 1916*. Buenos Aires: Universidad de San Andrés/Editorial Sudamericana, 1995.

INDEX

Figures are indicated by page numbers followed by *fig.*

Founded in 1893,
UNIVERSITY OF CALIFORNIA PRESS
publishes bold, progressive books and journals
on topics in the arts, humanities, social sciences,
and natural sciences—with a focus on social
justice issues—that inspire thought and action
among readers worldwide.

The UC PRESS FOUNDATION
raises funds to uphold the press's vital role
as an independent, nonprofit publisher, and
receives philanthropic support from a wide
range of individuals and institutions—and from
committed readers like you. To learn more, visit
ucpress.edu/supportus.

www.ingramcontent.com/pod-product-compliance
Lightning Source LLC
Chambersburg PA
CBHW030331270326
41926CB00010B/1585